Tinder

Digital Media and Society Series

Giota Alevizou, *The Web of Knowledge*
Nancy Baym, *Personal Connections in the Digital Age*, 2nd edition
Taina Bucher, *Facebook*
Mercedes Bunz and Graham Meikle, *The Internet of Things*
Jean Burgess and Joshua Green, *YouTube*, 2nd edition
Mark Deuze, *Media Work*
Andrew Dubber, *Radio in the Digital Age*
Stefanie Duguay, *Tinder*
Quinn DuPont, *Cryptocurrencies and Blockchains*
Charles Ess, *Digital Media Ethics*, 3rd edition
Terry Flew, *Regulating Platforms*
Jordan Frith, *Smartphones as Locative Media*
Alex Gekker, *Maps as Media*
Gerard Goggin, *Apps: From Mobile Phones to Digital Lives*
Alexander Halavais, *Search Engine Society*, 2nd edition
Martin Hand, *Ubiquitous Photography*
Robert Hassan, *The Information Society*
Kylie Jarrett, *Digital Labor*
Amelia Johns, Ariadna Matamoros-Fernández, and Emma Baulch, *WhatsApp: From a One-to-One Messaging App to a Global Communication Platform*
Mark R. Johnson, *Twitch*
Tim Jordan, *Hacking*
D. Bondy Valdovinos Kaye, Jing Zeng and Patrik Wikström, *TikTok: Creativity and Culture in Short Video*
Graeme Kirkpatrick, *Computer Games and the Social Imaginary*
Tama Leaver, Tim Highfield and Crystal Abidin, *Instagram*
Leah A. Lievrouw, *Alternative and Activist New Media*, 2nd edition
Rich Ling and Jonathan Donner, *Mobile Communication*
Donald Matheson and Stuart Allan, *Digital War Reporting*
Nick Monaco and Samuel Woolley, *Bots*
Jeremy Wade Morris, *Podcasting*
Dhiraj Murthy, *Twitter*, 2nd edition
Zizi A. Papacharissi, *A Private Sphere: Democracy in a Digital Age*
Julian Thomas, Rowan Wilken and Ellie Rennie, *Wi-Fi*
Katrin Tiidenberg, Natalie Ann Hendry and Crystal Abidin, *tumblr*
Jill Walker Rettberg, *Blogging*, 2nd edition
Patrik Wikström, *The Music Industry*, 3rd edition

Tinder

Stefanie Duguay

polity

First published in 2026 by Polity Press

Polity Press
65 Bridge Street
Cambridge CB2 1UR, UK

Polity Press
111 River Street
Hoboken, NJ 07030, USA

ISBN-13: 978-1-5095-6268-8
ISBN-13: 978-1-5095-6269-5(pb)

A catalogue record for this book is available from the British Library.

Library of Congress Control Number: 2026936016

Typeset in 10.25 on 13pt Scala
by Fakenham Prepress Solutions, Fakenham, Norfolk NR21 8NL
Printed and bound in Great Britain by Ashford Colour Ltd

For further information on Polity, visit our website:
politybooks.com

Contents

Acknowledgments

Life is far from an individual endeavor, and the same is true for writing a book. I wish to thank my editor Mary Savigar for listening when I said *this* was the book I wanted to write. I am appreciative of her support and the work of the rest of the team at Polity as well as the book's careful reviewers. This book was made possible with the funding and research time allotted through my Concordia University Research Chair as well as a year of sabbatical leave. The collaborative work of several research assistants has supported this book, such as the illustrations by Aliya Adamjee, the analysis of Tinder's newsroom posts co-conducted with Alex Chartrand, and Dunja Nešović's literature reviews. Thanks to the DIGS Lab for our discussions throughout this process and our exchanges about writing survival strategies.

As I mention throughout, this book is informed by my past research into Tinder and dating apps. While it references several of my past publications, the words and thoughts here are freshly written and synthesized. I am grateful to my former research participants and collaborators across those projects. Thanks to scholarly contacts and friends who have created meaningful space for discussing this book and our technosocial conundrums more widely, especially to Kath Albury, Paul Byron, and Brady Robards for their insights. Many thanks to the fantastic Digital & Social Media crew at the University of Technology Sydney for hosting my most chaotic book talk yet as I worked through the chapters' main ideas. I also appreciate the CODER team, collaborators across Canada and internationally, and digital media scholars who formed a key imagined audience for this book.

I appreciate Jo for being ok with me re-downloading Tinder ten years after we initially matched. I miss dearly the people we lost too early who would have had lively conversations with me about the book. Even so, I still feel their supportive presence in the search for more just, equitable, and loving ways to forge relationships, with or without technology.

Timeline

	Technology	Business & Governance
2012	Launch (iPhone)	Sean Rad as CEO
2013	Launch (Android)	
2014	Moments	#ITSTARTSHERE visual campaign Whitney Wolfe Herd sues Tinder Benchmark Capital investment Sean Rad steps down as CEO, replaced by Chris Payne
2015	Passport, Rewind Swipe limit Instagram integration Verified celebrity profiles Super Like Job & Education added to profiles Moments discontinued	Tinder Plus premium subscription First advertisement: Budweiser #*Whatever* USA Tappy acquisition Sean Rad reinstated as CEO
2016	Health Safety section Upload photos from camera roll Tinder Social Tinder Stacks Spotify integration Tinder Boost Smart Photos More Genders	Humin acquisition Hey! Vina launch 1 million paid members App becomes 18+ Swipe the Vote *All Types All Swipes* Match Group's CEO, Greg Blatt, becomes Tinder's CEO
2017	Tinder Online Tinder Social discontinued Tinder Reactions	Gold subscription tier added *The Menprovement Initiative*

	Technology	Business & Governance
2018	Loops Top Picks Bitmoji Swipe Surge push notifications	Elie Seidman becomes CEO *The Interracial Couple Emoji Project* Can request data for download TinderU Year in Swipe recaps begin annually
2019	Festival Mode Sexual orientation profile field Tinder Lite	Swipe Night
2020	Noonlight Photo verification "Does This Bother You?" Passport free (limited time) Video calling Election Center, "I voted" sticker	Safety Centre Jim Lanzone becomes CEO Platinum subscription tier introduced Guidelines on election behaviors Megan Thee Stallion partnership
2021	"Are You Sure?" Vibes Block Contacts Explore	Renate Nyborg becomes CEO Tinder Coins
2022	Background checks through Garbo Relationship Goals	Comparably's 2022 Best Places to Work Nyborg steps down, Bernard Kim becomes CEO
2023	Matchmaker Partnership with Garbo ends	*It Starts With a Swipe*™ campaign Select subscription tier introduced
2024		Faye Iosotaluno becomes CEO #theconnectionexperience on TikTok
2025	*The Game Game* Face Check video selfie verification Double Date	Partnership with OpenAI Partnership with World Iosotaluno steps down, Spencer Rascoff (Match Group's CEO) takes leadership

Introduction: Burning into culture

When I met my wife on Tinder, it was fun. I double-checked this with her the other day, trying to figure out what had been fun about matching more than a decade ago. She said, "I remember it being exhilarating" – don't worry, reader, this quote is not an ego-boost for me; she was referring to the entire Tinder experience of matching: "Just like, something new and interesting." Though this experience was also "nerve-wracking" because the moment matching opens the possibility of chatting, there is the pressure of saying something that lands with the other person, something relatable. Even so, when I asked her to sum up what made Tinder fun, she listed, "Connecting with people, the potential to date people and have it not work out and make friends, [and] seeing how interesting people can be." With this last point, she explained that it was always fascinating to see the range of people and their profiles, getting a glimpse of their identities, lives, and what they think is desirable, from fishing selfies to sunset beach shots. These glimpses reflect the different worlds we create, which an app like Tinder can bring together.

This discussion about Tinder's potential for connection – for sparking something new – resonated with my own experience and many of the experiences shared by people I interviewed about the app in the mid-2010s. While it was launched in 2012, Tinder's rise to popularity took only a few short years until the company reported in 2015 that it was topping the app store charts with an estimated 9.6 million daily active users swiping through more than 1.4

billion profiles each day (Gorman, 2015). Around this time, research also showed increases in digitally mediated dating participation, such as the Pew Research Center reporting a near-threefold increase between 2013 and 2015 in the number of 18–24-year-old Americans on dating apps and websites (Smith, 2016). Surveys showed that people found Tinder fun and entertaining (Carpenter and McEwan, 2016; Ranzini and Lutz, 2016) while Tinder success stories circulated on the app's website, among my friend circles, and in some of my research interviews. "Swiping right," as the focal gesture used to favor another profile on the app, even became a colloquialism for making a decisive decision in all sorts of scenarios that had nothing to do with dating, such as choosing auto insurance (The General, 2017).

Tinder in the 2020s carries a different affect. When I tell people I am writing about the app, they often go quiet. Some scrunch their faces while others, often women, adopt a tone of commiseration, "That must be really hard," alluding to sexist comments that circulate through the app or its implication in gender-based violence (Hess and Flores, 2018; Dugdale and Harjani, 2025). Still others have asked me if the research is making me angry, sad, or exhausted, thinking about reports of endless missed connections and dating app fatigue (Lindsay, 2024). Sometimes these questions reflect the feelings they experience when opening the app, as they share stories about wanting different things than those with whom they match, having difficulty telling fraud accounts apart from daters, blocking others for offensive behavior, and feeling bombarded with ads for premium plans. While some of these concerns speak to problems that have long been festering on dating apps, since spambots and harassment have been challenges for Tinder from its early years, some pertain to challenges that have steadily grown and shifted as Tinder has evolved. These challenges, relating to conflicting app uses, authenticity, safety, and commercialization are taken up in this book's chapters not just because they are on my mind, but also because they are often on the minds of the increasing volume of people who have encountered dating apps as they have become common technologies, whether these encounters involve direct use, hearing others' stories, seeing media coverage, or refusing to use them.

Dating apps have steadily risen in their ubiquity, even as the number of new users has stagnated in some regions in recent years (Match Group, 2024a; Ofcom, 2024). Beyond updated Pew Research Center statistics showing that about 30 percent of Americans steadily participated in digitally mediated dating from 2019 to 2022 (Vogels and McClain, 2023), the global dating app industry reportedly brought in $6 billion in revenue in 2024 (Global Dating Insights, 2025a). While 50 percent of this revenue comes from the North American market and 23 percent from Europe, it is also increasingly fed by dating apps' growing adoption in Asia-Pacific and African regions. According to those same reports, more than 300 million people are estimated to be using dating apps worldwide. Tinder's (n.d.-a) press materials boast that "today" (as of writing), the app is available in 190 countries, more than 45 languages, and still draws approximately 50 million users per month. Although a more modest number, industry statistics still impressively show that in 2024, Tinder was drawing more than 6.1 million monthly downloads (Statista, n.d.). When people become single or declare they are dating, it is often implied explicitly or implicitly by those around them that they should get on *the apps*, with Tinder remaining the most downloaded dating app worldwide (Dixon, 2025). Therefore, a shift in sentiment toward the app and the issues it reflects should be taken seriously, as Tinder's embedding in dating practices means that it cannot be brushed off as frivolous, expendable, or even optional for many individuals, as it represents a focal means for meeting people.

This book examines Tinder from its launch until the present to understand how this app has become integrated with sexual and dating cultures while also shaping them. It uncovers the opportunities that a new technology opens, such as the fun in expressing oneself in a profile or the creativity in repurposing or loosening Tinder's association with long-term relationships to spark friendships or realize other goals. But it also shows how this potential is couched within sociotechnical and economic arrangements that comprise the conditions for contemporary digital intimacy. These conditions give rise to particular norms, behaviors, and values being enacted with and through Tinder. As discussed in the chapters to come, such conditions give rise to expectations around displays of authenticity, such as by mandating the exchange of data for AI-powered verification processes, determine the levels of acceptability for harassing and discriminatory behavior, and facilitate the commercialization of intimacy into a booming digital matchmaking industry. While these conditions for digital intimacy are intertwined with broader societal structures, such as capitalism, and associated hierarchical systems that reinforce misogyny, racism, cisheteronormativity, and other oppressions that make their way through dating apps, looking closely at Tinder – its technological development, marketing, and governance – enables us to see that things do not necessarily need to come together in this way. The chapters ahead show how particular features, design choices, terms and guidelines, campaigns, and business strategies have made Tinder what it is today. For many people, especially women, racialized people, transgender people, and others, Tinder is not fun. Or, they find ways to make it fun and work for their purposes, but it is not as fun as it could be if they were not subject to conditions that unevenly distribute risk and ease of participation in digital intimacy. Even so, Tinder is an important tool that, for many, has become as prominent a social outlet as in-person venues where we are prone to make new acquaintances (Newett et al., 2017). As such, Tinder matters as a factor contributing to whether individuals can meet others, form relationships, participate in society, and even leave a generational legacy.

Ultimately, this book about Tinder is a book about relationships. It is a book about society's relationship with Tinder, thinking about the app as comprised of meanings about dating and the digital that become rendered material in a technology. It is also about individuals' relationship with the app, as they tap, swipe, and return to it time and again. Also discussed in these pages are the relationships formed through Tinder, whether brief or long-term, serious or jovial, antagonistic, complementary, dangerous, or loving. Tinder's relationships with other apps and platforms, the digital matchmaking industry, law enforcement and security companies, and governments also become relevant across chapters. Dating app companies and platforms alike throw around the phrase "meaningful connections" as those they aspire to catalyze. Beyond this marketingspeak, I am most interested in what enables and inhibits connections, with actual *meaningful* connections constituted by those that bring together people across the different worlds within which they are situated so that they may create a shared world, whether that shared world is constituted by a friendship, marriage, or the start of community-building. It is this potential for world-sharing and world-making that is fun, and this book traces where Tinder's potential lies and where this potential becomes foreclosed by how the app and its surrounding arrangements have taken shape.

Tinder's affordances and contextual dimensions

Anyone familiar with Tinder would mention that swiping to select profiles is the app's hallmark functionality. But there is something more going on here than a catchy design choice. Since users could just as easily tap checkmark or X buttons to sift through profiles, the swipe's notability points to the relationships that people develop with technologies and their features that shape their experiences and our understanding of the technology's significance more broadly. Scholars write about affordances not as inherent qualities of a technology but as routes of action that emerge relationally between the technology and its users, giving rise to common uses, practices, and norms (Baym, 2015; Evans et al., 2017). The opposite is true as well: the ways that people and technology come together can also constrain action, with technical limitations delineating the boundaries of behavior in relation to how several actors (e.g., marketers, regulators) view the app's proper role. These additional actors, beyond users, point to how an app or platform is never just a technology but is instead a social microcosm influenced by macro-level structures and forces, including culture, society, markets, and governing bodies (van Dijck, 2013; Nieborg and Poell, 2018). While the swipe lies at Tinder's technical core, there is much more to be said about the relationships that users form with the app across its functionalities and how these relationships feature in Tinder's corporate vision, its business strategy, and its governance approach. Further still, it is necessary to remember that as localized, rapid, and interpersonal swiping and chatting with a match might feel, this activity all happens within a broader app and platform ecology as well as a matchmaking industry bent on bringing people together.

Much research has been dedicated to identifying, defining, and categorizing the affordances arising from platforms and apps (Bucher and Helmond, 2017). Specific to dating apps, communication scholar Lik Sam Chan (2021) builds from his extensive research on dating app culture in China to identify the emergent affordances of mobility (dating anywhere and anytime), proximity (finding people nearby), immediacy (real-time communication), authenticity (modes of verifying identity), and visibility (the dominance of – mainly visual – self-presentation). Such affordances are, of course, contingent on user practices as much as they are on features and functions, for instance, with some users deciding to be less visible or verifiable than others (we will get into the complexity of authenticity within Tinder's context later). While I find this typology to be useful, I see it as an invitation to further specify which affordances are most focal to the Tinder experience. In the following sections, I briefly outline these affordances, posed as gerunds since they are routes for action, starting with swiping and algorithmic curating, which do not map easily on to this typology but are arguably important functions of Tinder. Then I move on to proximate partner-seeking, which encompasses mobility, proximity, and immediacy while placing geographic constraints on Tinder use. Then I briefly connect these affordances to the contextual landscape of Tinder's economic positioning and governance, which together with its technical updates have contributed to changes and evolutions in the app over time.

Swiping

> You are charismatic, you're loyal, you're a set of red hot lips and the body of a god
> Swipe right
> You are desperate, maybe for love, maybe to fuck, maybe to get over being alone all the time
> Swipe left
> You – You're trying to forget the sound of your heart breaking when loose hands let it fall to the floor
> – Lyrics from "Swipe Right" by Forest Blakk (2018)

This excerpt is from a poem by Canadian singer and songwriter Forest Blakk that never once mentions Tinder. However, by 2018, the connection between swiping and sorting through endless dating profiles was implicit. The poem critiques what Blakk reads into the swipe as a cursory judgment and ends with the lines, "So judge us not / Swipe left." To understand how the swipe has become entangled in such relationships, often fraught ones, it is necessary to take a step back to understand where swiping comes from and what it affords and constrains. In his apparent retelling of Tinder's origin story, one of the cofounders, Jonathan Badeen, mentions that Tinder's original version did not include swiping as a functionality when it launched. He explains that he "snuck it in a few weeks later" as something that "just made sense in this case and seems stupid simple in retrospect" (Rad, 2015). Swiping is indeed simple: Tinder presents profiles to users in what it calls the "Discovery" screen; users brush the screen to the right to select a profile and signal interest or to the left to discard that profile without it being shown again (unless the Rewind feature is purchased). In the 2025 version, the app displays the words Like or Nope over the profile as the swipe is happening (figures 1 and 2). When two users swipe right on each other, it triggers a "match," unlocking the ability for them to exchange messages. While swiping is optional, since Tinder's X and heart buttons serve the same function, it is a central activity within the app.

At first glance, the swipe does not seem particularly revolutionary. iPhone users were already swiping to unlock their phones. Other apps involved tactile user interactions, such as sliding a finger across the screen of a mobile game to target enemies or shaking the phone to reset text. The infinite scroll of social media apps already necessitated countless vertical swipes to consume new content. But swiping to sort through choices was relatively new. It deviated from the grid-like design, central to Grindr and common in similar apps, that displayed profile thumbnails in columns and rows organized by proximity with the nearest users at the top. This novelty invited multiple actors, from users to media commentators, to attach meaning and values to swiping that shaped their interpretation of it and associated practices. For instance, chapter 1 explores the ramifications of how Tinder's founders framed swiping as the key mechanism in viewing Tinder as a game, treating individual profiles as cards to be sorted.

Digital media and games scholar Stefan Werning notes how the swipe is a dismissal that invokes the interface to serve "the next best option" (2015, p. 63). He points out

Figures 1 and 2. Fictional screenshots from Tinder upon left swiping (left) and right swiping (right). Illustrations: Aliya Adamjee.

how engaging in this pattern, through which the victorious match screen provides a form of psychological reinforcement, associates the swipe with positive stimuli. This intermittent reward system is common in mobile games and video lottery terminals, designed to keep people wondering if the next swipe will be a winner. This suspense fosters sustained interaction with the app. Such consistent and tactile interaction can even generate a sense of intimacy between users and their devices (Mowlabocus, 2016). These design mechanisms have spurred accusations that Tinder and similar swipe-based apps are addictive (Hronis, 2024), with some users even filing a class-action lawsuit against Tinder and its parent company claiming that their app features lead to compulsive use (Hall, 2024). Whether direct psychological impacts can be proven, users have long found the swipe compelling, with Urban Dictionary entries lamenting "Tinder thumb" or "Tinder finger" as pain resulting from too much swiping.

The swipe, as a functionality, has certain qualities that shape users' interpretation of swiping. First, it is binary, forcing a yes/no choice before moving on to the next profile. This binary quality leaves no room for "maybe," precluding slow-burn forms of attraction or desire. This leads us to the second quality: the swipe is rapid. It is a quick gesture that enables sifting through many profiles at once. This leads to the interpretation that many Tinderers are unlikely to take the time to truly evaluate a potential match before selecting or discarding them. The app includes space for users to add a short biography to their profile and has steadily increased profile information fields over time, first including education and job information, expanding to information as far-ranging as height, drinking habits, zodiac sign, interests, and responses to prompt cards (e.g., "The key to my heart is …"). However, a user must stop their swiping flow to tap on an up arrow to see most of this information. In my current version, only a user's name and age and an excerpt of their bio are shown overlaying a full-screen photo. As such, the swipe's third prominent quality is its visual nature, with photos comprising a fundamental component of one's profile. This visual focus gives rise to the belief that when users are making rapid, binary decisions on profiles, they are basing their choices mainly on evaluations of physical attractiveness, leading to allegations that swiping is shallow and does not engage with individuals' inherent worth, comprised of qualities other than their looks – a key theme of Forest Blakk's poem. Artist Gaby David and visual sociologist Carolina Cambre observe how these qualities of rapid, binary, and visual interaction give rise to a "swipe logic" that complicates users' negotiations with screened intimacy, which involve "juxtapositions between depth and surface, solidity and ethereality" as well as juxtapositions between "duration and volatility, instability, and movement" (2016, p. 1). Swiping affords users a route of action for matching with other people through Tinder and, in relation to this activity, users exercise agency in how they interpret it and whether they conform, appropriate, refuse, or otherwise engage with the swipe's qualities.

Algorithmic curating

Instead of displaying users in the Discovery screen according to one specific and stated parameter, such as proximity or recent activity, Tinder serves up profiles using an algorithmic feed that takes into account many factors. As users swipe through profiles, Tinder recommends new people based on previous input, creating an "intensified dialogical relationship" between users and "taste profiling algorithms" (Werning, 2015, p. 63). Since Tinder has remained vague about the data it relies upon and prioritizes to tailor profile recommendations, users' interaction with these algorithms involves trying out different swiping and self-presentational approaches. There are many blogs, subreddits, and other resources in which people, from dating coaches to programmers, claim to have cracked the Tinder algorithm and unlocked the secrets of attracting more matches. As is common in public discourse about algorithmic technologies, many of these sources refer to "the algorithm" – referring to a singular algorithm as a powerful entity and developing conspiracy-like explanations for how it works (Kanthawala et al., 2023). However, Tinder functions through many algorithms, which constitute programmed processes or computational operations that handle inputs (data, commands) and produce outputs. Users' demands to know how "the algorithm" works reflect their desires more broadly to understand how the system intervenes in their ability to select and be selected by others. In attempts to figure this out, rumors have swirled as to whether Tinder provides individuals with attractiveness scores or "Elo ratings," a system initially developed for chess that pits players' skill levels against each other. In the context of Tinder, the Elo rating system that users and journalists dissected in the mid-2010s was presumably based on a user's number of likes received *and* the number of likes received by accounts who have liked the user, along with other factors (Carr, 2016). Such a system develops a hierarchy among users as it ranks and orders profiles.

Speaking directly to this coverage, Tinder (n.d.-b) made a newsroom post in 2019 (now a permanent page as part of the website's "A Guide to Tinder") declaring Elo was "old news." Without discussing the past ranking system in detail, the post continued, "Today, we don't rely on Elo – we have a dynamic system that continuously factors in how you're engaging with others on Tinder through Likes, Nopes, and what's on users' profiles." Among the top data points considered was how often people use the app, as active users are likely to be matched with each other. Tinder also divulged that proximity, interests stated in profiles, and – confirming users' hunches – the number of likes one receives all matter. Users with "similar photos" are suggested to each other too. While these admissions could actually confirm users' fears that they are being ranked based on their relative popularity or others' judgments of their appearance, Tinder was eager to assuage worries over whether its system overtly reinforces discrimination. The post asserted, "Our algorithm doesn't track social status, religion or ethnicity." Yet perceived qualities such as race or ethnicity still enter the constellation of data correlated with likes, or the lack thereof, making them proxies for determining a profile's ranking and visibility in terms of how frequently one's profile appears to others (Williams, 2024). While Tinder's blog post gives users some indication of how the app suggests profiles, it also reaffirms users' sense that developers' design choices have profound effects on who they interact with through this technology.

Proximate partner-seeking

Tinder rolls multiple affordances of mobile and geolocational apps into the same experience. Mobile phones and their software enable the possibility of digital intimacy on-the-go, as users are no longer tethered to desktop computers but can initiate connections wherever, enabling greater spatial and temporal freedom in partner-seeking (Nash and Gorman-Murray, 2014). Tinder's use of the phone's GPS allows for swiping on those nearby. Although apps with grid interfaces that show multitudes of users at once give a strong sense of co-presence with others across digital and physical environments (Blackwell et al., 2015), I have heard from my interview participants that Tinder can also provide a sense of having in common with other matches the same city, neighborhood, favorite venues, or even apartment building. Though Tinder's geolocational functionality also places a constraint on partner-seeking, limiting the search radius to 160 km (or 100 miles) or closer, unless one pays for the Passport feature, which enables swiping on users all over the world. My interview participants also spoke about how this limit can be particularly challenging if you are part of a specific niche (women seeking women) and looking for others in rural areas or to meet new people outside of existing tight-knit groups. Since matches are nearby, this facilitates meeting them in-person with immediacy, since it should be relatively easy to navigate the limited space between users. The text-based message screens that are unlocked through matching on Tinder and similar apps bolster this immediacy, since they encourage sending short and to-the-point messages (Licoppe et al., 2016). Therefore, multiple features (e.g., GPS, search criteria, texting) combine with user practices to encompass proximate partner-seeking on Tinder.

Among the most interesting aspects of proximate partner-seeking is the geographic localization it brings to dating. Since the app is only useful if there is a sufficient saturation of users who are proximate to each other, Tinder must be marketed in ways that persuade many individuals who are located in the same place to use it. As we will see in chapter 4, this marketing has involved a range of strategies, some of which align with local dating practices. This is not to say, however, that everyone who uses Tinder in a specific location is also living in that place long-term. Users have taken up the app's geolocational functionality for "Tinder tourism" (James et al., 2019), swiping on local singles when they visit a place. Further, Tinder can facilitate the intertwining of global and localized cultures, as media scholar Jason Vincent Cabañes and political scientist Christianne Collantes (2020) found in their study of how women in Manila used dating apps to connect with foreign partners and access "cosmopolitan global intimacies" (p. 97). Even so, Tinder tourism and associated practices can also exacerbate or seek to capitalize on racial and class-based disparities, reflected by white middle-class users depicting themselves in humanitarian or volunteer tourist scenarios to associate "sexiness and racialized benevolence" as a phenomenon brought to light by the mid-2010s Tumblr account *Humanitarians of Tinder* (Mason, 2016, p. 822). Thus, the ways that people use Tinder in specific places all over the world, while also taking up the app when traveling, migrating, or returning to one's homeland, hold multiple potentials to reinforce, disrupt, or bridge divides across geographical contexts.

Leadership and governance: Business and rules

Since apps and platforms are not simply technological tools but are also businesses and services that structure user activity and circulate content (Gillespie, 2018), this book also considers how Tinder's business arrangements and governance approaches shape its influence on dating cultures. Foundational to understanding the analysis that is to come, on the business side it is important to know that Tinder is owned by Match Group, a company that also operates other popular dating apps, such as Hinge and OkCupid. Reports about Tinder's founders are often variable in who they list but the focal names tend to include Sean Rad (who became Tinder's first CEO), Justin Mateen, and Jonathan Badeen, with some sources mentioning Joe Muñoz and Chris Gulczynski as also having roles in Tinder's development and conceptualization (Crook, 2014; Stampler, 2014). One of the more famous names, which was often left out in Tinder's early media coverage, is Whitney Wolfe Herd, who played a role in Tinder's early marketing but whose cofounder status was contested. She left Tinder in 2014 and filed a sexual harassment lawsuit against Justin Mateen through which she received a $1 million settlement and Tinder stock (Ellis-Petersen, 2015). Wolfe Herd went on to found Bumble, a dating app she has promoted as improving women's dating experiences, which has become a key rival to Tinder. In 2024, Tinder dominated with 25 percent of the US dating app market but Bumble was right behind at 24 percent (Curry, 2025a). Tinder exists within the broader app and platform ecology, interfacing with larger infrastructural platforms (van Dijck et al., 2018) to provide varied login options (e.g., signing in through Facebook) or data storage (e.g., using Amazon Web Services for cloud computing).

While a desktop version was eventually made available, the Tinder app is downloaded through app stores, such as Apple and Google Play. App stores require developers to ensure their apps meet certain requirements or else they reserve the right to pull them from their offerings, essentially removing public access to an app (Weltevrede et al., 2025). These store requirements logically influence app guidelines and policies, though their implementation can be nuanced and variable across apps. For instance, both stores prohibit violent and sexual content. While Bumble has banned profile photos that feature guns, with exceptions for depictions of competitive shooting or firearms held by military or law enforcement personnel while in uniform, Tinder has not followed suit. Instead, Tinder reserved the right to moderate such images only when the depiction of weapons "could be perceived as violent or threatening" (Flynn, 2018), with Tinder's Community Guidelines specifically prohibiting images that show the "use of weapons." This wording treads the line between understanding guns as potentially representing identity, such as affiliation with a hunting community, and seeing them as always symbolizing violence. App store requirements are sufficiently vague to allow this difference in interpretation.

Considering Tinder's uses, however, restrictions on sexual content and nudity may be even more difficult to delineate and enforce. Tinder's top guideline, "Consider boundaries," elaborates that the app does not allow "nudity, sexual content, sexual desires, or looking for sex on your public profile" and specifies that these topics should be kept to private discussions once matches have been made. Guidelines that leave the door open for moderating even the expression of sexual desire within a dating app are emblematic of a wider deplatforming of sex across social media (Tiidenberg and van der Nagel, 2020). Deplatforming can mean, broadly, removing or limiting one's ability to communicate in public. Applied in the context of social media, it involves restrictions on speech and self-expression that are enforced through multiple means, most commonly removal (i.e., censorship) or reducing the visibility of content or the account generating it (colloquially termed "shadowbanning").

While deplatforming sexual content reflects the spread of a puritan and right-wing ethos across Silicon Valley (Paasonen et al., 2019), it is also likely connected to shifts in platform regulation at national and international levels. US-based platforms have long benefited from the Section 230 "safe harbor" clause of America's Communication Decency Act, which does not make them liable for user content. However, the 2018 enforcement of dual legislation, the Stop Enabling Sex Traffickers Act and Fight Online Sex Trafficking Act (SESTA-FOSTA), holds online intermediaries responsible for the promotion and facilitation of "prostitution" or sex trafficking (Liu, 2020). SESTA-FOSTA not only conflates consensual and nonconsensual sex work, but has also invoked an expansive response from platform owners, resulting in heightened policing and removal of sexual content (Are and Briggs, 2023). In this context, Tinder's guideline, "Make personal connections, not biz ones," makes the most sense with its elaboration: "Tinder isn't the place for any sort of sex work, escort services, or compensated relationships. So, no – don't use Tinder to find your sugarmamma" (Tinder, n.d.-c). It also elucidates why a dating app would have such potentially expansive prohibitions against sexual expression, which could be applied at the first sign of content that could get Tinder into trouble with the authorities. In a similar vein, Tinder shifted from its initial age requirement of 13+ to 18+ in 2016, avoiding the concerns that surround teen sexuality and much of the debate that has subsequently been galvanized about whether teens should be banned from social media altogether (Livingstone and Sylwander, 2025).

Deplatforming of sexual content is also imposed by some governmental bodies, such as the Pakistan Telecommunication Authority, which banned Tinder and other dating apps for disseminating "immoral content" (BBC, 2020). Despite cultural taboos on dating and interaction between men and women outside of marriage in this predominantly Muslim country, Tinder was increasing in popularity among Pakistani users prior to its ban, many of whom found it useful for meeting friends and partners outside of traditional channels (Sohail et al., 2019; Malik, 2020). Aside from curtailed access for religious reasons, the Chinese government has periodically blocked or hampered Tinder for political reasons while Match

Group has restricted the app's use in Russia (Wu and Trottier, 2021; Race, 2023), discussed further in chapter 4. While geographic bans can be circumvented through virtual private networks (VPNs), national and region-specific influences on Tinder access, content, and policies certainly shape its uptake and use. These examples demonstrate how governance takes shape on Tinder in relation to three key levels: the company's governance measures, app stores' requirements, and broader governmental regulation or pressure.

The details of Tinder's design features, business strategies, and governance approaches are always changing. The Timeline at the front of the book charts changes from Tinder's launch until the present day, highlighting the technological features and functionalities as well as business and governance strategies discussed throughout these chapters. Tinder's dimensions shift in relation to one another. New business strategies, such as the launch of Tinder Plus as the company's first premium subscription plan, carry with them technical changes, introducing premium features like Passport and Rewind. Similarly, shifts in governance are supported by changes to the app, such as with Tinder's major safety update in 2020 that reinforced reporting processes while introducing multiple features under the umbrella of safety. The app's earlier years, from 2014 to 2017, involved especially rapid additions and changes as Tinder tried out new features and approaches. While the Timeline does not include all of Tinder's updates or depict every business or governance decision the company has made, it draws attention to how Tinder has remained anything but static.

But what's new? Situating Tinder in mediated sexual and dating cultures

While hyping an app's novelty is one way to sell a product or attract attention, rarely is a technology completely new. If we consider technologies to be scientific knowledge and cultural meaning channeled into a material form, as well as objects that convene cultures of use, then scholarly insight tells us that a single app is unlikely to pose a giant rupture from what has come before. Eminent cultural studies scholar Raymond Williams (1977) asserted that new cultural formations are emergent, as a recombination of residual and dominant cultural forms. When new worldviews and ways of being arise, these cultural formations involve elements of past and present knowledge, values, practices, and norms. This premise also checks out from a communication studies perspective, heeding Carolyn Marvin's (1988) illustration of how even communication technologies that date back to the advent of electrical media, such as the telegraph, were developed in relation to existing technologies. New technologies are understood and adopted, but clash with pre-existing communication expectations and habits. Indeed, feminist and critical race scholars provide the most vivid examples of how technologies are developed within societies amid existing and often longstanding gender and racial biases, which are then embedded in and perpetuated through specific devices and software (Benjamin, 2019; Wajcman, 2010). Given these continuities across cultural and technological shifts, I examine Tinder throughout this book as a cultural formation as much as a technology. This necessitates considering how Tinder features within, and shapes, pre-existing sexual and dating cultures as well as how the app relates to, extends, and changes technological mediations of dating and hooking up.

Residual and dominant cultures of dating and sexuality

Imagine you are in the grocery store, shopping in the produce aisle. Your hand reaches for an apple at the exact same moment as another person's hand and brushes it briefly. You look up only to smile into the eyes of someone you find to be dashing. They crack a joke and some common ground is established over your affinity for this particular type of apple. You exchange phone numbers and thus begins the romance story you will tell your children one day.

My students often chuckle when I conjure up this vignette as a contrast to two people swiping right and meeting each other through Tinder. I like to present this fantasy so we can laugh at just how strange it seems that the grocery store scene is easy to see as a wholesome and authentic experience, while swiping is often disparaged as artificial, cold, and shallow. The contrast speaks to how sex, especially casual sex, and relationships are understood. Media scholar Kath Albury (2017) outlines a history of heterosexual people engaging in casual sex long before Tinder and dating apps existed, tracing shifts in nineteenth- and twentieth-century social norms and technology (e.g., the development of the contraceptive pill) that allowed for an increase in sexual encounters outside of marriage. Despite this long history and the huge influence of women's liberation movements across the 1960s and 1970s, casual sex still garners moral and normative judgments. Albury points to anthropologist Gayle Rubin's (1993) foundational "charmed circle" as a still-relevant representation of the hierarchical value system of sexual acts. The inner charmed circle is comprised of permissible and even celebrated sexual acts, such as procreative sex among married, monogamous heterosexuals. The circle's outer limits identify acts that are stigmatized and seen as bad or abnormal, with casual sex among these acts. In these outer limits, Rubin's diagram includes a stigmatized element that, while not mentioned specifically by Albury, strikes me as highly relevant to Tinder: sex with manufactured objects. Rubin was likely thinking about the taboo of using dildos, vibrators, or other objects for sexual pleasure. However, this notion that an object between people during a sexual encounter, let alone a casual sexual encounter, is distasteful or takes away from the veracity of their connection maps onto interpretations of Tinder as inhibiting romance and creating artificial connections.

Charmed, acceptable, and valorized sexual encounters among good heterosexuals involve nothing coming between the (two) people involved.

The continued stigmatization of casual sex has gone hand in hand with the perpetuation of sexist gender roles within dating. Women are still subject to a sexual double standard through which they are expected to express sexual desire and exercise their sexual freedom but must also practice reputation management to avoid being devalued by accruing the label of "slut" (Farvid et al., 2017). Although this double standard has endured, shifts in media and public discourse can make it more or less salient. On one hand, postfeminist sensibilities and the rise of an individualistic, commercial popular feminism have generated discourses with an emphasis on women's choice in relation to sexuality (Gill, 2007; Banet-Weiser, 2018). Postfeminist media portrayals assert that women can be agentic in presenting themselves as sexually desirable and that such self-expression is not always for, or in response to, men. At the same time, the range of ways that women can self-present sexually is still limited and often subject to the Madonna/whore binary. The line between tasteful and distasteful sexual expression is easily transgressed, making women – especially those who are not white or of middle- to upper-class status – the targets of sexist and misogynist judgments.

Popular feminism has also been met with an intense backlash. Media scholar Sarah Banet-Weiser (2018) calls this "popular misogyny" and defines it as a highly visible enactment of rage and vitriol that wages "demands on women's bodies based on the entitlements promised by heteronormativity" (p. 33). This heteronormative entitlement points to the constraining role that gendered double standards of casual sex also carve out for men, encouraging hegemonic masculinity that constantly desires and expects sex while being devoid of emotion (never "catching feels"). Indeed, such forms of misogyny are laid stark when women come together in collective witnessing of their experiences of sexism and sexual aggression, such as on the @TinderNightmares Instagram account that hosts screenshots of explicit and threatening comments made by men on Tinder (Hess and Flores, 2018). As the internet and digital technologies have often been developed *by* men and *for* men as default users, women are frequently seen as unwelcome in online spaces and subject to harassment to diminish their participation (Jane, 2016). While the success of dating apps in heterosexual markets is contingent on the presence of women, men's sense of ownership over online spaces, the disinhibition afforded by digital environments, and the lack of immediate consequences for misogynistic behavior make Tinder a risky space for many women. The risk, however, is not solely due to the technology but is embedded in the gender inequities and power differentials constructed between men and women in heterosexual culture, especially in relation to sex.

I have been focusing on these heterosexual gender dynamics specifically because an aspect of Tinder that differentiates it from Grindr and other early hook-up apps is the company's focus on heterosexuals as target users. Despite this, lesbian, gay, bisexual, transgender, queer and other users of diverse gender and sexual identities (LGBTQ+) are still present on Tinder but their experiences are shaped by its entrenchment in heterosexual culture. The lesbian and queer women who I interviewed in past research discussed how they were not surprised to swipe past cisgender men even when their settings were configured to see "women only." Several interviewees hypothesized that these men felt entitled to change their gender to "woman," despite not being transgender, to question how it could be possible that any woman on Tinder could not be into men. Their experiences resonate with one lesbian's commentary in *Glamour* (2015), in which she estimates that one in ten of her matches were cisgender men. Despite this, the women I spoke with often found ways to ignore such profiles and connect with other women.

Further, some gay male users find that certain practices and norms on Tinder make it a better tool for finding a boyfriend in contrast to apps like Grindr that are more conducive to hook-ups (MacKee, 2016). Using Tinder to find "nice guys" (read: boyfriend material) is linked to how certain practices common to gay sexual cultures, such as sending nudes or specifying preferred sexual roles (i.e., top, bottom), are uncommon or not allowed within Tinder's design, norms, or policies, thus shaping partner-seeking behavior. These insights into gay men and lesbians' experiences with Tinder demonstrate how the app's embedded heteronormativity shapes its adoption across users.

Racism experienced within dating cultures can also be conveyed and exacerbated through dating apps like Tinder. Research by Distinguished Professor of Indigenous Studies Bronwyn Carlson (2020) found that Indigenous Australians who used dating apps frequently experienced sexual racism, as a form of racial prejudice and discrimination in others' partner-seeking practices. While sexual racism is often passed off as being *just not into* a certain kind of person, Carlson found that sometimes Indigenous users had flirtatious conversations with individuals who only rejected them after learning about their Indigeneity. She concludes, "So, for Indigenous people then, 'sexual racism' is just racism" (p. 141). Research shows that sexual racism is enacted through a range of dating apps, including those with heterosexual and queer user bases (Daroya, 2018; Carlson, 2020). It is often most visible in profiles that specify a preference in favor of, or excluding, a specific race or ethnicity. Communication and media studies scholar Apryl Williams (2024) examines sexual racism on dating apps as an extension and expansion of white supremacy and longstanding forms of discrimination. She views sexual racism through Patricia Hill Collins's (2022) "matrix of domination" as the interlocking axes of race, class, and gender oppression, noting how racism intersected with sexism and classism to disenfranchise people of color throughout history. She counters claims that dating apps make way for a "new" form of digital sexual racism, tracing instead how existing forms of sexual racism become automated and entrenched through algorithmic systems and dating app norms.

I have focused on emphasizing how heteronormativity, gender biases, and racism were already components of dating and sexual cultures prior to the use of dating apps while discussing how they continue to function through these apps. Other structural oppressions and forms of discrimination shape dating experiences and are mentioned throughout the book as they come up. By considering cultural contexts and structures, it is possible to understand how such power relations shape who feels the safest, sexiest, and most comfortable on an app like Tinder.

Technology matters in mediated dating

If we think about mediation as what something does when it comes between or liaises among people, then it is easy to see how dating and intimacy have long been mediated. I have discussed alongside Jean Burgess and Ben Light (2017) how, despite the purported ideal of an unmediated encounter (back to the grocery store), multiple forms of media and communication technologies have played a role in bringing people together, from letters to landline telephones, and watching a film on a date. Historian Francesca Beauman (2011) demonstrates the longevity of personal ads, identifying antique examples of lonely-hearts ads dating back to 1695, which morphed into personals littering the classifieds section of newspapers and print tabloids in the mid-twentieth century. Personal ads were sufficiently popular in the 1970s and 1980s to attract scholarly attention for clues about human desire much in the same way that trends in dating app metrics are reported today. For instance, examining hundreds of personals, researchers identified that men's ads focused on physical appearance while women stressed psychological criteria, noting the social influence of gender roles in shaping these differences (Deaux and Hanna, 1984). These decades also saw the advent of video dating, a service that allowed individuals to select VHS tapes of potential dates, watch them at home, and return the tapes along with their selection sheet specifying who they wanted to meet (Woll, 1986). This format was similar to some asynchronous telephone dating services through which individuals prerecorded messages for others, who could then call in to hear the recording and obtain that person's number if interested. A redditor in r/datingoverforty recalls participating in this service in the 1990s alongside a "party line" that enabled singles to call in and chat synchronously (CounselorWriter, 2022). This poster and others in the subreddit chime in with their memories of phone dating long before smartphones, remembering exchanges that led to in-person dates but could also result in no-shows or being on the receiving end of the dial tone for a disconnected phone number – an analogue form of ghosting.

Early digital technologies coevolved alongside these analogue routes. Technology historian Mar Hicks (2017) sheds light on how a British woman, Joan Ball, created the first successful computer dating service in 1964 to power her matchmaking business. Ball previously worked for a "marriage bureau" – a British firm for professional matchmaking, which reminds us that human matchmakers were among the earliest mediators of relationships – and she developed a large-scale matchmaking system for her spin-off commercial endeavor. In computer dating services, employees punched customers' preferences onto cards read by large mainframe computers. Hicks points out that although Harvard students are generally credited with creating the first computer dating service, Operation Match, they were about a year behind Ball in running a functional service. As online technologies developed into the 1980s and 1990s, individuals also took to early digital services, such as the Minitel in

France and Bulletin Board Services in North America, to meet strangers. Research traces how queer users, who had difficulty meeting people in offline spaces due to prevailing homophobia, were early adopters of these technologies as well as chatrooms, forums, and web portals (Correll, 1995; Livia, 2002; Campbell, 2004). Whereas these spaces were not often formally created for dating, often providing separate chatrooms or channels for dating or sexual encounters within a broader portal, dating-specific websites emerged in the 1990s and into the 2000s. Websites like Matchmaker and Match combined computer dating's focus on matching users according to their data with direct forms of communication, such as interacting with profiles and messaging. Mobile browsing extended the use of these websites to cell phones while many websites were re-released as apps alongside the debut of mobile-only dating apps into the 2010s.

While this brief history of mediated dating is far from comprehensive, it illustrates elements of continuity across dating technologies. One way to understand dating apps within this longer history is through the concept of convergence, which points to how particular media formats, technologies, practices, and uses come together through new media. Acknowledging both the term's overuse and enduring relevance, media studies scholar Jean Burgess (2017) explains that convergence is "a dynamic of new media that operates technologically, socially, and industrially" (p. 49). It is possible to understand convergence in relation to Tinder along these three axes. Technologically, text-based personals transform into profile biographies while data yielded through detailed computational dating questionnaires become algorithmically inferred through user behavior. While video dating provided a visual of a potential date, Tinder's emphasis on profile photos was more likely influenced by social media's visual turn and the rise of selfie-taking practices (Senft and Baym, 2015). Thus, Tinder's social convergence combines social media practices of self-representation and tactile scrolling through feeds while incorporating longstanding mediated dating practices of divulging intimate information to a third party. Even industrially, convergence is evident in Tinder's ownership by Match Group alongside a range of dating apps, across which similar features and policies have been rolled out over time. Recognizing convergence allows for identifying the novelty that dating apps like Tinder bring to mediated dating while understanding that this novelty emerges mainly through the recombination of preceding elements and practices.

Understanding Tinder

The lens I apply to analyze Tinder is formed from perspectives across communication and media studies, cultural studies, and science and technology studies (STS). There is a useful synergy in how cultural studies and STS both attend to how technologies are part of society and culture while also shaping them (Williams, 1974; MacKenzie and Wajcman, 1985). Across these fields, there has been increasing attention to materiality and the relationships formed between users/viewers and the *stuff* of a technology/medium (McVeigh-Schultz and Baym, 2015; Sharma, 2022). My research into gender, sexuality, and digital technology puts this STS-based relational approach into dialogue with feminist and queer scholars who have long interrogated structural and systemic power relations, such as patriarchy and heteronormativity, and questioned what may be done to counter the hierarchies and inequities they produce (including through technology) while forging relationships across difference (Fraser, 1990; Haraway, 1991; Warner, 2002). These scholars and I are indebted to Indigenous knowledges as well as anticolonial and decolonial calls for decentering humans, and human-centric endeavors (e.g., capitalism), in order to see complex relations across humans and nonhumans (Haraway, 2016; Simpson, 2017; Escobar, 2018; Liboiron, 2021). This broader way of thinking about relationality necessitates consideration of my multiple relationships to Tinder, as someone who once used it and formed a long-term relationship that began with a date arranged through the app, and as a researcher studying Tinder for more than a decade. These relationships are always situated (Haraway, 1988), especially in relation to relevant aspects of my positionality: I am a white queer woman (on the non-binary-to-masculine spectrum) and millennial who joined Tinder during its rise to popularity. I am located in Tiohtià:ke/Montréal where working on land unceded by the Kanien'kehá:ka Nation draws my attention to the need for, and the historical and structural limitations of, living out just relations. Therefore, the analysis that follows is my own perspective, which is grounded in research and yet inevitably (and intentionally) shaped by the scholarly and personal lenses I bring to this work.

This book integrates multiple forms of research. I have applied the walkthrough method for analyzing apps (Light et al., 2018) to Tinder multiple times, first in 2014 and again over the years with subsequent app updates. This method involves examining an app's environment of expected use – how the app owners and developers anticipate the app will be received, generate profit, and require the regulation of user activity – alongside its technical interface. Analyzing the environment of expected use involves examining the app's vision, operating model, and governance approach. To do so, I have consulted numerous materials produced and circulated by Tinder and Match Group alongside trade and industry reporting as well as media coverage and public discourse circulating on social media. As these materials and their analysis have accumulated, my approach has taken on elements of a platform historiography (Helmond and van der Vlist, 2019), turning to web archives, Tinder's newsroom posts, and forums to trace Tinder's business, technological, and cultural development over time, and platform biography (Burgess and Baym, 2020), examining the evolution of controversies and user cultures. The technical walkthrough has involved paying close attention to the processes, features, and design configuration of different stages of app use, from entry (e.g., login, profile creation) to everyday use (e.g., swiping, Discovery settings) and leaving (e.g., hiding one's profile, deleting an account). Although only using one research account populated with sparse details and a couple of self-portraits, I have corroborated my interactions on the app with depictions of features in Tinder press releases and user perspectives shared in the other sources consulted.

To the walkthrough, I add insights across several research projects involving Tinder. When I mention interviews, these took place with a limited sample of ten women who identified as lesbian, gay, queer, bisexual, and "homoflexible," ages 19–35, with two located in Canada and the rest in Australia, where I was based at the time (Duguay, 2022). The interviews are from 2015–16 with participants recruited through LGBTQ+ online networks and my social media. They speak to these individuals' Tinder experiences at a specific time and are not intended to be generalizable but are incorporated to add illustrative depth to broader analysis. At one point, I became preoccupied with users repurposing Tinder for activities other than partner-seeking. I interviewed four campaigners of sorts (e.g., a political campaigner, creators of anti-smoking and anti-sex trafficking campaigns, and a multilevel marketer) alongside analyzing 65 media articles documenting such behavior and in-app observation (Duguay, 2020). Chapter 1 mainly speaks to these findings, as they unveil perceptions of what Tinder is (and isn't) for. Alongside these methods, I draw extensively upon others' research. These sources also have limitations, since much existing research has taken place in North America, Europe, and Australia, with fewer studies in other locations despite Tinder's international reach. Even so, the resulting synthesis allows for consideration of foundational aspects of Tinder: its influence on notions of digitally mediated dating, identity and authenticity, risk and safety, and digital matchmaking markets.

This integration of approaches enables tracing smaller relationships, such as users' relationship to their profiles or algorithms, or Tinder's relationship with Match Group, to understand the bigger picture impact of this momentously popular dating app on people's relationships with each other. Understanding this impact matters because Tinder has become a focal mediator of digital intimacy, as I have said, shaping the conditions through which millions of people encounter each other through technology. Media scholar Nathan Rambukkana defines digital intimacies as comprising "the ways that digital tools, processes, and cultures enable and transform our connectivities and collectivities" (2023, p. 176). He connects this definition back to queer theorist Lauren Berlant's pivotal work on intimacy as being made up of connections, affinities, and affects that "*impact* on people, and on which they depend for living" (1998, p. 284). Berlant stresses that intimacy arises in spaces that are produced relationally through the connections we form with one another. In turn, intimacy is powerful: "intimacy builds worlds; it creates spaces and usurps places meant for other kinds of relation" (p. 282). When digital apps and platforms transform our connections, they shape how and whether intimacy can form among people and the kind of resonance this intimacy has throughout their lives and our societies. In exploring Tinder's sociotechnical, economic, and governance-related configurations in the following chapters, I also identify aspects of these configurations that potentially hinder intimate connections. These include arrangements that facilitate and exacerbate sexist biases, racism, and cisheteronormativity; set challenging and data-hungry expectations for authenticity performances; implement surveillance measures in the name of safety even if they imperil some users; and generate revenue from business strategies that may heighten all these problems. Berlant reminds us that intimacy is not always positive.

These problems in which Tinder is embroiled initiate forms of intimacy that can be violating, nonconsensual, dangerous, and some people's reason for disconnecting. They usurp the space for building worlds of intimacy that are fun and pleasurable, worlds that have been expanded through previous forms of digital intimacy and for which I hold out hope can be possible into the future.

Overview of the book

Now that this introduction has set the foundation for better understanding Tinder and its sociocultural impact, chapter 1 looks at what exactly Tinder is for. It applies the lens of interpretative flexibility to identify different meanings and associations that surrounded Tinder when the app was new, as well as the range of uses for which it was implemented. The chapter explores how public discourse galvanized around understanding Tinder as a hook-up app, raising moral panics associated with casual sex, while the company attempted to center interpretations on Tinder as a doorway to romance, long-term relationships, and marriage. I trace how these struggles led to narrower uses of the app and the stabilization of a melancholic understanding of Tinder as an app for pursuing, but not finding, love. This stabilization has emerged from the prevalence of gendered double standards and inequitable practices as well as safety issues that are often, unfortunately, framed as individual problems to be fielded by women and others who experience marginalization or discrimination through the app.

The following chapter considers how multiple notions of authenticity play out on Tinder. It first outlines three takes on authenticity, which differentially see it as: a reflection of one's true self, an indicator that a person is safe and trustworthy, and a performance in alignment with contextual norms. The chapter examines Tinder's mechanisms for facilitating displays of authenticity, from social media integration to more recent visual and data-driven forms of verification, asking whether and how such evidence can establish another's character or trustworthiness. These mechanisms are contrasted with how users self-present in ways they perceive as meeting expectations of authenticity and how they scrutinize others' self-presentations. Both Tinder's authenticity mechanisms and users' practices set particular expectations for displaying authenticity, which often reward performances that most closely align with normative notions of attractiveness. As such, the endless struggle to establish others' authenticity creates an environment that is hostile to some users who cannot satisfy these expectations.

Chapter 3 explores this hostility, identifying that, although Tinder's guidelines and safety measures function at the individual level, the threats to safety experienced on the app manifest as collective aggressions, often reflecting misogyny, cisheteronormativity, and racism. The chapter then examines how Tinder attempted to deal with the technocultures giving rise to these safety threats through successive campaigns, including *#All Types All Swipes*, *The Menprovement Initiative*, and *The Interracial Couple Emoji Project*. Such campaigns have since given way to built-in safety solutions focused on technology-driven surveillance, such as photo verification using biometric data, language detection filters, and background checks. Ultimately, these interventions reflect a patchy approach to safety. The campaigns attempted to target problematic cultural biases without effective or comprehensive technical changes, while technological solutions lacked efforts to shift biases and norms amid Tinder's cultures of use.

Despite variable experiences among Tinder users, the app still makes money. Chapter 4 takes up a political economy lens to examine how it does so. First, I analyze how Tinder's parent company, Match Group, has consolidated a large proportion of the digital matchmaking industry under its umbrella through horizontal expansion. Then I delve into how Tinder generates revenue for Match Group through premium subscriptions, advertising, and engagement campaigns. I consider how Tinder's marketing and engagement campaigns have gone global, identifying alongside other scholars how this marketing spreads neoliberal feminist discourses of women's empowerment while also finding that Tinder tailors its campaigns in many locales. A closer look uncovers unique regional content and local partnerships forged in key markets, such as Brazil and Southeast Asia. Overall, this chapter identifies how swiping has become a big business in which Match Group has set itself up for the long term. But Tinder's revenue generation strategies sometimes cost users, such as through paid features that enable top-tier subscribers to override the swipe's double opt-in and other mechanisms that would otherwise keep potential harassers at bay.

The book's conclusion operates from the premise that while Tinder's meaning, uses, and associations have stabilized over time, they have not reached closure. The app, along with its operating model and approach to governance, can, and likely will, continue to update and change. As this is true for dating apps more broadly, I close by considering how we can bring together different frameworks for change to approach a redesign of digitally intimate technologies – redesigning not only their interfaces but also the sociotechnical arrangements in which they are embedded. I merge increasingly popular human rights and digital citizenship frameworks with relational perspectives that call for creativity, autonomy, and localization in the creation of intimate technologies to consider how we can design for digital intimacy that is conducive to world-sharing and world-making.

CHAPTER 1

Hook-ups or romance: What is Tinder for?

In 2015, journalist Nancy Jo Sales penned an article for *Vanity Fair* that appeared in print as "Tinder is the night" and online with the much more provocative title "Tinder and the dawn of the dating apocalypse" (Sales, 2015a). The article describes a dystopic *end times* in which hot, young singles in New York City are out at bars but, instead of buying each other drinks, their faces are absorbed in the glow of their smartphones as they swipe through profiles with little resulting romantic spark. In chatting with these Manhattan "twentysomethings," Sales paints a picture in which the men are prowling for impersonal one-night stands and the women are looking for romantic dates but left deflecting sexually aggressive pickup lines. The article resonates with the research mentioned in the previous chapter about prevailing gendered double standards for sexual behavior, reflected in how the women Sales talks to express their desire to participate in casual sexual cultures but risk losing respect from men if they do so. Quips from men featured in the article confirm but also lament this situation, with one man noting that women "act like all they want is to have sex with you and then they yell at you for not wanting to have a relationship. How are you gonna feel romantic about a girl like that?" His question implies that women who have casual sex, facilitated through Tinder, are not relationship material.

Overall, the article illustrates an apocalyptic outcome of Tinder use in which the dating app's endless swiping leads to people always looking for the next best match. Men and women, so the story goes, cannot meet and form romantic bonds like they used to because men are driven to find new (and multiple) sexual conquests while women need to navigate sexual aggression and violence, finding a lack of pleasure in the casual sex they do have. These women are unable to find a romantic, long-term connection on Tinder because that is not what it is for. According to the article's testimonies, Tinder is for procuring sex and, even then, it is about "hit-it-and-quit-it" hook-ups rather than human connection.

The article reads as a direct affront to the app, with a standalone quote in the second paragraph stating, "Tinder sucks," to which Sales adds, "But they don't stop swiping." Such accusations did not go unnoticed by Tinder's media team nor its cofounder and on-again/off-again CEO Sean Rad. Shortly after the article's publication, Sales tweeted about a survey reporting that 30 percent of the app's users were married and the rebuttal from Tinder's Twitter account was followed by a slew of tweets contesting her article. Tech industry coverage of the exchange in *The Verge* (Toor, 2015) showcased the onslaught's highlights, including the following tweets:

> It's disappointing that @VanityFair thought that the tiny number of people you found for your article represent our entire global userbase 😉
>
> Next time reach out to us first @nancyjosales ... that's what journalists typically do.
>
> [Tinder is] about meeting new people for all kinds of reasons. Travel, dating, relationships, friends and a shit ton of marriages.

Later in the same year, Rad fumed to another journalist about how Sales's article was wrong about Tinder's role in hook-up culture (Edwardes, 2015). He talked about how the company was compiling data about "Tinder marriages" – marriages facilitated by the app – and conjectured that the divorce rate might be declining due to Tinder: "Now there is more choice, so people make the right decisions." The interview took a dark turn when he ominously mentioned "background research" he conducted about Sales that unearthed, "some stuff about her as an individual that will make you think differently."

Sales (2015b) responded directly to Rad with an open letter in *Vanity Fair*. She picked apart some aspects of Rad's interview, highlighting how his quotes about Tinder having 80 million users inflated the actual numbers and imperiled the Match Group's debut on the stock exchange as it scrambled to assert, officially, that Tinder had 9.6 million users in September 2015. Sales reminded readers that Rad and the company did not have the polished reputation he put forward, bringing up Whitney Wolfe Herd's sexual harassment lawsuit. Then she focused the rest of the letter on the importance of freedom of the press and how female journalists often have their careers threatened when they produce coverage that displeases tech moguls. She closed with an invitation for Rad and the head of Match Group to join her in a public forum about "female journalists and freedom of the press." While I am unsure whether the forum took place, this open letter, in which Sales defended her right to report on Tinder the way she saw fit, gave her the space to double down on her commentary about dating apps.

Sales went on to direct, write, and coproduce the documentary film, *Swiped: Hooking Up in the Digital Age* (2018). The film reiterates several themes from her article, and while it does not specifically take aim at Tinder, it emphasizes the ease of dating apps for facilitating casual sex, which she links to an unhealthy preoccupation (mainly for women) with appearance and beauty standards as well as a culture of sexual objectification. In 2021, she published a book titled *Nothing personal: My secret life in the dating app inferno*, as a memoir of her experience getting on dating apps in her late forties combined with investigative critique of the apps and her skepticism as to whether love can be found through them. Clearly, from the individuals that Sales has spoken with, her background investigations, and her personal use, she believes that much swiping is geared toward casual sex with the implication that this use of Tinder is frivolous and potentially harmful or even as unbearable as an inferno. This contrasts with the assertions made by Tinder's social media management and Sean Rad that love, marriage, and meeting the "right" person (and living happily ever after) can eventuate through its app.

But who is correct?

When a technology is new, there is rarely consensus about how to use it. Companies producing technologies often frame and promote them in a certain way, along with providing instructions, guidelines, and other indications of their potential uses. People interpret and evaluate tools when they encounter them but the uses and impacts of information and communication technologies are even less predictable than with other technological innovations, given that these tools convey a world of media to their users, which can carry multiple and shifting interpretations (Silverstone et al., 1992). Just as users are influenced by corporate rhetoric, media discourse, and others' practices, they are also subject to "expert" opinions exercised by journalists, power users, commentators, and other authoritative voices, who influence understandings of novel technologies and how they fit in our existing lives and social contexts (Marvin, 1988). This chapter explores how Tinder lacks a singular interpretation of what it is for as well as how certain interpretations shape how we understand the app's role in our intimate lives. It investigates how several different actors, including users, journalists like Sales, and Tinder's marketing team, have developed different framings of the app, some of which have stuck and others that have fallen to the wayside.

In exploring the tug-of-war surrounding Tinder's meanings and purposes in our lives, the chapter applies the lens of interpretative flexibility to consider variations of the app's use and interpretation among different actors within a wider sociocultural context. Interpretative flexibility is a concept that describes how meaning is socially constructed in relation to novel tools and technologies by different constituencies. These constituencies are described by science and technology studies scholars Trevor Pinch and Wiebe Bijker (1984) as "relevant social groups" who have a stake in asserting certain meanings that reflect their values or morals. Power struggles play out among these groups and shape users' orientations toward a technology as they come to share particular conceptions of it due to their social, political, cultural, and economic status, even if they do not otherwise have existing connections. These struggles play out until "stabilization" is reached: particular meanings and uses become dominant. Various factors intervene in this process of how meaning is ascribed, such as when a new version of the technology is released that instantiates a particular purpose or when a large population of users domesticate the technology into their everyday lives in a particular way. However, scholars raise questions as to whether "closure" is ever reached; that is, whether a technology's purpose is no longer contested and a single use case wins out (Clayton, 2002). While there are always likely to be creative appropriations and reuses of a technology, there are certainly technologies for which debates die down: *this* technology becomes known as being for *that*. A microwave is for reheating food. Their seamless domestication into our lives renders them nearly invisible in the sense of no longer being noteworthy. As such, the lengthy infomercials I watched as a child that tried to sell all sorts of apparatuses for creative microwave baking and gourmet cooking have become scarce.

Tinder is not a quiet technology in our lives, even after more than a decade. While it is no longer as interpretatively flexible as during its early years, the controversies, debates, and contentions that rage on about the app reflect a lack of interpretative closure. Neither Sales nor Rad has the winning interpretation of Tinder: some people view it as a hook-up app while others view it as a means for finding a long-term partner. Still others convene all sorts of situationships, from friendships to friends-with-benefits, and other modes of intimacy that blur any defined lines. Many people use Tinder for entertainment purposes and, at one point in its popularity, health campaigns, marketers, and individuals tried out all sorts of surprising uses. Throughout this chapter, I examine the most prominent interpretations of what Tinder is (and has been) *for* and reflect on how they shape individual and societal reactions to the app as well as its actual uses. Then I discuss how Tinder's relative stabilization (but not closure) over time has congealed into a melancholic notion of "swipe culture" (Orchard, 2024). This culture builds on, and is fueled by, many of the gender biases and inequalities from which Sales recoiled in her exposés of dating app practices. While this stabilization is much more complicated than pointing to Tinder as the cause of these problematic practices, the app has become inextricably entangled in them through its framing and the public's interpretations.

Tinder is for fun (?)

One logical way to investigate what Tinder is for is to simply ask people why they use it. Several academic studies have done just that. For instance, a 2016 online survey of US-based respondents found that they used Tinder for a variety of purposes, including hooking up, finding friends, looking for relationships, meeting people when traveling, and self-validation, while finding that entertainment was a pronounced motivation for using the app (Ranzini and Lutz, 2016). This last finding echoes another survey of US-based university students, with more than 80 percent on Tinder, which asked broadly about dating app uses and concluded, "generally, people tended to indicate that they used the app for entertainment more than they wanted to use it for dating or sex" (Carpenter and McEwan, 2016). The finding that people often turn to Tinder for entertainment has also been demonstrated elsewhere, for instance, with some South

Korean interview participants remarking on their motivation to use Tinder for the fun of chatting with new people or for its game-like swipe (Kim et al., 2024). Interviews with men seeking men in Argentina found that Tinder offered "a personal and conversational experience, often more enjoyable, compared with Grindr" (Suenzo, 2025, p. 6217). A survey of 1,498 young adults (18–29 years old) across Turkey that found Tinder was their preferred dating app, especially among users in metropolitan areas, and uncovered that alleviating boredom was the top motivation for dating app use, followed by satisfying social curiosity and finding new friends (Sunam Audry et al., 2023). Working across media studies and psychology, Elisabeth Timmermans and Elien De Caluwé (2017) combined findings from studies in the United States and Belgium to develop and validate what they call the "Tinder Motives Scale" (TMS), consisting of 13 motivations that reflect high levels of user agreement with certain phrases associated with particular uses (e.g., "I use Tinder to get an 'ego-boost'"). Among the 13 motivations, "Pass Time/ Entertainment" and "Curiosity" were the strongest in their studies. Across this research, using Tinder for entertainment or "for fun" – as Timmermans and De Caluwé include in this category – appears to be a dominant purpose.

Tinder's fun factor, however, is no accident. Sean Rad provided insight into his vision for the app in an interview with *Time Magazine*, stating, "We always saw Tinder, the interface, as a game" (Stampler, 2014). He noted that people "join because they want to have fun. It doesn't even matter if you match because swiping is so much fun." Rad focused on the innovation of swiping as a way to make choosing among many different options "fun" within a software interface. The swipe-to-choose mechanism was something that Tinder bet on being popular from a corporate and technology development perspective. The company even later introduced an iMessage add-on called "Tinder Stacks," which allowed people to send each other "stacks" of options (e.g., photos) to swipe through (Tinder, 2016a). Although Stacks never quite caught on – it was discontinued in 2018 only two years after its release – swiping was a hit, and many other apps quickly adopted this design feature that prioritizes the gamification of choice.

This push for gamification was strong in the early 2010s. I recall it all too well as I was at the tail end of my time working for an institution that tried to entice its employees to start working with digital platforms (e.g., precursors to Microsoft Teams) through gamified features like points systems and virtual badges. Philosopher Karim Nader neatly defines gamification as "the process by which we use game design strategies to encourage people to reach their aims in real life" (2024, p. 3). He explores how, despite Tinder's marketing as a dating app, its design reorients individuals to the goal of matching with as many other users as possible. Within the game of Tinder, the goal is not meeting up, per se, but the much simpler aim of maximizing matches, which provides rewards: validation and the metrification of "success" in the visible number of matches accrued. Nader argues that Tinder's monetization mechanisms point most starkly toward this gamification, as the Super Like, Boost, and other features are geared toward maximizing matches. Such features, therefore, are not much different from power-ups or other bonuses available as in-app purchases across popular smartphone games.

As Tinder's algorithmic sorting of users has become more sophisticated, the game has also increasingly involved interaction with this algorithmic system toward the goal of matching with others. Users strive to influence the matches that are algorithmically curated in their feeds and to raise their algorithmic visibility in others' feeds. Media scholar Carolina Bandinelli (2022) observes these negotiations among individuals in the United Kingdom and Italy who use a range of dating apps with similar designs. She surmises, "Dating apps turn sexual and romantic evaluation into a game in that they organise it within a structure of quantifiable losses and gains, bonuses and maluses" (p. 914). She and other scholars observe how this game can be played alone or together with friends and acquaintances, swapping strategies on how to win (Bandinelli, 2022; Sobieraj and Humphreys, 2022).

If people merely garnered an abundance of pleasure from swiping and matching cards, this book might instead be about an app version of the Chinese tile-matching game Mahjong. Or Tinder Stacks would not have met its end as a software widget. But Tinder's immense popularity raises the question of what propels this fun. What exactly do users find entertaining about the app? This question brings us back to the reality that users are not swiping among options for pizza toppings but are instead presented with profile pictures – mainly selfies and full-body photos – of other people. This aspect of Tinder's design was not novel at all. It follows from other, much older attractiveness-rating websites, such as HOTorNOT, which launched in 2000 and allowed users to rank each other's photos on a *hotness scale* from 1 to 10 (ABC News, 2014). Illustrating the absorption of attractiveness ranking into digital dating, the online dating website Badoo bought HOTorNOT in 2012, seeing an opportunity to pair its ranking functionality with features for connecting users (Lunden, 2012). Perhaps more famously, Facebook's early iteration – Facemash – was a Zuckerberg creation that imitated HOTorNOT by compiling photos of other students from their online "facebooks" and putting them side by side for others to submit comparisons of who was hotter (Kaplan, 2003). In this way, Tinder replicates a game that has been around for a long time: evaluating others according to conventional norms of attractiveness.

This game can be fun when one is winning, resulting in the sense of validation and self-esteem boost reported in some of the studies mentioned earlier. However, Nader (2024) points out that it can be fairly easy to lose at this game, especially for people whose desires, preferences, or embodiment fall outside gendered and racially biased norms of attractiveness. It also becomes a losing game when users treat each other as pawns toward reaching the goal, seeing others not as people but merely as virtual conquests. Nonetheless, so many messages that individuals receive from other people, advertising, and celebrity culture continue to emphasize the importance of being attractive in terms of normative beauty ideals. Therefore, it can make us feel good – or at least relieved – when others deem that we have attained such ideals. Within this hierarchical rubric of attractiveness, it is also possible to imagine a sense of fun being garnered by assuming the powerful position of judging. A mixed-methods study of young daters in Buenos Aires, Argentina, who mainly used Tinder, Happn, and OkCupid, found that these individuals experienced the apps' visually focused swiping and algorithmic sorting as similar to navigating a competitive video game (Linne, 2020). Confirming Nader's perspective that such conditions lead individuals to strategize to avoid "losing" at this game, these users enacted daily self-management practices that ranged from comparing and optimizing their profiles against others' to consulting with peers and online tutorials about how to maximize matches.

Fun is gleaned not only through this validation in-app but also through the anticipation of what might happen off-app. Sex and love in heterosexual culture have long been interpreted as games (Albury, 2017; Mackinnon, 2022), from the protagonist in a romantic comedy negotiating hurdles to *get the girl*, to pickup artists trading tips on how to take a woman home (notably, these are stereotypically gendered games). These kinds of instrumental gamification live on, illustrated on the long-running thread "Weekly Profile Review" in the Tinder subreddit on the discussion forum platform Reddit. Here, users post screenshots of their Tinder profiles while others provide feedback, often giving tips to nudge them closer to normative ideals of attractiveness. Elsewhere on the subreddit, users post screenshots of conversations with matches, often framed triumphantly as examples of pickup lines that sealed the deal. These screenshots are met with multitudes of upvotes (a key metric on Reddit and an aspect of that platform's gamification) as accolades confirming that, if the point of the game is to have sex, then the prize has been attained.

Tinder is for sex (?)

An April 2013 screen capture by the Internet Archive's Wayback Machine unearths one of the earliest homepages from the Tinder website (Tinder, 2013). A blurry photo of four adults in their early twenties fills the page. All of them are light-skinned and two shirtless men sport chiseled abs and pectoral muscles with their arms casually around the skinny waists of two women in bikinis. An animated smartphone screen with the outline of a Tinder profile slides across these figures, bringing each one's face into view when it lands. As it does so, the profile populates with a fictional name, age, and number of mutual connections.

Tinder's early marketing strategies leaned into interpretations of this technology as a hook-up app through which sexual connections could be forged with (potentially) sexy people. As the app gained traction, a series of launch parties in 2013 and 2014 solidified its associations with sexual nightlife cultures. A YouTube video from the venue The Backroom Sydney (2013) shows people Tindering all night long while the liquor flows at the bar and models from the men's magazine *Maxim* pose with partygoers. A photographer who attended the London launch party that same year documented a similar sexual ethos, though perhaps with queerer potential, as the party took place at the circus and burlesque themed club Cirque Le Soir (Andy Tyler Photography, 2013). Later, Tinder's party for the launch of its subscription model, Tinder Plus, featured the theme "Tinder takes off," with the models this time wearing tight-fitting flight attendant outfits next to snapshots of Stella Artois taps and Cîroc vodka displays (Getty Images, 2015). It is no surprise that alcohol companies are prominent alongside Tinder's promotion, since they invest heavily in social media advertising and often see a payoff in increased sales among early adults (McCreanor et al., 2024). Given these companies' legacy of selling their product through sexual narratives, whether the narratives involve women's sexual objectification or empowerment (Ramšak, 2022), their involvement in the app's marketing heightened Tinder's sexual framing.

While launch parties serve as a form of networking among investors and tech elites, and garner media coverage through celebrity appearances, Tinder's on-the-ground early promotion strategy centered on college campuses. Like other technology companies, Tinder recruited student brand ambassadors who were then unpaid but received free swag and sometimes even the promise of internships. One such ambassador described to the *Huffington Post* how he held parties that required attendees to download Tinder to gain entrance and then offered free drinks and prizes throughout the evening (Bosker, 2013). As chronicled by several sociologists, expectations of engaging in casual sex are prevalent on American campuses and often fueled by binge drinking (Bogle, 2008; Wade, 2017). Many ambassadors belonged to fraternities and sororities in which traditional gender roles tend to be entrenched and sexual double standards are prevalent (DeSantis, 2007). Tinder saw rapid uptake in this context, eventually introducing a TinderU program that included in-app features for finding other students at one's own university and nearby campuses, and formalized the ambassador program. While ambassador roles are now advertised with hourly pay and are much more akin to influencer gigs, with the majority of the role centering on social media promotion (Archrival, n.d.), the early days of Tinder marketing tapped into college drinking, partying, and associated casual sexual practices already taking place.

Through this framing and popular discourse about the app's quick swiping being more conducive to casual sex than to long-term partner-seeking, Tinder gained notoriety as a hook-up app. In the early years following Tinder's launch, entertainment media reinforced this understanding, such as through comedy skits that laid bare the less-than-subtle subtext that a Tinder match meant a potential sexual encounter. When celebrity television host Conan O'Brien filmed a segment with actor Dave Franco about Conan's first time on Tinder, he introduced the app as, "A social networking site where you can find people in your area you've never met; they're in your vicinity and they're ready to meet and maybe hook up" (Team Coco, 2014). Conan's awkward definition belies Tinder's novelty in 2014, as an app that still required explanation, even while he decisively indicates that hooking up is Tinder's purpose. While using technology for sexual purposes is common (as I mentioned in the previous chapter, relations between people have long been mediated), this purpose becomes an issue in public discourse due to societal associations between sex, risk, danger, and stigma. The stigma is palpable when Conan adds, "Naturally, because I'm a creep, I'm intrigued," implying that using Tinder for hooking up is creepy.

Thus, Tinder's media coverage has sounded the alarm about the app's multiple risks. Highly publicized cases of dating violence have put Tinder front and center in their reporting, such as an Australian case in 2016 that dubbed a man the "Tinder killer" when his date died after falling off his apartment balcony (Sky News, 2016). While this case had many factors upon which to focus, such as allegations of intensive substance use, Tinder endured in headlines as the trial went on while other factors that could have exacerbated risk or violence fell to the wayside. Different "Tinder killers" have made headlines in the United States (Ramos, 2023) and New Zealand (Vlessing, 2024), with this sticky label providing attention-grabbing headlines for cases. Instead of focusing on the prevalence of sexual violence against women, these stories' focus on Tinder plays into concerns over *stranger danger*, which place the responsibility upon women to avoid and be fearful of men's potential for violence. It wraps these society-wide issues into a cautionary tale about the women who eschewed these responsibilities in the pursuit of desire and were met with terrifying consequences. More recent media depictions follow a similar framing, such as the Netflix true crime documentary *Tinder Swindler* (2022) that highlights the app's use by a financial fraudster who took advantage of many women. The work these media depictions do to interlink app usage and, by extension, women's engagement in casual sex with grave consequences elides structural problems that enable harmful behavior to be perpetrated without due punishment, as the swindler remains free at the end of the film and sexual aggression remains an often-celebrated trait of hegemonic masculinity.

More fearful reporting about Tinder has focused on associations between the app and increases in the spread of sexually transmitted infections (STIs). A highly publicized 2015 report from the US state of Rhode Island associated increases in the rate of syphilis and gonorrhea with "using social media to arrange casual and often anonymous sexual encounters" (Rhode Island Government, 2015). Although the report did not name specific apps, its media coverage drew direct associations between STI transmission rates and the use of Tinder, Grindr, and hook-up apps more generally. Even with the original report identifying that some statistical increases could be attributed to more effective testing measures, and similar increases in the state of Utah were associated with abstinence-only education, media coverage pointed the finger at dating apps (Gabbatt, 2015). Sexual health-related organizations also ran with this association, as the Los Angeles-based AIDS Healthcare Foundation created a billboard and poster campaign depicting the word "Tinder" across one silhouetted face pointing toward another face with "chlamydia" printed on it as a visual metaphor for the app introducing individuals to STIs (BBC, 2015). In Australia, the company HERO Condoms created fake Tinder profiles embodying STIs, with names like "Chadmydia" and "Gonorrheeta," with whom users could match to receive a free pack of condoms (Lieu, 2016). Tinder reacted strongly to this coverage and the billboards, sending a cease-and-desist letter to their originator, while also adding a "health safety" section to its website with functionalities to help US users find STI testing clinics (Dias, 2016). Beyond my observation of Tinder-related media articles over the years, a study of news media reporting about hook-up apps in Australia, the United Kingdom, and the United States similarly found many headlines that emphasized harassment, scams, or privacy breaches as well as articles conflating app use with STI transmission and other health risks without evidence (McCosker et al., 2019). This study also found a significant volume of articles taking a pedagogical stance, attempting to educate users on how to negotiate hook-up apps, as well as articles focused on play and non-risk-related aspects of well-being. However, the tendency for news media to foreground risk often frames dating apps as a public health problem, overshadowing reporting about their everyday use and people's agency in managing such risks (Albury et al., 2020).

While I am in favor of dating app companies helping to increase awareness of healthy sexual practices, I echo complaints about the lack of evidence regarding direct health risks, since the causal association drawn across these reports between Tinder use and acquiring an STI does not add up. Although the risk of infection can rise with an increase in the number of one's partners (no matter how a person meets them), infections do not jump through phones. The threat of health dangers serves as another way to stigmatize, discourage, and constrain app use. As famed French theorist Michel Foucault (1982) observed, with society's shift toward secularization, the religious regulation of sexuality (and populations more broadly) has given way to regulation by medicine and associated institutions in the name of health and well-being. Dating apps, through their association with sexuality, become framed as vectors for infection and counter to a healthy lifestyle.

These associations of Tinder use with risk and danger point to a moral panic that has surrounded the app throughout its popularity. Media scholar Nancy Baym (2015) highlights that moral panics often surround new technologies, and are undergirded by technological determinism as people worry about, and overinflate, what a new technology can or will do (or *make* people do). She cites Stanley Cohen (1972), the sociologist who coined the term "moral panic" in relation to concerns over Britain's youth cultures, defining moral panics as situations in which anxieties over uncontrollable forces (e.g., violence, infectious disease) become displaced onto new cultural trends. Further, youth are often the locus of moral panics, given societal efforts to control what young people do and worries that youth may become deviant or out of control. With Tinder's rapid uptake by early adults, leaving boomers like Conan O'Brien referring to it archaically as a "social networking site," the dating app itself became the threat or danger as institutions (governments, health organizations) and shapers of public discourse (media commentators) attempted to make sense of how it shifts and interfaces with sexual cultural trends.

The intersection of sexuality and technology also fuels the enduring quality of moral panics surrounding Tinder, even as the app is no longer novel. Experts in social media and sexuality Katrin Tiidenberg and Emily van der Nagel understand moral panics in this realm as reflecting a "trifecta of anxieties" at the intersection "where sex meets public life, where public life meets the internet, and where the internet meets sex" (2020, p. 21). Sex gives rise to panic in relation to morality and regulation when its practices and attendant issues are taken up in public life. The internet and its technological advances expand access to new and potentially threatening realms of public life, necessitating shifting negotiations over privacy and publicness, and largely structure contemporary access to sexual media while shaping sexual practices. This trifecta of anxieties is evident in relation to Tinder as it opens new avenues for identifying sexual partners and influences sexual practices. It overlays public space through a digital interface that shifts interactions in terms of when, where, and how people are likely to meet. And it does so through a mobile app that introduced several novel affordances. Thus, we see longstanding fears about sexual morality, death, disease, corruption of youth, and threats to traditional relationships displaced to Tinder. When these anxieties are channeled into moral panic, Tiidenberg and van der Nagel underscore that they give rise to shame, which can take on multiple forms, such as gendered shame in which women feel bad for their sexual desires or shame in relation to sexual interests (being a “creep”) or technology use (falling victim to “Tinder addiction”).

I heard the shame and stigma in relation to Tinder use repeated by my research participants in their assurances that they were not on the app for hooking up. Several of the queer women I spoke with told me that, although people they know associate Tinder with sex, they were looking for a wider array of connections: friendships, potential relationships, and even just getting to know their neighbors better. Those who had formed relationships with matches on the app downplayed its role in sparking their connection when introducing their significant other to family or friends. Even interviewees who were looking to arrange casual sexual encounters asserted that their situations were different from what was being portrayed in the media, noting that women seeking women tended to be on more even ground than heterosexual couples dealing with patriarchal hierarchies of power. They did not necessarily view Tinder-facilitated hook-ups as transactional or emotionless, and there was not the same kind of gender-specific pressure to make or deflect advances. It was not that these women did not encounter challenges in communicating clearly about why they were using Tinder – one individual remarked to me that lesbian sex was sometimes a difficult project in itself because women were not socialized to make the first move – but that their sexual encounters were less encumbered by the heteronormative and gender-biased double standards prevalent in heterosexual cultures, such as the ones that so strongly circulate on college campuses. These less-than-desirable outcomes of Tinder's entrenched association with sex for heterosexual users raise questions about the app's real dangers, such as gender-based violence, to which I return in chapter 3. While meeting a partner on Tinder has become increasingly normalized through the proliferation of dating apps and their massive uptake, the evolution of Tinder's marketing has also worked to shift the range of possibilities when it comes to the outcomes of swiping.

Tinder is for romance (?)

Operating an app that is seen as the gateway to violence, infection, or creeps is bad for business. Beyond the panics outlined in the previous section, a slew of opinion pieces, personal testimonies, and investigative articles like the Sales piece that opened this chapter simply concluded that Tinder was not useful for finding love. In a 2016 essay for the *New Inquiry*, Alicia Eler and Eve Peyser (2016) describe what they call the "Tinderization of feeling" as the reduction of intimacy into an abundance of binary choices that instantiate a cold process: "Swipe right, match, date, fuck, unmatch, rematch, repeat." Their assessment of how the app renders interactions into emotionless ("chill") exchanges resonates with scholars writing about dating apps' transactional qualities. Tinder's swipe is, indeed, binary and rapid – qualities through which the app's focal interaction can be understood as instrumental (David and Cambre, 2016). Media and communication scholars Steffen Krüger and Ane Charlotte Spilde (2020) identify trappings of commodity culture within Tinder, reflected in the "objectifying tendencies" they note are built into the interface. These tendencies include the swipe's binary logic alongside the app's emphasis on the visual – profile photos occupy most of the swipe screen's real estate – and the app's seemingly bottomless database of users. It can be argued that these features set users up to interact on and through the app as though it is a marketplace (the stereotypical dating "meat market" made digital, to which I return in the book's conclusion). As scholars run with this metaphor, identifying how user profiles convey "value" to others (Peetz, 2024), their analyses often seem to affirm op-ed accusations that meaningful relationship formation cannot happen through such a disembodied, abstracted, and market-driven digital environment. However, even if Tinder is perceived as only being good for hook-ups, sociologist Christian Licoppe (2020) notes that its dominant heterosexual user base is invested in patriarchal and heteronormative scripts that call for rationalizing sexual encounters through romance and the potential of forming a relationship. He finds that users negotiate direct messages on Tinder in a way that enables setting up "quick, but still 'proper'" (p. 86) hook-ups through the plausibility that they may lead to a relationship. To provide the conditions for this plausibility, and to retain a market base that holds strong to the traditional valorization of long-term relationships, Tinder needs to make it believable that its app is a tool for romance.

Tinder's "It Starts with a Swipe™" marketing campaign reflects the company's ongoing efforts to keep this belief alive. The campaign includes a series of short advertisements that mimic scenarios in the romantic comedy film genre. For instance, one advertisement named "Rescue" (Nudd, 2024) features actors Lana Condor and Evan Mock in a traditional-looking library (think, "dark academia" Tumblr aesthetic). Condor is balanced on a stool, reaching for a book on a high shelf. When she stumbles and falls, Mock catches her and gently returns her to the ground. As they stare into each other's eyes, she says, "Hey, thanks for making my day with your hace [*sic*]." He responds, "What?" and she shakes her head, quickly adding, "Typo – I meant, face." It is evident that they are using text messaging vernacular, especially when Mock adds "smirk emoji" later in the conversation. As the two appear to hit it off, their dialogue emerges in message bubbles around them while a narrator announces, "Meet cutes happen every day on Tinder, just not like they do in the movies." The screen goes dark as closing credits notify the viewer that the scene was "Inspired by the real Tinder® messages of Samantha & John," who have been a "couple since 2020."

Tinder's (2024a) press release introducing this video and a series of similar ones describes how they reflect users' contradictory desires. It explains that the ads fulfill the "nostalgic affinity" of the "younger generation of singles who came of age in virtual spaces" for meet cutes. However, it proceeds, these same singles might find such in-person scenarios to also be silly and awkward. The solution? Tinder. The ads, this press release, and the very definition of "meet cute" – as a charming or amusing "first encounter between romantic partners" (Merriam-Webster, 2024) – indicate that these exchanges are the first sparks of a romantic relationship and not a hook-up. The messages from real couples, which were provided to the ads' creative team, testify as evidence that Tinder can be used to find relationships and that the relationships it sparks will last.

Or, at least, the relationships Tinder initiates last more than three months. This is the fine print associated with the press release's claim (in bold) that, "A new relationship starts every three seconds, thanks to Tinder." This data point is apparently reflected in a 2023 survey commissioned by Match Group, though little information about it is available on the linked host site (at the URL aptly named tinderlove.com).

This site instead centers around the photos and stories of 22 couples who met through Tinder. Including snapshots from a variety of heterosexual and same-sex couples of multiple ethnicities who are based in different locations across the world, their stories walk the reader from the first swipe through to their relationship steps of cohabitation, proposal, and marriage. Real user stories serve as a one of Tinder's dominant promotional themes, also highlighted in Tinder's 2024 YouTube "Long story shorts" campaign in which the company recruited social media influencers to act out the first-date stories of couples who met through the app. Prior to these initiatives, the Tinder (2015a) website hosted a page of success stories, circulating them across its social media with the hashtag #swipedright. This hashtag campaign's central message (reflecting Sean Rad's excitement about "Tinder marriages") conveyed that the right way to swipe was one focused on meeting the "right" person (singular) for a long-term, romantic relationship, with marriage as the ultimate goal.

Tinder has further emphasized marriage through its support for the weddings of couples who met through the app. In fact, the company's FAQs include a question, "Will Tinder sponsor my wedding?" with the response: "While Tinder has sponsored weddings in the past, we can't make any promises, but we are always down to celebrate your nuptials" (Tinder, 2024b). The response lets users know they could receive free swag if they write to tinderstories@gotinder.com. A 2024 campaign on Tinder's Australian YouTube channel (2024) entitled *Big Tinder Wedding* shows how the company's interest in matches turned into marriage has expanded to feature LGBTQ+ users more prominently. The nine-episode mini-series follows two same-sex couples through the steps of planning their Tinder-sponsored weddings, from initial storytelling about how they met on the app all the way to their ceremonies and luxury cruise receptions. The press release announcing the series noted how it commemorates the five-year mark since Australia's marriage equality vote (Tinder, 2024c). The series could be lauded for featuring gay and lesbian couples with diverse ethnic backgrounds, as their ceremonies reflect elements of Indigenous and South Asian cultures. However, the series also conveys what scholars have noted is a double-edged sword about marriage equality struggles and their seamless progress narratives: rights are often earned through conformity to normative lifestyles and relationship formats as well as commercial consumption (Duggan, 2002; Richardson, 2005). The *Big Tinder Wedding* rewards these couples for engaging in an inherently heteronormative ritual and, from the clothes to the cakes and rings, focuses on the couples' choices about commodities framed as essential for celebrating the beginning of a marriage.

Fairly recent updates to Tinder's interface have also ushered users toward relationship-seeking, such as a category in the Explore section (introduced in 2021) titled "Looking for Love" that shows the profiles of others who have also selected this category. In 2022, Tinder also began to roll out the "Relationship Goals" feature – a profile field enabling users to announce that they are searching for one of the following: long-term partner; long-term, open to short; short-term, open to long; short-term fun; new friends; or still figuring it out. Many of my interviewees longed for such a feature, since they often had trouble telling if women on the app were looking for relationships with other women or only selected 'seeking women' to make friends. Note, however, that these options focus on relationships, with three indicating the possibility of a long-term relationship, and casual sex presumably euphemized as "fun."

Aside from the handful of users that Tinder places in the spotlight through its marketing campaigns, there are indeed those in the broader dating population who use the app for relationship-seeking. A survey of 1,038 Belgian Tinder users found that although the most common outcome of Tinder matching was not meeting up at all (sadly, ghosting is the common reality), more than 25 percent of offline Tinder encounters resulted in a committed relationship (Timmermans and Courtois, 2018). Between these outcomes, Tinder use also often leads to recurrent sexual encounters (i.e., friends with benefits and related arrangements). The study's authors, one of whom developed the aforementioned Tinder Motives Scale, trouble the line between these ongoing interactions and official relationships, noting casual sexual arrangements can and often do develop into long-term relationships. However, since Tinder emphasizes long-term relationships, the common development of intimate arrangements that do not fit squarely into one designation or another is not foregrounded in its promotional campaigns.

Even as the swipe and several of Tinder's affordances may appear to counter or limit romantic outcomes, users also have agency in how they negotiate the app and find relationships, if that is what they are seeking. Despite its "objectifying tendencies" (Krüger and Spilde, 2020), users can reinterpret the app's features, such as by viewing the asynchronous swipe as providing a longer opportunity to evaluate a potential future partner. While dating app users often lament how these technologies commodify intimacy and how their algorithmic sorting and data-driven filters can make it difficult to spark relationships, digital media scholar Łukasz Szulc (2025) draws on interviews with Polish LGBTQ+ people in the United Kingdom to highlight how they also often overcome these hurdles through reappropriation, creativity, and mixing their app use with offline flirtations (Szulc, 2025). In interviews with Tinder users in Cape Town, South Africa, anthropologist Leah Junck (2021) found the metaphor of the "rabbit hole" (think Lewis Carroll's *Alice's Adventures in Wonderland*) as appropriate to understanding their experiences, since their outcomes were never fixed – anything could happen. Her participants discussed Tinder as a gateway to that which was beyond the familiar and, despite sometimes feeling pressure to conform to sexual and relationship scripts, felt they had several access points to an emergency exit from the figurative rabbit hole: "'creeps' can be blocked, parameters adjusted, or a break from the pressures of the erotic instantly commenced with the 'delete' button" (p. 215). Deletion and account recreation offer not only a reset on one's Tinder profile and algorithmic feed but also a chance to enact different dating practices.

Tinder was for everything

Tinder's broad interpretative flexibility was evident in its early years in the playfulness with which different actors approached the app. Several culture writers made throwaway accounts, constructing profiles as – for example – a dog (Veix, 2014), a cupcake (Breslouer, 2015), or a strawberry milkshake (Bans, 2015), writing about people's amusing reactions while capitalizing on Tinder's buzzworthiness to attract readers to their magazines and online outlets. When I first started spending time on the app in 2014 and the next couple of years, a range of uses outside the conventional purposes of dating or hooking up caught my eye as forms of technological appropriation, understood as instances in which people domesticate a new technology by shaping it to their everyday lives and purposes (MacKenzie and Wajcman, 1985; Silverstone and Haddon, 1996). Ron Eglash (2004), a scholar who brings together anthropology and design with his background in cybernetics, identifies how appropriation can involve shifts in the balance of power, as those who are generally situated outside processes of technological development can claim and (re)shape a technology for their own purposes. He identified three categories of appropriation: "reinterpretation," when users redefine a technology's meaning; "adaptation," when a technology is repurposed for something aside from its dominant use; and "reinvention," as a structural or design change to the technology.

Tinder users have engaged in all three kinds of appropriation. Reinterpretation and adaptation combined as people recognized the vast possibilities of Tinder's interface. I observed users posting items for sale, such as by making a profile for an old laptop with the price and specifications in the bio, or promoting local events and music gigs by making profiles and then sending the party coordinates to those who swiped right. These users redefined Tinder as a marketplace and a local newsletter or flyer board. As I have described elsewhere (Duguay, 2020), individuals and nongovernmental organizations engaged in very specific repurposing of Tinder's affordances. Politically passionate campaigners used the app to promote their candidate of choice in the 2016 US presidential election while health and human rights organizations found that Tinder's interpretation as a hook-up app made their messages about sexual education or anti-sex trafficking especially relevant. Simultaneously, some commercial brands surprised users with profiles that were really advertisements. Perhaps most famously, a Tinder bot at South by South West (SXSW) promoted *Ex Machina* (2014) by enacting the persona of a robot character from the film (Lee, 2015).

Several other actors engaged in reinvention. Developers built third-party add-ons, such as the app Bonfire, which replaced Tinder's swipe screen with a proximity grid, much like Grindr's home screen. Individuals with programming skills developed scripts to automatically swipe right on every user profile, enabling everyday users to implement these "auto-liker" tools regardless of their coding skills, boiling the matching process down to truly a "numbers game" (Seals, 2014). One user even found that Tinder's application programming interface (API) allowed him to create a program that made users think they were talking to a match when they were simply talking to other swipers. He used this program to deceive men who thought they had matched with a woman, leaving them to confusedly hit on each other until they worked out that something was amiss (Zelenko, 2015). Beyond repurposing, these programming endeavors changed the very way that Tinder worked. They challenged how it arranged people and data, endeavoring to offer different options or enact hacks, raise problems, and play pranks (as well as engage in ethically dubious and privacy-threatening activities) in ways that revealed the technology's logic and potential weaknesses.

When appropriation happens with a tool in isolation, it can be a fairly straightforward process: no one cares much if you redefine a hammer as paperweight, use it to keep a beat, or reshape it into a metal sculpture. But apps and platforms are not isolated tools. They are simultaneously environments that engage multiple user populations as well as commercial systems, which are steered by developers, managers, and investors. For this reason, I have found it helpful to think about platform appropriation as "off-label use" (Duguay, 2020), encompassed by the range of uses that fall outside of a technology company's intended purposes for its platform. Building from the pharmacological meaning of "off-label" as a purpose not included in a medicinal drug's packaging, this concept has helped me to identify uses that contravene or exceed Tinder's prescribed use, especially when they may garner public reactions and invoke scrutiny from Match Group or privacy watchdogs. While some forms of off-label use are to be expected, such as auto-likers or sex education campaigns, those that generally attract the most attention are the uses that most starkly defy dominant expectations of what a technology is for. They challenge interpretations that are most prominently beginning to stabilize around a new technology. Therefore, political campaigning and film promotion hijinks that played on users' imaginations (and potential fears of a cold robot future) featured prominently in press coverage.

Tinder initially invited a broad understanding of its app, with the company and its spokespeople often referring to it as a tool for "social discovery" (Hess, 2014; Recode, 2016), which could include all sorts of networking purposes. However, Tinder eventually made design, policy, and discursive moves to narrow this perception. As the company began to monetize through Tinder Plus and its own authorized advertisements (discussed in chapter 4), Tinder tightened API restrictions and introduced the swipe-limit, shutting down auto-likers while attempting to constrain the app's abundance of bots. Tinder's Community Guidelines now specifically prohibit individual users from advertising, fund-raising, selling items, or campaigning, and the company has instilled pathways for organizations and brands to use its now-official marketing channels. Political engagement in relation to the app has also been funneled into "Swipe the Vote" quizzes that incorporate the swiping functionality to help users determine their political preferences. Ahead of the 2024 US election, Tinder introduced a new "Take Action Center" that included features to help users register to vote, find polling stations, and add "I voted" stickers to their profiles (Tinder, 2024d). Tinder is still involved in several aspects of consumer and public life through these kinds of commercial and civil society partnerships. However, these corporate shifts make it clear that when it comes to users, the prescribed use is dating and there are limited, official avenues for other activities. Moves to limit appropriation therefore are also efforts to shift the balance of power over Tinder's purpose back to its developers and owners. On the other hand, when it comes to brand partnerships that signal potential profits and the company's public role, off-label uses are transformed into on-label, well-defined uses if they promise to be manageable (easily overseen and controlled through specific procedures) and beneficial to Tinder's reputation or revenue.

While these stabilization mechanisms were well in place by 2020, the COVID-19 pandemic generated controversy about the role of dating apps in people's lives. When countries went into lockdown and social distancing protocols were implemented, it raised a key question: what was the purpose of an app for meeting potential sexual and romantic partners in person if you were not supposed to see people face-to-face?

Controversies are known to destabilize established meanings in relation to technologies and the sociocultural arrangements that they mediate, and a variety of actors are involved in this destabilization (Venturini, 2009). Across several countries, governments, health authorities, and public commentators warned against in-person sexual contact, with many pointing a finger at using dating apps as a high-risk activity (Belmonte, 2020; Violet Blue, 2020; Garwood-Cross et al., 2023). With fellow researchers David Myles and Christopher Dietzel (2021, 2022), I traced the response of Tinder and several other dating app companies to this controversy to see how they restored meaning and purpose to the use of their apps. One of the first moves that Tinder made was to specify directly through the app and a press release that users should keep their matches "digital" by refraining from meeting in person. In doing so, Tinder asserted that it "has always aimed to help connect people who may never have crossed paths – to break the limitations of who you would meet in the physical world" (Tinder, 2020a). The company made its Passport feature free for a period during the first wave of North American lockdowns to reinforce this notion that Tinder was for forming connections regardless of the potential of meeting in person. It further strengthened this framing by normalizing the idea of "virtual" dating in social media posts and rolling out a video chat feature for interacting synchronously in-app.

While some posts are no longer available, at the time we chronicled how Tinder's discourse about dating during the pandemic joined with the promotion of other Match Group properties and rival popular apps to (re)emphasize the search for love (Duguay et al., 2022). Using new video chat features erotically or turning to direct messages to have cybersex in place of in-person sexual activity did not come up in Tinder's pandemic era promotion. Instead, Tinder's marketing spotlighted users who noted that the pandemic was an opportunity to get to know others more deeply before getting physical. Just as the company's longstanding promotion of its app for forming long-term relationships and marriages staves off the stigma of it being used for casual sex, its pandemic promotion helped to distance Tinder further from associations with sex, an already risky activity rendered more dangerous at this time. Furthermore, messaging about finding love oriented users toward traditional notions of courtship that held the potential of stability through heteronormative monogamy (Ahmed, 2006), even within a highly unstable time. As this stability was transferred to Tinder, the app found a place within the pandemic crisis, reflected by Tinder's announcement that it saw surges in swiping and matching throughout 2020 (Hahn, 2021). Research confirms that users turned to dating apps during the pandemic to look for romantic, monogamous relationships that would restore their sense of security (Portolan and McAlister, 2022). The success of Tinder's crisis maneuvers helped the company to double down on the premise that its app is for romance, insisting that Gen Z was still using video chat and other digital means to practice "slow dating," matching, and interacting online for a prolonged amount of time before meeting in person, long after lockdowns subsided (Hinchliffe, 2022). Overall, the COVID-19 pandemic raised a particular set of circumstances during which it was possible to see multiple constituencies draw Tinder's meaning into question and to observe the company's approach to restabilization through marketing and features backing claims that the app's predominant use (especially during crisis) was for finding love.

Conclusion: Tinder's melancholic stabilization

Picking up Treena Orchard's (2024) book about dating apps, I am struck by how she describes using these apps – including Tinder – for several of the purposes I have discussed in this chapter. A medical anthropologist conducting an autoethnography, combining her life experiences into a mix of memoir and cultural critique, she describes joining several apps in mid-life, initially hopping on them out of curiosity and as a means of sexual and self-discovery. As she recounts a range of encounters, from fun and lighthearted dates to sexual escapades and eventually falling in love, she also discusses the misogynistic and sexually aggressive encounters lamented by Nancy Jo Sales and others. These negative experiences win out as the book's main theme, represented in the title, *Sticky, sexy, sad: Swipe culture and the darker side of dating apps*. Orchard does not provide a succinct definition of swipe culture but discusses its components as (1) sex – sexual activity that is fraught with gendered expectations brought by men and women, leading us to (2) gender – mainly in terms of gender inequities and patriarchal attempts by men to reclaim power over women through their behavior on apps, and (3) technology – as these apps and their swipe functionality are programmed to retain users for corporate benefit. The definitional struggles, debates, discursive framing, and moral panics discussed in this chapter belie that these components have stabilized into a common popular understanding of what Tinder is for as well as its sociotechnical impact in sexual and dating cultures. It is an app with fraught gender relations through which people often look for sex but find themselves immersed in the cogs of a cold matchmaking industry. Even if this interpretation elides users' agency and creativity in their actual dating practices, it entrenches sadness as "a by-product of the rationalization and efficiency logics embedded in dating app design" (p. 2), giving rise to what Szulc (2025) critiques as "emotional technological determinism." He uses this term to reflect the deterministic thinking through which people come to hold the belief that technologies make us feel a certain way: Tinder makes us sad. Despite experiences that counter this interpretation, such as the formation of friendships or elating sexual and romantic relationships, swipe culture and its negative connotations represent a dominant stabilization of meaning in Tinder's process of interpretative flexibility.

Even so, a contradiction often arises in discourses surrounding this disenchanted swipe culture. Although touching on cultural constructions that emerge collectively, such as gender relations, discussion of swipe culture and what to do about it often focuses on individuals. For instance, Orchard leaves readers with "key takeaways" that are presumably meant to speak to readers who are similar to her and not the bros she laments throughout her pages. She advises that we should "invest more in each other and ourselves" and "craft our unique sexual destinies" (p. 225) among other actions we can take to "make our dating galaxy more satisfying, fun, and dripping with glitter" (p. 226). Sales (2015a) similarly implies that users could or should change their behavior, such as when she marvels that they "don't stop swiping." While these authors make points about gender inequities in relation to dating apps, their focus on individual behavior resonates with postfeminist rhetoric that responsibilizes women for taking action in relation to society-wide gendered issues. British cultural theorist Angela McRobbie points out a "pathologisation of femininity" within popular culture that "is asking young women to get used to gender melancholia, and to recognise themselves and each other within its terms" (2008, p. 115). Women's feelings of depression, alienation, and immense pressure to embody femininity or womanhood in particular ways are dismissed as individual struggles, with the resulting struggle or state of melancholia located with individual women, rather than being recognized in the political and sociocultural conditions that surround them. Digital media scholar Amy Dobson (2015) builds on McRobbie's lens to identify how young women's expression of their discontent with such conditions is often dismissed as a reflection of "personal and psychological grievances to be managed individually" (p. 42). I see much of dating app commentary as illuminating gendered experiences that stem from longstanding systems and structures, which Orchard eventually locates within patriarchy, but these pieces often shift the focus to individual solutions targeting women's sadness or frustration with dating apps in ways that erase this bigger picture.

This is why, if we are to acknowledge swipe culture as the enduring interpretation of what Tinder has wrought, we need to take this stabilization as an indicator of a much larger problem. This problem becomes buried under moral panics about sex or recourses to traditional marriage as an escape from the meat market. As I have underscored throughout this chapter, the stigmatization of casual sex in heterosexual culture prevails as a means to regulate, shame, and steer people's behavior. This stigma is often brought to bear most heavily upon women, who are still faced with gendered sexual double standards and made to shoulder responsibility for not only their sexual actions but also men's sexual actions. Heterosexual culture's baggage also spreads out in ways that affect those subjected to racial and colonial hierarchies of eroticization as well as heteronormativity. In this way, longstanding, historical, and systemic gender inequities merge with the ways that sex is used to subordinate others.

Tinder is not the cause of these issues. Nor was it just naively dropped into these sociocultural arrangements. Feminist science and technology scholars assert that technologies are developed within existing gender relations and, as such, often recreate and interface with gender relations in ongoing and mutually shaping processes (Wajcman, 2010; Noble, 2018). As is evident from Tinder's origin stories, the company was born from sexual and dating cultures in which picking up was viewed as a game – one that the male cofounders admitted to losing but thought could be won with technology. Further, Tinder's promotional strategy envisioned that the app would thrive in environments with existing gendered sexual double standards, such as sororities and fraternities. The logic of capitalizing on the gender-inequitable game into which our society has rendered casual sex is indeed built into Tinder's technological design, reflected in the central swipe, algorithmic and visual assessments of attractiveness, and matches as success metrics. Though, in pivoting toward the profitability of offering the heteronormative dream of marriage and a monogamous *happily ever after*, Tinder has found reputability and longevity in its framing as an essential tool for what many people have been led to believe is a logical and necessary rite of passage. The company's shift toward romance discourse, however, further reinforces notions of shame and stigma associated with casual sex. Therefore, gender melancholia becomes dating app melancholia as think pieces and commentary accuse these technologies, often deterministically, of being cold, dark, and sad while giving rise to experiences of dating discussed at the individual or interactional level as difficult or apocalyptic – particularly for women, who are told to invest in themselves more, craft their destinies, or simply stop.

I take up the fallout of these gender relations further in chapter 3, since the structural conditions of patriarchy and misogyny experienced through Tinder and reflected, even if often reductively, in swipe culture threaten women's well-being and safety. However, the discussion needed to begin here to point out that this stabilized interpretation highlights how individual users have limited recourse when such dating app melancholia actually stems from broader societal, political, and industry-specific issues that need to be addressed on more collective levels. Importantly, although swipe culture has become a stabilized interpretation of Tinder, the debates over whether Tinder is just for fun, hooking up, or finding relationships rage on in ways indicating that closure has yet to be reached. A lack of closure means the possibility of change remains open in terms of shifting Tinder's meaning and use at both individual and societal levels.

Chapter 2

Strangers and catfish: Establishing authenticity

"Catfish," as a label for people who present themselves deceptively online, has become part of everyday vernacular. However, the term was relatively obscure prior to the debut of the documentary *Catfish* (2010) and its spin-off MTV reality show of the same name. The documentary traced the saga of Nev Schulman, filmed by his brother and best friend in an often-grainy reality style (think *Blair Witch Project* shakiness when moments get tense), as he sought to determine whether the woman with whom he formed a relationship through Facebook was really who she claimed to be. Over the course of 87 minutes, the three men examine evidence that leads them to the home of a woman nearly twice Nev's age who posted photos of someone else to gain his interest and lied about nearly every biographical detail. After the reveal, the woman's husband summarizes the situation through a story he tells the cameras:

> They used to tank cod from Alaska all the way to China. They'd keep them in vats in the ship. By the time the codfish reached China, the flesh was mush and tasteless. So this guy came up with the idea that if you put these cods in these big vats, put some catfish in with them and the catfish will keep the cod agile. And there are those people who are catfish in life. And they keep you on your toes. They keep you guessing, they keep you thinking, they keep you fresh. And I thank God for the catfish because we would be droll, boring and dull if we didn't have somebody nipping at our fin. – Vince Pierce, *Catfish* (2010)

While this parable lacks evidence as to whether catfish and cod were ever really shipped together and media commentators have traced the story's origin to a 1990s preacher whom Pierce may be paraphrasing (Travis, 2022), this story sets the stage for the documentary's title. Through this prominence, catfishing has become a term for a specific form of deception that happens online through digital media platforms and technologies. Notably, catfishing most frequently relates to deception in interpersonal relationships – those intended to form friendly, romantic, or sexual relationships – and not other kinds of exchanges in which one party's identity is unknown. In contrast, an unsolicited email requesting money or advertising services from an unknown sender is simply "spam." Online attempts at identity theft are often referred to as "phishing" – a term that is closer to metaphors about lures or that view the internet as a vast sea in which we are all swimming. However, catfish has stuck as a term for more personal online deception in the process of getting to know someone.

Catfish: The TV Show (2012–present) transforms the documentary's phases into a repeatable narrative template that depicts the intricacies of online deception, attracting viewers by bolstering their fear of falling prey and through the spectacle of identifying the elusive catfish. Each episode begins with an individual – dubbed "the hopeful" – coming to Nev Schulman, who has been propelled from his documentary fame into a television career, and his cohosts with concerns that they are the victim of deception. Schulman and his team then investigate the situation, scrutinizing the potential catfish's photos and correspondence, eventually arranging an in-person meeting between the catfish and the hopeful. This meeting is the episode's climax as an often-emotional scene in which the hopeful realizes they have been fooled and the catfish comes clean, sometimes only apologizing after Schulman admonishes them for lying.

Although these productions bring another layer of mediatization to such situations, the documentary and the television show reflect aspects of digital displays of authenticity that are highly relevant in relation to Tinder and dating apps more broadly. Media scholar Michael Lovelock (2017) observes, "the catfish has come to circulate as a cultural myth that fixes certain meanings and norms of usage to [social networking sites]" (p. 208). The shocking reveals reinforce the notion of an online and offline divide in which the offline version of oneself is taken to be the most authentic version. To be authentic across this divide is to ensure that the online self and the offline self match. When individuals fail to convey this congruence, not only are they are depicted in the show as using social media in the wrong way, but they are also conveyed as failing to come to terms with their "true" self. Schulman often walks the catfish through a process of reflective self-acceptance. In follow-up episodes, former catfish are depicted as now fully self-realized, authentic individuals who love themselves for who they are and act with total congruence across online and offline realms of their lives. Thus, this congruence is expected when it comes to self-presentation on dating apps.

Even so, this neatly packaged reform story glosses over the way that catfish on the show often conceal details or deceive interlocutors concerning particular qualities that are more broadly understood as unattractive and undesirable. Several catfish choose personas and photos that match normative beauty ideals, such as being youthful and skinny, and that evade the punishing hierarchies of erotic capital that valorize white supremacy, cisgender expression, high socioeconomic status, and other privileged identity categories (Daroya, 2018). Their deceptive self-presentations do not reflect a lack of self-acceptance so much as knowledge and, perhaps, lived experience of the lack of others' acceptance toward certain bodies and positionalities. The show centers these individuals' failure to attain such standards of attractiveness through what media scholar Alicia Kozma (2018) terms "shame as entertainment" or "shametainment" (p. 468), ignoring the social structures that render certain identities normative and attractive while others are discarded with a left swipe as stigmatized, deviant, and undesirable. Outside the show's framing, catfish could be understood as exercising an ingenuity for connecting with others despite prevalent biases and prejudices – even if such connection is short-lived. Although their strategies of deception are often more extreme than the little lies daters may tell on an app, they illustrate the intense pressure people feel to depict themselves in alignment with rigid parameters of desirability.

In a reality where certain behavioral norms have become expected on social media and apps, especially dating apps, and in which desirability is often conflated with trustworthiness, this chapter takes up the complexity of authenticity in relation to Tinder. It considers two ways that Tinder has attempted to alleviate authenticity concerns: first, by importing social media data into user profiles and, second, through the more recent implementation of profile verification and modes of visual authentication. There is, however, a mismatch between the app's avenues for establishing authenticity and the approaches that users take. The chapter later raises this contrast by exploring how users convey authenticity, often through self-presentations that put them in alignment with ideals of attractiveness, and how others evaluate such displays and discern the overarching authenticity of their matches. These processes of verification that users take upon themselves are especially important, as they foster a sense of safety and familiarity in advance of meeting in person. Before considering Tinder specifically, I first lay the groundwork for this chapter by discussing popular and scholarly definitions of the very slippery but common concept of authenticity in relation to digital interactions.

Authenticity: Selves, safety, and situations

With the prevalence of public, online displays within contemporary internet culture, there has been an increase in popular and scholarly discourse concerning authenticity. The rise of microcelebrity, as an imperative toward digital self-branding in the 2000s and 2010s (Senft, 2013), has given way to an influencer industry wherein one's paycheck depends upon the construction of a seemingly authentic digital persona. In full circle, everyday people feel compelled to mimic influencers' self-presentational styles to gain any notice within the impoverished digital attention economy (Abidin, 2018; Bishop, 2023). One's self does not seamlessly translate to online contexts; scholars have long made the point that it is necessary to write, post, or (now) record and livestream oneself into being (Sundén, 2002; boyd, 2014). For these reasons, viewers and followers question the authenticity of others' online self-presentations: Can I trust this person? Is she depicting who she really is? Is he relatable? Do I *get* them?

These seemingly digital-age concerns also touch on longer-running philosophical and sociological debates about the nature of the self, the considerations involved in constructing a public persona, and the context-dependency of authenticity. While a proliferation of understandings surrounding the *what, how,* and *why* of authenticity and its many meanings abound (Abidin, 2023), the following subsections focus on three particular conceptualizations of this phenomenon and their relevance for dating as well as digital sociality. As we will see, these conceptualizations are entangled in how Tinder mandates authenticity as well as how its users present and evaluate others based on overlapping notions of authenticity.

A true self

Authenticity as a reflection of one's true self is the most prominent understanding of this concept in popular culture. Many celebrities and influencers refer to being "real" and are adamant that they convey authenticity despite the pressures to perform for press, cameras, or social media fans. However, social theorist Anthony Giddens (1991a) observes that the notion of an individualized identity, or self, is a modern development. With the establishment of impersonal industrial and capitalist systems that structure everyday life, trust between people no longer stems from "personalised connections within the local community and kinship networks" but rather "becomes a project to be 'worked at' by the parties involved, and demands the *opening of the individual to the other*" (p. 121, emphasis in original). Giddens describes this opening as a "mutual process of self-disclosure" (p. 121) but, to engage in this process, one must have specific, seemingly unique qualities and characteristics to disclose. Cultivating these qualities involves the work of picking them from among various options provided by systems and structures in modern and late modern times, among which a range of *experts* – from self-help gurus to wellness instructors – provide advice for self-optimization. In this way, building an identity becomes what Giddens calls a "reflexive project" (p. 114), and while it has the capacity to always be in flux, we develop a coherent and well-practiced narrative through our repetition of choices and their expression in daily routines. Giddens (1991b) declares, "The authentic person is one who knows herself and is able to reveal that knowledge to the other, discursively and in the behavioural sphere" (p. 187). As a person's sense of self becomes routine and solidifies, it becomes possible to express identity in a coherent biography that looks and feels true – truer than the options that have been eschewed – to the individual expressing it and those surrounding them.

It is possible to consider more deeply how this conceptualization of authenticity has developed in relation to political and economic structures. As neoliberal approaches to government have reduced social programs and support for community structures, individuals have been encouraged to develop independence and resilience. Simultaneously, as that independence is gained through financial stability stemming from participation in the workforce and by purchasing one's needs, it positions most people's primary role in society as consumers. Since consumers make many choices about what they purchase, branding has become a means to tap into and shape people's sense of identity. As media scholar Sarah Banet-Weiser (2012) explains, "the process of branding impacts the way we understand who we are, how we organize ourselves in the world, what stories we tell ourselves about ourselves" (p. 5). Through the mechanisms advertisers use to convince consumers that products are an expression of the self, purchasing practices and showing off commodities (when not seen as overly done or *selling out*) become a central mode of expressing what we believe to be our true selves. Hence, those who work in the personalized sphere of influencer advertising (or even just influencers who must advertise to sustain their main creative practice) must espouse with conviction how the products they sell align with their passions (Cunningham and Craig, 2017; Duffy, 2017). For everyday people, brand culture renders the things we own and the products we favor into reflections of us.

These social, political, and economic dynamics have solidified the notion of identity into a singular self, comprised of a unique combination of interests, tastes, hobbies, products, expenditures, and dispositions. Such a nuanced self is difficult to represent online, since it can become fragmented through text boxes and static selfies. When a disparity is perceived between what an individual displays online and how that person may act offline, their true self is assumed to be the offline, unmediated version. Such an assumption persists despite evidence that people use digital technologies to emphasize and express aspects of themselves that may be constrained in their offline contexts, such as transgender people feeling more empowered to assert their pronouns and chosen name online (Dame-Griff, 2023). Nevertheless, longstanding assumptions about mediated communication bolstering deception and having less veracity than in-person communication have endured into the internet age (Baym, 2015). These assumptions are reflected in the realm of mediated dating, spanning from researchers' preoccupations with the degree of frankness in newspaper personals to studies seeking to gauge the levels of deception in online dating profiles (Laner and Kamel, 1978; Ellison et al., 2011). Into the 2000s, research found that the negative sentiment attached to online dating stemmed from the suspicion that deception was rampant on these sites and that those who were willing to subject themselves to such a risk had to be desperate to find a partner (Anderson, 2005). Deception across these studies has been consistently operationalized as a discrepancy between online and offline self-presentations.

Safety

Authenticity's coupling with safety has become solidified through public and corporate responses to the affordances and qualities of digital interaction. Worries about not knowing who you are talking with online abounded in relation to the early internet, with public discourse propelling fears about strangers in cyberspace. In one sense, these reactions were legitimate responses to a communication form that was very different from in-person interaction, and scholars set about examining how reduced or altered social cues in early online environments affected sociality (Walther, 1992). The possibilities and pitfalls of early online interactions were reflected in Peter Steiner's iconic 1993 *New Yorker* cartoon depicting a dog at a computer explaining to a canine friend, "On the Internet, nobody knows you're a dog." The cartoon reflected a preoccupation with the inability to verify one's identity online, about which Nancy Baym observes, "Whether this cartoon represents a dream or a nightmare depends on whether one is the dog or the fool unknowingly talking to the dog" (2015, p. 38). The dream of cyberspace comprised the possibilities it posed for expressing oneself beyond physical boundaries and in different modalities, reflected in creative usernames, avatars, emoji, and lively internet speak comprising digitally infused identity presentations (Livia, 2002; McCulloch, 2019). However, the public frequently latched on to the nightmare interpretation, tapping into and fueling fears of being something much worse than a fool: a victim.

Cultural artifacts beyond contemporary depictions of catfish have perpetuated the notion that anonymity is dangerous. One that stands out starkly in my memory is Dateline NBC's television show *To Catch a Predator* (2004–7), which aimed to identify what its host, Chris Hansen, called "potential sexual predators" (NPR, 2007). The producers sought to fulfill this mission by having individuals in chatrooms pose as minors and, when adult men initiated sexual discussions with these minors, the men were invited to meet at a physical location. When the men arrived, Hansen then confronted them, and they were often detained by police. Although this show was accused of engaging in entrapment and follows a reverse format to the catfish broadcasts (those developing the show are the ones engaging in deception), it undoubtedly conveyed the message that predators were lurking everywhere online and bolstered fears over children's safety. Justine Cassell and Meg Cramer (2008) note similarly strong messages in public service announcements airing in the 2000s, which depicted young women as especially at risk of internet predation. These scholars argue that fears about safety have long been used to curtail girls' and women's access to, and use of, technologies – from landline telephones to computers – and to justify their surveillance.

Many women have internalized these messages about the need to be fearful and risk-averse when using digital technologies. As women are often told that they must manage their own behavior to remain safe, especially from the threat of sexual violence, they are overburdened with the responsibility to make decisions in hopes of avoiding culpability for their own harm. For instance, interview research with Australians on dating websites in the mid-2000s detailed how women felt they were more at risk of physical violence than men, whereas men reported few fears of physical threats (Couch and Liamputtong, 2007). One participant, Eliza, elaborated the many steps she took to ensure her safety when meeting up with strangers from the dating website, from having her daughter photograph her date's license plate to ensuring that several other people met her date before she spent time alone with him. Similarly, interviews with female Tinder users demonstrate an awareness of the need to take responsibility for their safety, deflecting invitations from men who feel perfectly comfortable having them over to their houses on the first date, and avoiding behavior that could invoke victim-blaming in the face of unwanted sexual advances or assault (Farvid and Aisher, 2016). Further, Katherine Angel (2021) observes that women's expression of desire, such as by joining a dating website or app, can be perceived as abandoning their responsibility to guard against sexual violence from men. She notes how women's use of dating apps is often galvanized as evidence against them in rape and assault trials: "You can't be raped, in other words, by someone you met on Tinder – by someone you are thought to have met out of a confident desire for sex" (p. 11). While women encounter real threats to their safety through Tinder, as explored in the next chapter, this call for them to be unrelentingly vigilant about their safety shapes their decisions about whether and how to use the app.

With Tinder marketed as an app for *everyone* – the majority of whom are assumed to be heterosexual – notions that Tinder is unsafe can threaten its bottom line. Without women, heterosexual men have no need to be on the app. In efforts to bolster perceptions of user safety, social media and tech corporations have demanded an ever-expansive amount of information from their users. This contrasts with the majority of early internet websites, forums, and chatrooms, which required little identifying information, widely affording pseudonymity through usernames (van der Nagel, 2017). This design choice of pseudonymity aligned with ideals about the internet as a new frontier for free speech – famously celebrated in John Perry Barlow's (2019) "A declaration of the independence of cyberspace," which was originally penned in 1996. It was complemented by online communities' social norms for regulating behavior without requiring the use of legal names (Kennedy et al., 2016). However, many social media platforms were developed with the intention for individuals to be recognizable in ways beyond online self-referentiality. MySpace, Friendster, Twitter, and Facebook encouraged connecting with individuals not only based on their online self-presentation but also because of information known about them offline, urging users to connect with – for instance – offline friends, distant ties, journalists, and known celebrities. With the internet's visual turn, as photos and streaming video became widely integrated into platforms due to greater technical capacity, visual self-presentations became expected on social media and dating apps alike (Gosine, 2007), with the lack of a face photo indicating that a user has something to hide.

Alongside platforms requesting increasing amounts of data from users to facilitate these connections, multiple modes of verification were integrated into online spaces. Authenticating users through their email addresses, third-party verification (e.g., logging in to one account through a different account), and, eventually, two-factor authentication through mobile phones became prevalent. While platforms often justified these forms of verification as safety measures, the ability to consolidate information about individuals under real names and visual likeness also allows for building more comprehensive databases, which can fuel the profits of technology corporations relying on data-driven advertising or data reselling. Through panics about online strangers and platforms requiring that no one remains a stranger, authenticity is often taken to mean congruence across, and knowledge of, an individual's singular identity that is linked to their legal name and physical likeness.

Contextual performances

Authenticity is also a performance in relation to a specific context. This understanding of authenticity is less prominent in public consciousness, perhaps because of its contrast with notions that authenticity reflects a true self. However, the choices that one makes about their identity – the hobbies, tastes, and preferences they build it with – only become legible through their congruence with the surrounding circumstances. Sociologist Erving Goffman (1959) developed the idea that we perform the self and that these performances differ across contexts. He observed that individuals performed in certain ways among specific audiences in public settings, which he referred to metaphorically as the front stage. In contrast, these same individuals performed very differently when away from these public audiences in what Goffman called the backstage. For example, in the classroom, I wear somewhat formal clothing, speak loudly, and gesture toward my slides with (sometimes too much) enthusiasm in front of an audience of students. This behavior is different from when I return home, change into sweatpants, and relax on the couch with my cat and the latest Netflix reality show. It might be easy to assume that this backstage is the most authentic but Goffman defines the backstage as "a place, relative to a given performance, where the impression fostered by the performance is knowingly contradicted as a matter of course" (p. 114). In this backstage, I can be thoroughly entertained by a consumption-focused semi-scripted real estate television show depicting faux female empowerment even though my amusement may contradict the lesson I just taught critiquing such discourses. However, I am just as authentic in both spaces because my performances – as a teacher and, later, as cat mom and reality TV fan – respond to the cues surrounding me. Since the backstage is conducive to developing impressions for the front stage, I might scribble some critical notes when the show's credits roll and work them into my next lecture. After all, what makes a performance read as authentic is the ability to give the sense that one is not performing at all. This is another reason why internalizing a solid and static sense of self makes it easier to convey authenticity because then the performance can become invisible to the one enacting it. Dating profiles often reflect a polished front stage performance, which can be augmented through photo editing or stretching small details, but such embellishments can make the performance difficult to recreate on a first date since in-person performances often give off more than a profile lets on (Ellison et al., 2011).

As a symbolic interactionist, Goffman often wrote about people in their immediate environments. He discussed norms, modes of speech, and details about people's settings as they performed aspects of their identity for each other. However, his work was not always attuned to the broader ways that culture, as a shared set of values and worldviews that are often reflected in media, artifacts, and people's broader contexts, provides the substance and scaffolding for performances of authenticity. In his search for authenticity in Chicago's urban blues clubs, ethnographer David Grazian's (2003) consideration of culture led him to boil authenticity down to two related attributes: the ability of a place, event, or – I would add – a person to conform to "a set of expectations regarding how such a thing ought to look, sound, and feel" (p. 10) and the credibility of a performance to appear natural and effortless. The bars that seem the most authentic to those immersed in blues culture are ones that align with fans' expectations while not appearing contrived. These bars are starkly different from those catering to tourists who, in their lack of blues savviness, are easily taken in by try-hard replicas.

Thinking about Grazian's takeaways for authenticity in the context of dating, individuals who meet others' expectations and who do not seem to be trying too hard are likely to be seen as authentic. I see the expectations for appearing authentic on and through a dating app as stemming from two layers of context: the app's immediate pretense and affordances as well as the broader sociocultural context in which daters are situated. Social media and apps have dominant uses and norms that arise with their popular uptake, which constitute their platform vernacular (Gibbs et al., 2015). Within this platform vernacular, individuals signal that they belong by following these norms and using the platforms' features in expected ways. In my study of off-label uses of Tinder, mentioned in the previous chapter, it was evident when individuals contravened this platform vernacular because others had strong reactions to their expectations being violated as they were aghast at – for example – being sold a detox tea when they were looking for love. *Catfish: The TV Show* further illustrates notions of a correct and authentic way to use social media when the host shames catfish for lying in their profiles or stealing others' photos.

The wider contextual layer to which individuals' authenticity performances must conform is that which makes people legible as social, political, economic, and cultural beings. Individuals are interpreted through the lenses of gender, race, financial status, age, and other factors that are socially constructed and imbued with differential value along hierarchies of power. When individuals are not legible in normative categories, such as by defying heteronormativity through LGBTQ+ identities or violating normative sexual expectations through kinky practices or polyamory, they may violate others' expectations of who an acceptable sexual or romantic partner is. Since the contexts that scaffold hierarchies of desirability and normativity are often beyond an individual's control, people tend to self-present in ways that are congruent with expectations in these contexts and that enable them to be perceived as authentic. In this sense, authenticity can be thought of as achieving conformity or belonging. Though, when one's self-presentation cannot fulfill others' normative expectations, or when conforming becomes unbearable, it becomes difficult to blend in without altering details about oneself or leaving the context altogether.

Tinder's authenticity solutions

Tinder launched at a time when heterosexual daters were still more accustomed to sparking new acquaintances in public spaces than online (Bergström, 2021). The app was released into an existing context of concern over online strangers and doubt that online connections could ever be as real or trustworthy as those formed offline. Tinder's design followed suit with platforms' trend toward demanding identifying information from their users. Its features for swiping on those nearby heightened the potential to meet others in person at an accelerated pace compared to practices on websites that were not proximity-based (Quiroz, 2013). For these reasons, Tinder has had a stake in proving that its users are authentic in all three senses of the term: they are who they say they are offline; they are safe to interact with and to meet; and they fulfill normative expectations of behavior and attractiveness – they are hot! To achieve this, Tinder has centered particular design choices and rationalized them as means for establishing users' authenticity. This section examines how key app mechanisms of social media integration and visual verification are positioned in service of establishing user authenticity.

Authenticity through social media

Tinder launched with the requirement for users to log in using their Facebook account. In 2015, it added the ability for users to connect their Instagram account (Tinder, 2015b), followed by the integration of theme songs and favorite artists from Spotify in 2016 (Tinder, 2016b). From its earliest days, Tinder has been intertwined with users' social media presence, reconfiguring their networked connections, tastes, and social media self-expression to attest to who they are as daters.

When I ran my first walkthrough of Tinder in 2014, I was met with a large blue button upon opening the app, prompting me to log in through Facebook. Doing so not only initiated the creation of my Tinder account but also pre-populated my profile with data from Facebook including my first name, age, and gender, and information about my likes and friends to display when I encountered other users with those same preferences or connections. Photos could also only be added once they had been posted to a Facebook album that was public or, at least, visible to my friends on that platform. Tinder's (2014) FAQs from that same year asserted that this integration was necessary: "We use Facebook to make sure you are matched with real people who share similar interests and common friends." This explanation speaks to the notion of authenticity in terms of having a coherent identity characterized by specific interests, rendered legible through their instantiation as categories on Facebook but also with the implication that such interests – hobbies, music tastes, etc. – are enacted offline, allowing for their congruent discussion with potential dates. Associating being real with having friends in common also seeks to establish connections that bridge perceptions of an online/offline divide, since people have been known to often add people with whom they interact in person as Facebook friends (Hogan, 2013; Baym, 2015). Centering friends of friends as ideal potential dates, such as through Tinder's use of this Facebook data to indicate mutual friend connections on profiles, also reinforces the assumption that friends can vouch for the authenticity and trustworthiness of those in their network. Even so, the users I spoke with were more likely to avoid friends of friends than to swipe right on them. One of my interviewees found it particularly suspicious if someone was shown as a mutual friend but she had never been introduced to that person, noting that perhaps it was a red flag because if her friends thought they were compatible then they would have already been introduced.

Facebook was the logical platform of choice for integration due to its emphasis on users adhering to a singular expression of identity that could be cross-checked with information offline and from other sources. The first form of this verification showed up in Facebook's initial requirement for new users to have university-issued email addresses, providing proof that they were known to an institution under this same identity. When Facebook expanded to include users with any kind of email address, the platform's emphasis on identifiability was underscored through its "real name" policy requiring people to use "the name they use in everyday life" (Meta, 2025a) on their profiles – notably, this phrasing has remained the same across years (Haimson and Hoffmann, 2016). While this criterion implies that the names used in a social context are sufficient, Facebook specifies that a user's name should appear on official identification documents, such as government-issued IDs, like driver's licenses, or IDs issued by third parties, such as employee IDs or student cards, which are also likely to be granted based on legal documentation. These forms of identification are required to clear up contestations between Facebook and users about profile names.

Numerous scholars have documented how Facebook's real name policy has led to account removals and privacy breaches for people whose legal identities are stigmatized while putting them at risk of discrimination or violence. Studies have considered the policy's repercussions for abuse survivors, drag queens who may not be 'out' to others in their lives, transgender users in states where their identities are not legally recognized, and people for whom their legal names simply defy the assumption that last names must conform to white Anglo-Saxon conventions, such as Indigenous users (Lingel and Golub, 2015; Haimson and Hoffmann, 2016). Such policing and emphasis on presenting a singular identity harks back to Mark Zuckerberg's notorious philosophy:

"Having two identities for yourself is an example of a lack of integrity" (Kirkpatrick, 2010, p. 199). Privacy and data ethics scholar Michael Zimmer (2010) points out that not only does this philosophy ignore Goffman's (1959) observations that it is completely reasonable and common for people to present different versions of themselves in different contexts, but it also encourages people to share everything seamlessly and equally with everyone they know. This philosophy undergirds the very structure of Facebook, giving rise to an architecture designed to garner vast amounts of user data, leading to its success as an advertising behemoth.

While Meta – the parent company of Facebook, Instagram, and WhatsApp – has shifted away from "real names" in its discourse, much of this ethos remains more than a decade following Zuckerberg's declaration. Although Meta's (2025b) Community Standards now include a section entitled "Integrity and Authenticity," this shift in terminology still designates "authentic identity" as associated with the name that one uses in everyday life, once again centering a person's name as the crux of their identity and assuming that it is unchanging. Over time, Instagram and (more recently) Facebook have integrated features that allow users to create multiple linked accounts (Meta, 2023), though these accounts are intended to be connected to one main account through which a user remains identifiable to the platform (remember, treating users as singular entities makes for a more accurate back-end database). Even so, media scholar Taina Bucher (2021) discusses how Zuckerberg's assertions that Facebook is "grounded in reality" have imbued this ideal of authenticity throughout Facebook and not only in its naming policy. Facebook demands this singular version of authenticity through the biographical narratives that user timelines generate, the profile template with fields for real-life details about work and education, and – as others have also observed (Cho, 2017) – the platform's default publicness that encourages unitary self-expression across audiences and contexts.

Facebook's association of authenticity with "real" offline selves has also spilled over to Instagram. Scholars studying this platform observe that while its norms and design have accommodated the creation of multiple accounts for much longer than Facebook, Instagram comes with the "aesthetic expectation" that users display a curated and polished self-representation (Leaver et al., 2020). Users may create Finstas – "fake Instagram" accounts – to depict a backstage self-presentation to close friends and family while maintaining a prominent and public account – the Rinsta – to represent them more widely. It is this prominent account, which often includes variations of a user's legal name, visual likeness, and other identifiers (e.g., a link to one's personal website), that circulates most widely and is most likely the Instagram account that a user will connect with Tinder. Within the dating app, Instagram photos display under the Facebook-imported information on profiles as additional evidence of a user's attractiveness, showcasing selfies, travel photos, and other trappings of life that are commonly shared on Instagram.

The social media platforms that Tinder integrates into its design shape normative expectations for user profiles. In essence, users must date with their Facebook and Instagram selves and any violation of the self-presentational standards on either of these platforms (once connected) sets off red flags when spotted through Tinder. Facebook is not a very sexy platform. Users manage the information and photos they post in relation to multiple audiences and often only share the "lowest common denominator" (Hogan, 2010) of acceptable content across their Facebook friends, who often include colleagues, acquaintances, and family members. Tinder photos can also be scrutinized through this lens: if someone shares a particularly sexual image, then others are likely to see it through a Facebook-defined lens of (un)acceptability. Instead of thinking, "Oh, that's hot" in a dating context, a user evaluating another's profile is more likely to think, "Wow, that person posted this to Facebook, what kind of judgment do they have?" Similarly, the basic information that Tinder has pulled from Facebook, alongside Tinder's prominent placement of education and employment fields, mimics how Facebook's ideal authentic user is "reflective of a white, middle-class, affluent and liberal life trajectory" (Bucher, 2021, p. 85). Individuals who come across as authentic and desirable through data and templates ported from Facebook are those who have normative and impressive information to fulfill these categories.

To an even greater extent, Instagram's platform vernacular and aesthetics cater to aspirations of what Alice Marwick (2015) calls "Instafame," with users seeking attention through highly edited content that reflects displays of celebrity and luxury. These practices highlight how glamour has become a dominant Instagram aesthetic, as everyday people mimic the highly stylized content of influencers (Hearn and Banet-Weiser, 2020), showcasing brands and striving toward normative beauty ideals in ways that are made to appear effortless although they are highly stylized (Abidin, 2016). Raising the bar even further, amid the saturation of seemingly flawless displays on Instagram, influencers have learned to draw attention through careful performances of calibrated amateurism (Abidin, 2017), which foster authenticity through contrived displays of unscripted, raw, emotional, and messy sides of life. While these practices trickle into the lives of everyday and aspirational users hoping to accrue attention, they demand emotional and aesthetic labor to achieve raw but carefully deployed displays that others feel are relatable and convey a sense of intimacy (Reade, 2020). Therefore, the integration of Instagram photos into Tinder profiles – alongside and not replacing the app's main profile photos gleaned from Facebook – raises the stakes of self-presentation. It asks users to display how adept they are at deploying the complex stylized platform vernaculars that Instagram demands, proving that they too can be desirable on a platform alongside celebrities like the Kardashians and the latest popular influencers while still coming across as relatable. Together, appeasing Tinder's once-mandatory Facebook integration and opting into displaying Instagram photos allows a user to assert authenticity on multiple levels. It conveys to others, "Here I am as a safe, Facebook-friendly individual with a singular coherent biography" and, simultaneously, "Look at how I can meet Instagram's contextual affordances and demands for adherence to the standards of attractiveness propelled by popular culture." Displays of Facebook interests and Instagram photos showcasing travel or time spent with friends also provide photographic evidence of an offline self that is consistently depicted online. Desirability on Tinder is conveyed by the ability to satisfy these multiple levels of authenticity.

The permeation of Meta's approach to authenticity into Tinder's design is further demonstrated through Tinder's developers choosing certain platforms to integrate while others have been omitted. Given that Facebook has a close partnership with Spotify (Vonderau, 2019), which enables data-sharing and the ability to login using one's Facebook account, it makes sense for Tinder to allow Spotify content in user profiles as an extension of dating with one's Facebook self. In my observations spanning 2014–16, I noticed many users sharing their Snapchat handles in their profile biographies. However, Snapchat was never officially integrated into Tinder profiles, not as a login option nor a profile field. Snapchat has radically different affordances from Facebook: it enables pseudonymous communication and its content is ephemeral, since photos and chats disappear after a limited amount of time. While Instagram's Stories feature also allows users to post images or videos for a short duration, an affordance often employed by users to showcase more banal and ordinary aspects of life (Reade, 2020), Instagram still prominently displays enduring posts in the app's central feed – and this static feed is visible through Tinder while Instagram Stories is not. In terms of user practices, Snapchat's affordances for sending spontaneous and silly content have contributed to its uptake, mainly among teens and younger adults, for entertainment and enjoyment (Bayer et al., 2016; Alhabash and Ma, 2017). These uses align well with Tinder's common uptake for entertainment, as discussed in the previous chapter. However, with less information conveyed through profiles and ephemeral content, user identities can be difficult to ascertain and content challenging to regulate. A thread on the Tinder subreddit reflects that these tensions have endured over time (Dry_Conversation7090, 2022), as users share their experiences with Tinder matches asking to be added to Snapchat. Some warned that this request often indicated that a user was a sex worker looking to sell nude photos and sexual content, or a "scammer" watching for those susceptible to financial fraud. However, other posters noted that the intentions and uses of Snapchat by Tinder matches differed by region and age, as they found that it was more common among younger daters to use Snapchat to get to know romantic connections and Snapchat was more commonly used for socializing in certain countries. Some individuals attested to using Snapchat as a safer way to get to know a match than giving out a phone number and that it allowed for more sexual chatting than what felt permitted or comfortable on Tinder.

Given that Snapchat enables users to interact without grounding their profiles or expressions in a "real" self that can be held accountable through moderation as well as social expectations, it is unsurprising that Tinder has not integrated Snapchat. Tinder did, however, once experiment with offering users similar functionality in 2014 as a feature called Moments (Rao, 2014). This feature allowed users to share photos, which could be playfully edited through text, drawing, and filters similar to Snapchat's photo-editing functions, and post them for 24 hours. Differing from the ability to target certain audiences or send one-on-one Snaps, Tinder

Moments were broadcast to all of one's matches, who could swipe right to like them or left to dismiss them, reporting back to the poster the number of total likes. This requirement for Moments to be viewable across matches perpetuated the notion of authenticity as a true self that should be equally expressed across audiences, contrasting with design choices allowing for tailored self-expression. Despite then-CEO Sean Rad reporting that Moments sparked "a massive increase in conversations and post-match engagement" (Crook, 2015a), the feature was quietly retired the following year in 2015. While no reason was given for its removal, it is notable that even when Moments was functional, people did not stop relocating their conversations to Snapchat and elsewhere, indicating that the existing social media integration was not enough for many users when it came to their efforts to truly get to know a match.

Visual verification

Toward the end of the 2010s, Tinder no longer required users to create an account through Facebook. Articles gave advice on how to protect one's privacy by logging in with a phone number and two-factor authentication (Ellis, 2019), eventually showcasing a range of options for logging in through Google or Apple ID, Facebook, or with a phone number (Johnson, 2021). The move away from requiring Facebook verification coincided with the same change in other popular dating apps, such as Hinge and Bumble, as well as the first murmurs that Facebook planned to launch its own dating functionality (Perez, 2018). Dating app companies may have been preparing for competition with Facebook or perhaps simply adjusting to a landscape in which their users were stratified across platforms, especially with younger users' uptake of Instagram and Snapchat (Perrin and Anderson, 2019), making a single platform login counterintuitive. From 2020 onward, authenticity within the app became less contingent on the use of social media and more focused on consistent visual self-representation.

Tinder has always showcased users in the swipe feed by featuring their profile photos, shifting the app's design over time so that photos stretch across the smartphone's screen with minimal textual information superimposed on them. In 2024, I observed that Tinder profiles included space for up to nine photos, uploaded from the phone's library or taken with the camera (discarding the Facebook photo album requirement entirely). Users could also upload "loops," similar to Instagram's "boomerangs" in which videos play backward and forward on a continuous loop. Below the upload buttons, users are notified that the "Smart Photos" feature "continuously tests all your profile photos and picks the best one to show first." The app swaps the first photo that other users see, testing out which one will garner the most positive reactions, and prioritizes the photo that others right-swipe on most. Tinder's (2016c) Newsroom announcement launching Smart Photos boasts that this "brand new algorithm" led to a "12% increase in matches" for users during testing. The images in this announcement and throughout Tinder's promotional materials model the practice of mainly posting profile photos of one's face.

Selfies, as digital self-portraits often taken with a phone's front-facing camera, have become a primary mode of self-presentation across platforms and apps as the internet has increasingly accommodated visual media. However, selfies have a fraught and ambivalent relationship with authenticity (Senft and Baym, 2015; Tiidenberg, 2018), since they are subjectively evaluated for their form, content, and context. Others consider how much a selfie has been manipulated, from using a filter that touches up blemishes to the major fabrication involved in creating deepfakes. Onlookers also evaluate how, where, and with whom the person in the selfie is posing, and how appropriate the selfie is in the context of its staging (e.g., the acceptability of a funeral selfie compared to a wedding selfie) as well as the platform where it is shared. While Tinder users evaluate others' profile photos on these multiple levels, the Smart Photos feature promises to put the most successful (read: most seemingly authentic) photo first, delegating to algorithms a task that is already challenging for humans. Meanwhile, the loops functionality encourages users to post short video content that provides more visual information about their appearance and context. Video-based self-presentations that involve movement and multidimensional perspective and remain consistent are likely to be perceived as more difficult to fake than static images, even if loops are capped at just two seconds.

Tinder further promises to confirm others' authenticity through their photos in relation to safety. The app's "photo verification" mechanism was rolled out in 2020 alongside a handful of other "safety-focused updates" (Tinder, 2020b). Tinder's (n.d.-d) website explains that the photo verification process "allows you to show that the photos on your profile look like you." While it goes on to describe the process as involving the user taking a "video selfie," when I tried it out, I was prompted to take two selfies that mirrored poses displayed by the app. Tinder also offered me a reward of 125 coins of in-app currency, which can be used to purchase extra features like "Rewinds," as an incentive to get verified.

According to Tinder, the images taken during this process are then compared to the user's profile pictures using what the in-app instructions call "the super cool AI stuff to prove the authenticity of the photos." If the visuals match, a blue verification badge is added to the user's profile. Originally ushered in on platforms like Twitter to signal the authenticity of celebrity accounts, eye-catching (and often blue) verified badges now proliferate across platforms, setting the expectation that users should be willing to undergo a process of identity verification (Caplan, 2024). According to platform governance scholar Robyn Caplan, blue checkmarks have been used to regulate who can make money through platforms (e.g., Pornhub's model verification program), to designate certain individuals as experts qualified to disseminate information during a crisis (such as through platforms' factchecking protocols during the COVID-19 pandemic), and to convey the social status of celebrities and influencers. Given this legacy, Tinder's verification badges communicate that a user is safe, reliable and – perhaps – more desirable than others, even though the process merely involves photo matching.

The data exchanged in this process and the role of technical systems in verifying users' photos tie into issues surrounding artificial intelligence and machine vision more broadly. Tinder's (n.d.-d) website describes the aforementioned "cool AI stuff" in more detail as a "liveness check" determining that the video (or photo) was taken by a "real, live person" and not digitally manipulated. In Tinder's privacy policy (n.d.-e), this process is described as involving the collection of "facial geometry data," and the policy notes that in some jurisdictions, facial geometry data may be considered biometric data, a classification that may be subject to different regulatory constraints in various countries or economic regions. AI scholars stress that facial recognition technologies do not work equally well for all people. These technologies tend to work the best for individuals who look like the programmers developing them, who tend to reflect the overrepresentation of white men in the tech industry, and are less effective for those underrepresented in the tech industry, such as women and people of color (Buolamwini, 2023). However, when facial recognition and data-driven technologies *work* for people who are underrepresented or marginalized, or hold less power in society, they can often be used to subject them to surveillance and social control, and to police them (Benjamin, 2019). Tinder's (n.d.-e) privacy policy notes that "face geometry data" is used to "keep you and other members safe" and may be accessed in the process of detecting and fighting violations of their terms of service or illegal activity. Given the prevalence of false positives and inaccurate profiling of racialized people when AI technologies are used to fight crime (Benedict, 2022), Tinder's use of this data in cases that may involve law enforcement raises greater cause for concern than simply whether photo verification will work well for people of color, however much this lack of consistency may shape their ability to obtain a blue checkmark and its legitimizing associations.

Since biometric data raises many privacy concerns, it is not surprising that the information Tinder provides about the photo verification process is followed up with details about how the data produced in this process is stored. One's facial geometry data is retained for as long as the verified individual has an account, with deletion of the data occurring only after account closure, unless one is located within the European Economic Area (EEA) or Switzerland, where users can delete this data while retaining an account – though they will lose their verified status upon deletion (Tinder, n.d.-f). For those without this option or who choose not to access it, Tinder's verification data for active users are stored indefinitely through a third party: Amazon Web Services (AWS). As such, handing over data about one's visual likeness to Tinder for ongoing storage on AWS servers is the price of verification, and this price may be higher for some whose data is in danger of being misread.

Even in terms of the user's role in this process, requiring users to hold and capture photos in certain poses may be challenging for some people with physical disabilities or mobile impairments. Jenny Cavallero (2021) shares about her difficulty getting verified due to her rheumatoid arthritis that makes it difficult to mimic the selfie prompts. This creates a barrier to her being seen as authentic on Tinder and connecting with matches. Despite these risks and challenges, Tinder makes it clear that this process has usurped Facebook in terms of authentication. The company's updated 2024 FAQs respond to the question, "Are Tinder profiles real?" with "Tinder offers Photo Verification to make sure the person you're talking to matches the photos" (Tinder, 2024b). The FAQs "strongly suggest" that users obtain the blue checkmark because "they look good on everyone and help keep our community safe." In other words, obtaining the blue checkmark is now the bar to clear for asserting realness and those without this profile badge should be considered potentially dangerous.

Tinder has introduced a third major functionality for users to interact visually: "Face to Face" video calls. Video calling was first piloted with users in some locations in 2020 to help matches get to know each other when meeting in person posed a threat to public health during the COVID-19 pandemic (Tinder, 2020c). Both users are required to switch on the Face to Face feature in the match messaging screen before they can call each other. While originally launched to facilitate virtual dates, Tinder's (n.d.-g) Dating Safety Tips now suggest that a "video call can be a useful screening tool before meeting." Therefore, video calling is associated with authenticity in the sense of establishing that another user is safe to interact with before being physically co-present with them. With much more information expressed than in a two-second loop, video calls can also enable consideration of whether an individual is authentic in terms of their consistent self-presentation, allowing users to see if tendencies conveyed on one's profile also come through in video format. However, video interaction requires users to give an authentic performance in terms of the video call's context, demonstrating suaveness in a communication format that may be unfamiliar to some people, while also being subject to greater scrutiny concerning visual desirability. Within video calling, it is possible not only to judge whether someone's video self-presentation matches their profile selfies but also to evaluate another person's physical environment, including their house, car, and other people in the background. This additional information could actually increase the risk to one's privacy and security. This has been demonstrated, for instance, in the increased visibility work required of livestreamers, who find that the abundance of information conveyed through video can threaten their domestic privacy (Tran, 2024). Some people may also judge others as less attractive if they have not attained the kind of house or other commodities that convey a desirable socioeconomic status or stable domestic life.

Across all three forms of visual authentication, a central question emerges: what can one's visual likeness convey about authenticity? As I have noted, these mechanisms seek to confirm consistency as reflective of a true self. If a user posts multiple photos, if these photos are consistent, and if the photos can be supported by video evidence, then this emphasis on visuality fulfills that notion of authenticity. In terms of safety, if one's visual likeness can be clearly established, then this may be used to hold individuals accountable, allowing for their later identification through legal documents (e.g., matching a profile photo to a driver's license). However, it is most likely that Tinder users browsing through the swipe screen are going to judge others based on their contextual authenticity: how well does this person meet expectations of desirability within Tinder's context and in a broader sociocultural context of normative attractiveness? A focus on visual self-presentation means that users whose bodily qualities and comportment meet such normative ideals are most likely to come across as being authentic and trustworthy. Such norms are also built into the verification system, such as a norm that assumes all users are able-bodied and easily able to pose as directed for photo verification, or norms that render some users' biometric data more machine-readable than that of other users.

The privileging of visual data and AI-driven processes supported by advancements in machine vision, however, channels authentication efforts in this direction not because knowing what someone looks like means that they are indeed an authentic person (and, by extension, genuine and safe) but because these are the routes that the current technology renders possible. Tinder is following suit with other companies that have become reliant on AI and data-oriented solutions to user profiling that recreate biases and assumptions from the past (Chun, 2024). In particular, Luke Stark and Jevan Hutson (2022) note how machine learning systems are recreating the damaging pseudoscience of physiognomy – the discredited assumption that someone's character can be ascertained through their facial features. They define "physiognomic AI" as "the practice of using computer software and related systems to infer or create hierarchies of an individual's body composition, protected class status, perceived character, capabilities, and future social outcomes based on their physical or behavioral characteristics" (p. 922). Tinder's visual features and functionalities enable the app and users to categorize (e.g., verified versus unverified) and sort others based on imagery and behaviors through which assumptions can be made about a person's trustworthiness, attractiveness, personal traits, economic status, and more. However, outward appearance cannot confirm character. It is impossible to know just by looking at someone if they are a good, safe, and trustworthy person (and I list these qualities knowing that they are highly subjective, polysemous, and fluid), even by looking at nine of their verified selfies or watching their video stream. While these visual technologies appear to propose a solution to authenticity, they recreate hierarchies concerning *who* is authenticated and seen as authentic while leaving qualities associated with authenticity altogether unverifiable.

How do users convey and evaluate authenticity?

Aside from the main functionalities that Tinder has made available and framed as mechanisms for establishing authenticity, users have developed practices for conveying and evaluating each other's authenticity. In interviews with Tinder users in the Netherlands, researcher Janelle Ward (2017) found that users selected profile photos to convey an "ideal yet authentic self" (p. 1644). Talking to people at a time when Tinder still relied on importing data from Facebook, her interviewees discussed choosing photos that especially resonated with their Facebook audiences. They strategically picked selfies that showed them in a good light while conveying realistic details, such as whether they had children or lived the lifestyle of a university student. Ward's study aligns with other research that finds dating app users, including Tinder users, implement small lies or embellishments to manage impressions and boost others' perceptions of their self-presentations (Markowitz and Hancock, 2018). Ward notes that her findings resonate with previous research about the users of dating websites. They are especially resonant with Nicole Ellison and co-authors' (2011) notion of "profile as promise" in which "the profile constitutes a promise made to an imagined audience that future face-to-face interaction will take place with someone who does not differ fundamentally from the person represented by the profile" (p. 56). Users stretch the truth in online dating profiles more when there is a longer amount of time between connecting online and meeting offline, such as by listing the occupation one hopes to attain by the time they meet their match. Individuals also fudge details that might otherwise lead others to quickly reject them in online contexts, such as by listing their age as a few years younger when this is a prominent profile field.

While Tinder users can convey themselves with some malleability in their photos and accompanying job or education information, I would argue that the app has intensified the notion of "profile as promise" in two ways. First, Tinder's integration of an abundance of precise data from platforms (and the lasting norms stemming from this functionality) has limited users' leeway for stretching details that social media and the app's requirement for visual evidence now put a forensic spotlight upon. Second, Tinder's proximity-based dating and quick instant messaging gear users toward meeting in person much more quickly than on dating websites of the past (Quiroz, 2013). Therefore, there is little room to implement aspirations (e.g., get that job, bulk up by 20 pounds) before meeting face-to-face, which heightens the expectation of seamlessness between online and offline self-presentation.

Several studies have shown that dating app users implement an iterative process of getting to know each other, aiming to establish their authenticity in terms of presenting a singular, consistent self and being safe to meet in person. In an ethnographic study of dating app users – including Tinder users – located in Berlin, media scholar Fabian Broeker (2023) found the prevalence of "rituals of transition" as individuals matched within dating apps and then connected through multiple other means before meeting offline, finding each other on Instagram, Facebook, or messaging apps like WhatsApp and Signal. Messaging apps enabled matches to incrementally increase their access, connection, and frequency of exchanges to cultivate intimacy and move interactions beyond dating apps' compartmentalization, spreading exchanges to other realms of life (e.g., calling while someone is in the middle of their daily routine). By communicating through these different means, potential partners and their exchanges spilled out into mundane and more expansive aspects of life.

I understand this spillage and overlap as providing matches with the ability to observe and evaluate each other's consistency and self-presentations across multiple contexts and to cross-verify information beyond Tinder profiles. The queer women I interviewed told me as much when several described processes of friending matches on Facebook, following them on Instagram, and talking on the phone before meeting for a first date (Duguay, 2022). One woman even showed me long text message exchanges, which more closely resembled love letters, that enabled her to feel comfortable spending the evening at a match's house. These practices for evaluating authenticity are not new, as users of dating websites frequently googled each other to determine the veracity of profile information (Gibbs et al., 2011) or added connections on social media prior to meeting up (Cassidy, 2018). We can also recall Eliza's multiple checkpoints prior to the social media era, which highlight how women are often compelled to implement various forms of communication and gather more details as a safety protocol (Couch and Liamputtong, 2007). But the persistent need for rituals of transition in relation to Tinder attests that the mere data imported from Facebook or Instagram into the app's interface is not sufficient for users in their evaluation strategies. Nor are selfies and videos enough. Users who implement these rituals are looking for consistency and reliability of information across multiple contexts and exchanges, drawing conclusions from dynamic interactions beyond Tinder's curation.

While these practices can be implemented once two people have matched, evaluations of others' authenticity start much earlier when users are swiping on each other. However, evaluating authenticity within Tinder's swipe context proves to be difficult due to the app's framing and understandings of it within broader sexual and dating cultures. Tinder's marketing to heterosexual users and framing as both a hook-up app and potential outlet for romance (see chapter 1) means that the gender-biased scripts involved in hooking up and dating are reinforced and sometimes even amplified through this technology, reflected in research – for instance – from Italy and Spain (Comunello et al., 2021; García-Gómez, 2025). To be viewed as authentic and desirable within Tinder's context, women and men often feel pulled toward traditional gender scripts and roles, compelling men to show off their muscles or pressuring women to toe the line between "sexy" and "slutty" in their photos. On American college campuses, where expectations that individuals engage in casual sex are riddled with sexual double standards, researchers found that within Tinder's game-like structure "the app helped to encourage racist, classist, sizeist, and misogynistic swiping behavior and created a space for people to draw unapologetically on stereotypes to explain their preferences" (Berkowitz et al., 2021, p. 499). Norms of attractiveness and hierarchies of desirability do more than stipulate favorable or "proper" expressions of gender and sexuality. Instead, they function in intersecting ways to designate only certain bodies, identities, and self-presentations as swipeworthy. Within such contexts, users that appear to be the most authentic in terms of belonging on Tinder are those at the top of inequitable and punishing erotic hierarchies. These hierarchies are reinforced not only through Tinder's architecture as a quick swiping game, in which judgments rely on heuristics and stereotypes, but also through the app's legacy of privileging normative Facebook-friendly displays and emphasizing visual attractiveness.

Even when users manage to somewhat shift the context of Tinder, norms within and outside the app shape who is seen as authentic in terms of belonging and attractiveness. When I combined my interviews with those that Lindsay Ferris conducted with queer women on Tinder in the United Kingdom, we found that our participants managed to configure their swipe algorithm to the extent that they experienced a less heteronormative context for Tinder: a "gay Tinder" of sorts (Ferris and Duguay, 2019). With their settings configured for "women seeking women" and within the flow of profiles on "gay Tinder," our interviewees judged other users' authenticity in relation to signals of LGBTQ+ identity rather than rigid heteronormative displays of masculinity or femininity. They looked for visual indicators of queerness in selfies, such as plaid shirts or rainbows, and statements in user bios, such as claims to lesbian or gay identities or simply including the iconic 'two women holding hands' emoji that users have appropriated as representing sapphic/queer/lesbian identities. However, these evaluations of authenticity, in terms of searching for women who are authentically attracted to other women and potentially datable, also defaulted to stereotypes. Women with feminine gender presentations found that they did not reliably ping on other women's gaydars, while our findings also uncovered biphobia that other researchers have documented on Tinder (Pond and Farvid, 2017), with bisexual users often not seen as *really* being into women. Again, wider biases and forms of discrimination prevalent in LGBTQ+ communities seeped into evaluations of others on Tinder, while the app's interface facilitated easily dismissing those who fell outside stereotypical expectations at first glance. Overall, our research and the other studies discussed in this section show that Tinder's affordances as well as contexts within and outside the app present barriers to many users in terms of conveying the kind of authenticity associated with belonging and attractiveness.

Conclusion

This chapter has considered three understandings of authenticity and their relation to digitally mediated dating, locating how they play out in relation to Tinder. Authenticity is a slippery concept that often loses its meaning in the many scenarios in which it is referenced, whether through influencers' appeals for audiences to believe that their authentic selves are on display or in platform Terms of Service that reward "authentic behavior" constituted simply by that which follows the rules. Nonetheless, I have discussed how authenticity is often translated through Tinder as (a) the display of a *true self* that remains consistent online and offline, evidenced through social media and visual displays; (b) being *safe* to meet due to the premise of accountability associated with the programmed and automated compilation of data, especially data related to legal, visual, and biometric elements of identity; and (c) *belonging* through the ability to meet norms and expectations cultivated through Tinder's affordances and broader sexual and dating contexts. Tinder has provided specific mechanisms for establishing authenticity, first through the integration of Facebook and eventually Instagram and Spotify, and secondly through an emphasis on visual self-presentation, foregrounding the role of selfies, videos, and AI verification in authentic self-presentation. While Tinder promises that the app's algorithms and AI mechanisms reinforce and aid users' evaluations of authenticity, users put much effort toward choosing how they present themselves and evaluate others' self-presentations. With the app's central swipe screen privileging quick decisions based mainly on visual assessments and users' positionality within gendered, sexual, and racial dating scripts, individuals' determinations of others' authenticity are technologically and culturally shaped.

While *Catfish: The TV Show* often sides with "the hopeful" – the person deceived by a romantic prospect – a study by Bronwyn Carlson (2020) provides a glimpse from the perspective of some Tinder users who could be accused of catfishing. She describes three Indigenous Australian women living in a remote community, who did not think that other dating app users would swipe right on them if they made profiles resembling their likeness. Instead, they chose to use profile photos from elsewhere online that depicted blonde-haired, blue-eyed women (characteristics shared with several models in Tinder's marketing materials), allowing them to chat and have text-based romances. Carlson explains, "Such performative acts are indicative of knowledge regimes of surveillance," meaning these women are aware that their presence on the app is subject to surveillance by their own community, who do not necessarily approve of dating apps and their potential for initiating relationships with non-Indigenous users, and surveillance from users outside the community who are ready to judge through gendered and white supremacist biases. Carlson further notes that these women "demonstrate knowledge of what *needs to be done* in order to fulfill the basic requirement of 'hooking up'" and produce "a desirable self through intentional misrepresentation" (p. 144, emphasis in original). Her analysis considers norms of desirability and segregated community formations in Australia's racist history as factors that prompt these women to depict themselves as non-Indigenous and in alignment with white supremacist beauty standards. She also underscores how these factors are linked to present-day threats of violence faced by women, especially Indigenous and racialized women, in their use of dating apps.

While authenticity is often depicted as a means for establishing safety, especially by platform and app companies, it turns out that self-presentations commonly perceived as authentic, which are singular, traceable, and often triangulated to legal information, are not the safest ways of showing up for everyone. Instead, demands for authenticity are often made by those in power, such as tech CEOs, and those in privileged identity categories that are rarely or never used against them. Alternatively, some identities are treated as grounds for avoiding, marginalizing, and excluding altogether the participation of those who cannot convey themselves according to norms and criteria conflated with authenticity. Amid these demands, catfishing becomes a survival strategy, as it is sometimes the only viable route for participation on an app that has become a staple in many people's everyday dating lives. Catfishing could also be understood as a set of self-protective practices taken by those rendered most vulnerable within technological and sociocultural structures of inequity, discrimination, and violence.

Chapter 3

Your safety, your problem: Weak interventions and strong surveillance

An expert in researching gender-based violence, Rosalie Gillett (2023) has interviewed numerous women about their experiences on Tinder, especially in relation to what she calls "intimate intrusions" – encounters with other users that make women feel "uneasy, uncomfortable, or unsafe" (p. 200). Exploring how women reacted to intimate intrusions, Gillett shares this quote from one of her interviewees, Kimberly, which reflects a tendency among her research participants to ignore other users' sexual aggression and misogyny rather than reporting these actions:

> Yeah and you know what? I didn't even think to report it. Like, it's not that uncommon for, sort of, similar things to happen. Like, if he had said, "I'm going to fucking kill you" or something more serious, in inverted commas, maybe I would have, but I should have, but I don't know, it just didn't cross my mind at the time.

Gillett reflects on how misogyny has become ordinary online to the point where it shapes decisions of whether to report this behavior and, by extension, whether women believe that reporting it will make it stop. She builds on the work of others, such as Emma A. Jane (2016), who have been pivotal in bringing to light how the internet's development and uptake within masculinist technocultures has given rise to online misogyny's expansiveness today. Uploading an archive of explicit phrases amassed during her fieldwork investigating online misogyny, Jane and Nicole Vincent (2017) once created a "random rape threat generator" software program, which emulated a slot machine as it spliced and recombined real comments endlessly to illustrate how common, repetitive, and mundane threats of sexual violence made toward women have become. According to Kimberley, these now-common threats were not sufficiently remarkable to warrant reporting so long as they fell short of death threats.

This quote and others from Gillett's participants leapt off the page for me because I recognized them in my interviews with Tinder users. While the women I spoke with only noted a couple of encounters with sexually aggressive female matches who made them uncomfortable, the queer and bisexual women who matched with men frequently found the need to deflect misogynistic and sexually aggressive comments. They similarly discussed unmatching but not reporting these men since Tinder felt like a common place for these kinds of interactions. One of my interviewees, Caitlin, said, "I'm kind of sure that it's perfectly appropriate to some people" (Duguay et al., 2018, p. 243), reflecting on how Tinder felt like an environment conducive to sexually aggressive behavior while her desire to not be objectified, threatened, and pushed beyond her boundaries seemed inappropriate in this space. In other words, as Gillett's research demonstrates, intimate intrusions have become normalized on Tinder.

Since I imagine some readers may be crafting advice to bisexual women to stick with dating other women, I will underscore that men are not intrinsically the problem. Sex is also not *the problem* because sexual relationships can be proposed, initiated, and negotiated in consensual ways that do not lead to harm. Rather, as I have been writing about across these chapters, problems of bias, harassment, discrimination, and unsafety stem from Tinder's situatedness within gendered and sexual cultures that are inequitable. Pre-existing gendered sexual double standards, sexism, misogyny, and the intersection of these oppressions with racism, classism, and other systemic forms of violence, carry over to Tinder since interactions there are not blank slates. People who meet on

Tinder are also situated in sociocultural environments and bring their past and present experiences, knowledge, and preconditioning into conversations with matches.

The flip side of this, as we have also seen, is that Tinder plays a role in reinforcing and perpetuating certain understandings, relations, and scripts within the mediated environment it provides for users. When Tinder is perceived as being an app for straight, cisgender, normatively attractive users to find hook-ups or true love – a perception bolstered by how it has been discussed in the press and sold through promotion, and its integration of particular features – then those who fall outside the range of these identity categories and who deviate from these aims are seen as fair targets for behavior that makes it more difficult for them to be on the app. Ultimately, the app itself fosters a particular culture. Communication studies scholar Adrienne Massanari (2015) coined the term "toxic technocultures" to describe "toxic cultures that are enabled by and propagated through sociotechnical networks" (p. 333) and illustrated how Reddit's features, interface design, and other factors collided with toxic masculinity to render a distinctly misogynistic technoculture on the platform. Tinder may not have the same concentration of gamers and nerds as Reddit, but its reputation as a means for fulfilling the sexual double standard that expects men to "score" regularly in the bedroom has attracted men embedded within misogynistic cultures.

Massanari emphasizes how app or platform governance greatly influences the online cultures that emerge and are sustained. She highlights how Reddit's governance decisions enabled toxic technocultures to fester, such as by acting slowly and retroactively when women's nude photos were shared nonconsensually or allowing communities to bond over plans for doxing female journalists. In his book *Custodians of the internet*, Tarleton Gillespie (2018) argues that the duty to moderate is platforms' focal service: moderation is simultaneously platforms' duty of care and a mundane task equivalent to mopping the floor to ensure the utility of a space. Moderation reflects governance decisions about what kind of content can circulate, how users can behave and interact in relation to each other, and what behavior or content is refused or prohibited. Gillespie notes that criteria for these decisions are often developed in light of competing values, which span the company's interests, advertisers' expectations, and a vast range of users. I have noticed how platforms often ignore or overlook these values and the cultures of use to which they give rise. In fact, Nicholas Suzor, Jean Burgess, and I emphasized this tendency in our analysis of patchwork platform governance as an approach to governance that "relies on formal policies and content moderation mechanisms" but constitutes a patchwork as it "pays little attention to dominant platform technocultures (including both developer cultures and cultures of use) and their sustaining architectures" (Duguay et al., 2018, p. 237). We observed that Tinder, Instagram, and the now-defunct short video app Vine had detailed Terms of Service and buttons for flagging content or blocking other users, but the companies running these apps paid little attention to the kinds of cultural understandings, norms, and perceptions that determined whether and how people abided by rules or used protective features. This patchwork platform governance contributes to users like Kimberley and Caitlin feeling as though Tinder's reporting feature is not a viable option even though it exists within the app.

In the years following my interviews, however, Tinder has rolled out a series of campaigns and initiatives that seem to target culture in attempts to shift values, beliefs, biases, and associated behaviors. After considering how Tinder's community guidelines and safety tips perpetuate an individualizing discourse of safety even in light of harms on the app stemming from more structural issues of misogyny, transphobia, and racism, this chapter examines campaigns as symbolic gestures that appear to address a bigger, (techno)culturally shaped picture. It considers the messages and steps taken in Tinder's campaigns about transgender and non-binary inclusion, gender-based harassment, and interracial dating, looking at how these issues are framed. Noting exclusions and patchwork that have persisted despite the campaigns, the chapter then analyzes Tinder's more recent approaches to safety that rely on heightened levels of surveillance. These approaches feature tools that enable users to keep tabs on each other and normalize dataveillance, which may generate safety for some users while posing privacy risks for others. Overall, this chapter follows Gillett's (2018) lead in considering how violence and abuse remain ordinary and everyday experiences on Tinder despite formal policies, moderation mechanisms, campaigns with inclusive messages, and technological "solutions" all established under the umbrella of safety.

Individualized responsibility and user-led moderation

From a liability perspective, it makes perfect sense for any app to assert that it has no responsibility regarding its users' behavior. Tinder (2024e) does just this in its Terms when stating, "Though Tinder strives to encourage a respectful user experience, it is not responsible for the conduct of any user on the Service." US-based apps and platforms are not legally liable to moderate user content under Section 230 of the Communications Decency Act (Gillespie, 2018). While these companies do inevitably become involved in the custodial duties of moderation, Tinder's policies and messaging make it clear that, ultimately, individuals must ensure their own safety. The terms continue: "Use your best judgment when interacting with others and review our Safety Tips." These Safety Tips (Tinder, n.d.-h) provide actions (or prohibitions) to be followed, such as "never send money or financial information" and "be wary of long distance and overseas relationships" – advice presumably aimed at curbing the romance scams and financial fraud experienced by some users and often spotlighted in public discourse (recall Netflix's *The Tinder Swindler*). These Safety Tips even extend into advice for in-person dates, such as the need to "know your limits" when it comes to drugs and alcohol and "be in control of your transportation" when getting to and from a date. It is possible to see how, if someone decided to meet a date in a semi-private place or to accept a lift home (let alone share details about their "daily routine" such as "that you go to a certain gym every Monday" – something Tinder advises against but that seems like a normal topic to discuss with a match), it would be easy for that person to feel as though they did something wrong by not following the tips. In turn, if something harmful happens in relation to these choices, users may feel as though they have little grounds for enlisting Tinder to help confront or ban the perpetrator, let alone pursue any other recourse.

However, Tinder's Safety Tips do emphasize blocking and reporting as key responses to "suspicious and offensive behavior." This section of the page mixes further appeals to individual judgment – "you know when someone's crossed the line and when they do, we want to know about it" – with direct instructions to "block and report anyone that violates our terms" alongside a list of potential violations that include harassment, threats, and offensive messages, among others. In contrast to these instructions, however, the Community Guidelines do not depict Tinder as a first port of call when a user has experienced harm. They read:

> If you have been hurt by someone on Tinder: first, please take care of yourself, and second, take some time to decide what you need to heal, whether that be accountability measures, disclosure, support, or all of the above. If this includes reporting the harm to us, please reach out. We are here for you. (Tinder, n.d.-c)

Taking care of oneself is the first step on this list, followed by numerous avenues for which Tinder's role is ambiguous:

What accountability measures? Disclosure to whom? Support from which professionals? Since reporting is the only action for which the user is encouraged to "reach out," the implication is that these other recourses do not involve the company. Reporting is also optional, meant to be pursued *if* reaching out to Tinder is part of "what you need to heal." Consideration of users' collective safety, such as by removing dangerous individuals before they have a chance to repeat their behavior or stopping these kinds of actions from spreading as a trend, are not discussed as grounds upon which one should reach out.

Blocking, flagging, and all mechanisms of reporting through apps set users up for negotiating safety between each other. Users become interpreters of app policies and terms, deciding whether a phrase in a profile violates a clause against hate speech or if a comment is harassing *enough* to constitute harm. User-led moderation often puts conflicting sets of user values and worse – biases and views rooted in discrimination – at odds with each other. In the context of dating apps, these values and biases are often depicted as personal and sexual preferences, such as when Grindr users assert racial exclusions in their profiles as *preferences* but these expressions actually reflect racism (Liu, 2015; Shield, 2018). While Tinder's guidelines prohibit racism and other forms of identity-based hatred or violence, the section detailing these prohibitions also tells users, "If you see someone who doesn't meet your personal criteria, don't like them or unmatch and move on. Don't report them unless you think they've violated our policies." While such an invocation can be helpful in encouraging users not to target others based on their identity or self-presentation, its placement blurs the line between racism and bigotry on one hand and, on the other, "personal criteria." Although user reporting has become a mainstay for tackling moderation at scale, enabling apps to govern large user populations, flagging mechanisms are simplistic and blunt tools that often fail to reflect the complex and ongoing negotiations concerning the public issues to which they are applied (Crawford and Gillespie, 2016). Nonetheless, reporting is a central channel that Tinder offers to users for preserving safety, since its Community Guidelines assert, "By reporting, you can help us stop harmful behavior and protect others."

Harmful technocultures

There is a stark contrast between Tinder's Terms, Community Guidelines, and Safety Tips, with their focus on individual responsibility for safety, and the harm experienced by large numbers of people who could be understood as collectives or, at least, belonging in a collective way to certain identity groups and categories. Gillespie (2018) notes that platform statements "do important discursive work, performing but also revealing how platform companies see themselves as ambivalent arbiters of public propriety" (p. 46). Indeed, it is possible to imagine that Tinder would rather not get involved in the intimate conversations, first dates, and relationships that spark from its technology. However, the risks and harms associated with dating app use make it impossible for the company to ignore user safety. One survey of more than 1,000 US-based university students, with nearly 84 percent using Tinder exclusively, included reports of having to navigate a range of other users' negative behaviors, such as stalking and deception (Fansher and Eckinger, 2021). Another survey with a similar demographic, though with a smaller number of Tinder users (34.8 percent), uncovered that 54 percent of dating app users reported experiencing some type of technology-facilitated sexual violence (TFSV) (Porter et al., 2024). The study draws on Henry and Powell's definition of TFSV as encompassing interconnected "civil, criminal, or harmful sexually aggressive or harassing behaviors" (cited in Porter et al., 2024, p. 2965), including online sexual harassment, cyberstalking, image-based sexual abuse, or using technology to carry out sexual assault. In a mixed-methods study of dating app users across Australia, in which Tinder was popular among many participants, 44 percent reported experiencing discrimination when using dating apps (Albury et al., 2019). These are just some of the many studies that find that dating app use involves multiple risks, from breaches of privacy to threats to bodily safety and varied forms of sexual violence, which turn into harms when they are experienced.

However, not all risks and harms are experienced equally across dating app users. The Australian study tells us that LGBTQ+ people were more likely than straight respondents (57.3 percent vs 26 percent) to report experiencing harassment through dating apps, while those who identified as culturally and linguistically diverse experienced higher rates of discrimination than those who did not (67.9 percent vs 44.5 percent). Among the US university students who experienced TFSV through dating apps, the study reports that "women and non-heterosexual students experience significantly more TFSV than male and heterosexual students" (Porter et al., 2024, p. 2965). This reality resonates in non-Western contexts too, as research shows that Chinese women's experiences of dating apps – including Tinder – were riskier than men's, with women reporting the need to protect themselves from male users' slut-shaming and unsolicited nude photos, and the use of women's identity-related information for harm, such as to stalk or threaten them (Wu and Liu, 2024). In fact, a scoping review of studies concerning sexual violence and abuse in relation to dating websites and apps asserts, "The broader evidence base on technology-facilitated sexual violence indicates that certain population subgroups are disproportionately at risk, most notably women and girls, sexual and gender minorities (e.g., gay, lesbian, bisexual, trans, and gender-non-conforming persons), and people of colour" (Filice et al., 2022, p. 12). For these categories of users, Tinder-specific studies provide much evidence of these higher risks.

Tinder experiences that spill out to other platforms tell of the ways that gender biases and sexual double standards shape misogynistic speech, threats, and discrimination on the app. In digital culture scholar Jin Lee's (2019) study of r/Tinder, the popular Tinder subreddit dedicated to discussing the app, she observed discussions that linked Tinder's visual focus and emphasis on physical attractiveness to hook-up culture's gender-based scripts. With similarities to earlier cultures of heterosexual casual sex (Albury, 2017), this digital hook-up culture compels both men and women to play it "cool" in terms of restricting emotion and emphasizing visual self-presentation toward the goal of sexual interaction that accords men with bragging rights and women (often) with less respect. With Tinder's features conducive to this "cool" self-presentation alongside the heightened visibility of women on the app – and this heightened visibility garnering waves of hatred toward women in the form of popular misogyny (Banet-Weiser, 2018) – Lee (2019) reflects, "Popular misogyny's collusion with heteronormativity gradually intoxicates both men and women by taking the form of what is seen as *reasonable* criticism toward women" (p. 9). Thus, open expressions of objectification toward women and undermining their sexual agency, such as through "no means yes" attitudes that steamroll over women's consent, have become dominant within heterosexual exchanges on Tinder (Thompson, 2018). In turn, this combination of heteronormativity and misogynistic attitudes shapes perceptions of how women should act and what behavior they should tolerate.

A 2023 Pew Research Center report provides empirical evidence of these harmful norms, depicting them as collective trends rather than one-off altercations (Vogels and McClain, 2023). The report shows that female dating app users under age 50 are much more likely than male users (of any age) to have been: sent unsolicited sexually explicit images or messages (56 percent), contacted after saying they were not interested (43 percent), called an offensive name (37 percent), or threatened with physical harm (11 percent). Scholars such as Lee and Gillett, whose research has focused specifically on these harms experienced through Tinder, remind us that sexually explicit messages and misogynistic insults should not be disregarded but can instead shape women's well-being on a day-to-day basis while potentially erupting into more severe forms of violence. Gillett (2018) notes that while media accounts are quick to focus on cases in which women are murdered (the "Tinder killers" mentioned in chapter 1), focusing on physical violence "can distract us from cultural norms that produce abusive behavior" (p. 216). While these cultural norms vary, from popular misogyny in the United States arising from backlash to women's empowerment movements to a combination of liberal views with more traditional and religious gender roles that circulate in India, Turkey, or the Philippines, they underpin the shaming, objectification, and punishment of women for using an app associated with sexual desire (Das, 2019; Cabañes and Collantes, 2020; Cöbek and Ergin, 2021). The normalization of this gendered abuse contributes to more women than men feeling unsafe on dating apps.

These gender dynamics and Tinder's embedding in heterosexual culture, and – by extension – expectations of cisheteronormativity, also affect the safety of LGBTQ+ users. These users find themselves in a bind when choosing dating apps: sexuality or gender-specific apps like Grindr or Her can provide safe spaces away from homophobia or cisnormativity, but mainstream apps like Tinder are more common and provide access to a greater volume of users (Sharabi et al., 2023). In my interviews with queer women, some participants discussed how their dating pool was already restricted to those who were *out* enough to use dating apps, and even then they easily ran out of options on Tinder (Duguay, 2019). However, Tinder's larger user population comes with a price. Transgender, non-binary, and gender-non-conforming users are often seen as not belonging within Tinder's gender-binary design and framing, which can have severe implications for their participation and safety. In interviews with transgender and non-binary dating app users in the United Kingdom, many of whom used Tinder, Griffiths and Armstrong (2024) found that several participants experienced "double discrimination" as othering and rejection enacted by cisgender heterosexual people and other LGBQ+ users. While their interviewees recounted some positive aspects of using dating apps, such as being able to easily disclose their gender identity in profiles, some users also experienced fetishization, sexual coercion, and fears that proximity-based features would make them vulnerable to transphobic assaults. Researchers in Australia uncovered similar findings in relation to transgender dating app users, most of whom were using Tinder at the time of research, with these individuals reporting instances of feeling unsafe, being exposed to transphobic profiles or chats, experiencing fetishization, or encountering cisgender men when they elected not to be matched with them (Albury et al., 2021). These researchers point out that dating apps like Tinder that (now) allow users to choose from among different gender identity options but sort profiles by only "men," "women," or "both" place transgender and non-binary users in an uncomfortable bind of deciding whether to disclose difference in their profiles or omit their gender identity and risk being accused of deception.

Although not specific to Tinder, I was struck by an installation in Montreal, Canada, by the artist Ianna Book titled "Hello" – the name of a fictional dating app – which displayed messages with matches reacting to her coming out to them as transgender, ranging "from cruel indifference to explicit violence, interspersed with comments marked by misplaced hypersexualization" (Book, n.d.). In the middle of a circle of screens depicting these messages stands a statue of a feminine figure whose arm lies broken on the floor holding a smartphone. While Book notes that the work blurs the line between fiction and reality, having been inspired by her personal experiences, she intends it to shed light on "the judgements, stereotypes, and power dynamics that continue to weigh on LGBTQ+ identities in our society." Indeed, as we will see in the next section, transgender people's experiences of being reported and harassed have been so widespread and severe that Tinder has had no choice but to attempt to intervene.

Racism is so prevalent on dating apps that I have already mentioned it several times throughout this book. Studies going back to dating websites have chronicled "racial homophily" – people searching for partners of the same race – and "racial hierarchy" in terms of biases and discriminatory logics through which people rank those of different races according to differential levels of attractiveness or desirability (Lin and Lundquist, 2013). While racial biases and hierarchies shift in relation to people's context, history, and location, they often endure and are present on Tinder, for instance, in South African daters' tendency to rely on Tinder's heavily visual interface to facilitate intra-racial dating over interracial dating (Tanner, 2024) or in the erotic capital that Chinese gay men attribute to white foreigners on Tinder (Wu and Trottier, 2021). In her book *Not my type: Automating sexual racism in online dating*, Apryl Williams (2024) demonstrates how historical factors and longstanding racism – specifically, in her research, American anti-Black racism – have carried over to today's dating apps. Pointing directly at swipe-based apps like Tinder, she argues that racial bias has become embedded within their sorting mechanisms in ways that reinforce users' racism. Analyzing Match Group's patent for its algorithmic sorting technology, she notes how the system's facial recognition and other inputs may be used to detect users' ethnicity, hair color, eye color, and other characteristics that taken together can be used to categorize people by "race" as a "socially constructed and contextually specific" classification that nonetheless has consequences "because we treat it as though it is a real, biological unchanging truth" (p. 64).

Alongside categorization by appearance, Tinder's curation of profiles by how many likes they have received interfaces with users' racial biases pertaining to attractiveness to reinforce racial hierarchies of desire. Williams argues that this gives rise to "automated eugenics" in terms of favoring and selecting for certain qualities (she also finds that the patent discusses matching users by IQ – a classic eugenicist goal), leading to certain categorizations of users finding greater success at matching. And more success within a dating app can indeed mean continuing one's lineage throughout a population. Throughout the patent, she finds ample evidence that swipe-based algorithmic matching systems automate and reinforce sexual racism.

Even if racism is not always overtly apparent, it functions in the background of dating app practices. Interviews with white, heterosexual, American college students on Tinder unearthed discourses of color-blind racism that attempt to speak neutrally about race and frame race-based selections as a preference (Peck et al., 2021). These students justified rejecting Black users by applying stereotypes and generalizations, conflating race with social class, and attributing racial "preferences" to family values and cultural incompatibility ("we don't have much in common"). When conducting interviews with a range of American app users, Williams (2024) asked her white research assistant, Rachel Keynton, to interview the white participants so that they would feel freer sharing their views on race and dating apps. Together, they similarly uncovered color-blind racism in participants' claims of racial sexual preference and that dating someone of a different race felt uncomfortable. Their participants tended to respond in ways that naturalized racial segregation, perpetuated cultural racism through faulty stereotypes, and minimized racism to suggest that it no longer impacts people of color. Williams notes that these views are also part of a bigger picture: "Individuals' seemingly personal, 'natural,' neutral choices about racially unacceptable partners collide with the Whitening machine that is Silicon Valley to produce automated sexual racism" (p. 83). Indeed, the whiteness of Silicon Valley and the tech industry more broadly has given rise to the characterization of communication technologies as being for white people and digital spaces as white spaces (Nakamura, 2002; Brock, 2020). Tinder's integration of Facebook and the dominance of whiteness on that platform (boyd, 2012; Bucher, 2021), alongside the centering of white users in Tinder's early promotion (e.g., the Tinder Plus announcement depicting a skinny, young blonde woman as she dates across Europe), have contributed to forming an app that white users are likely to feel is for them.

The experiences that people of color have with matches are often characterized by racial sexual objectification (Lundquist and Curington, 2019). A study of Black and African American women, some of whom spoke about using Tinder, showed that although they had some positive experiences on dating apps, many received racially fetishizing comments in conversations with white matches, including expressions of colorism that fetishized women for the shade of their skin (Banks et al., 2024). Even outside of conversations with users, women in this study discussed how stigmatization and hypersexualization from others shaped how they constructed their profiles and who they swiped right on. Moving beyond the Tinder subreddit, Jin Lee's (2021) in-depth interviews with two users, "Greek-Black biracial Betty and Korean-Asian Rose," show how different racial stereotypes play out on the app, as Betty experienced sexual fetishization associated with stereotypes of Black women while men assumed that Rose would be sexually submissive and inexperienced, applying stereotypes of Asian women. With the pretense of color blindness or "post-racism" in which "race is considered as non-existent or consumed as the 'flava' of diversity in media" (Lee, 2021, p. 455), both women had difficulty countering these men's stereotypes and instead shifted their personal approaches, with Betty dismissing her irritation and Rose restricting her sexual expression. Lee (2021) points out how ignoring or denying racism leads to it being dealt with as a personalized or depoliticized matter rather than a collective problem. Other research shows that another likely outcome is for women of color to delete Tinder altogether (Christensen, 2021).

This section has illustrated that precisely because the risks and harms on Tinder stem from collective problems, including misogyny, cisheteronormativity, racism, and their intersection, individual solutions and safety tips are like trying to stop a wave from crushing a boat by using a tiny umbrella. It will not work, but if the wreckage is noticeable enough, then eventually someone must do something about it.

Tinder's campaigns in relation to technocultures

App and platform companies feel the heat of negative attention and respond to it. A longitudinal study of negative media attention toward Facebook, Twitter, and YouTube found that – across nearly two decades – flagrant news stories have been followed by shifts in platform policies and governance approaches (Marchal et al., 2024). These changes are often accompanied by public relations campaigns in which platform CEOs or other influential individuals make statements intended to reduce the buzz over an issue, much like how platform discourses more broadly serve to situate users in relation to each other and naturalize governance decisions (Hoffmann et al., 2016). These ad hoc and reactive campaigns and policy shifts are not unfamiliar in relation to dating and hook-up apps. For instance, sexuality and media studies scholar Sharif Mowlabocus (2020) examines Grindr's "Kindr" initiative, which sought to address discrimination enacted through the app. While the campaign included extensive multimedia content featuring people discussing their experiences of being discriminated against alongside rebranding efforts and policy updates, Mowlabocus notes that it devolved into backlash and resulted in little apparent change. Spoiler alert: his observations about the campaign pressuring users into the labor of moderating each other's discriminatory behavior without making meaningful changes to the app's design are also apparent in the campaigns I discuss in this section. While Tinder's public relations strategy spans a range of initiatives, from its campus engagement to voter registration efforts, it is worth taking a deep dive into three campaigns seemingly directed at the toxic technocultures involved in the app's prominent problems of cisnormativity, misogyny, and racism.

All Types All Swipes

By the mid-2010s, reports about transgender users being flagged by others for their gender identity and subsequently banned from Tinder were hitting the media (Villarreal, 2015). In 2016, Tinder unveiled its #AllTypesAllSwipes campaign to introduce more gender options in the app and popularize a message of inclusivity toward transgender and gender-non-conforming users. The campaign involved a press release announcing changes to the app, strongly asserting that these updates aligned with Tinder's emphasis on authenticity: "Starting today, no matter how you identify, you can express your authentic self on Tinder" (Tinder, 2016d). The press release was accompanied by a moving promotional video on YouTube (Tinder, 2016e), which showcased clips from trans, non-binary, and gender-non-conforming activists, celebrities, models, and media professionals, including Zackary Drucker, a producer on the television show *Transparent* (2014–19). Throughout scenes, these individuals share about negative experiences, such as Tinder users asking them questions about their genitals or being reported simply for sharing about their gender identity. The video also includes then-CEO Sean Rad, two consultants from the LGBTQ+ media advocacy organization GLAAD, and trans filmmaker and advocate

Andrea James explaining the problem of trans users being targeted on the app. At one point, Drucker praises Tinder's changes as integral to "having trans people integrated into the world," while Rad closes the video by declaring, "Everyone has the right to be who they are and meet someone great who loves them for who they are." Text on the screen then fills in the phrase, "I am ..." with a variety of gender identity terms, ending on the statement "I am welcome" before Tinder's logo flashes and the campaign hashtag is shown.

Tinder's changes were generally met with positive media coverage (McNamara, 2016; Steinmetz, 2016), with some media outlets even supplementing Tinder's announcement to inform users about the meaning of all 37 new gender options (Clarke-Billings, 2016). Since Facebook had already collaborated with GLAAD in 2014 to implement a similar range of options (GLAAD, 2014), Tinder's move was perhaps unsurprising given its close integration with Facebook at this time. The announcement was largely absent of backlash or controversy and, although it took place prior to the intensification of anti-trans discourse later in the 2010s (Butler, 2024), it is possible that – for the most part – Tinder's average user may not have noticed a difference. As displayed in the press release, this updated version of the app still listed the standard options of "Man" and "Woman" prominently in the gender screen. These were now followed by a button that read "More," which users could tap to enter another screen and search for other gender identity options. The original gender screen now included a button to toggle "Show my gender on my profile" on or off, with the default set to "off" and a hyperlinked line that read, "Learn more about Tinder's gender feature." The app still sorted users through the binary options of seeking men, women, or both, with no option to curate profiles in the browsing screen specifically by other gender identities.

Just less than six months following the introduction of Tinder's gender options, Sean Rad featured in a panel titled

"Swiping Right on Inclusivity with Tinder & GLAAD," with GLAAD representatives and Zackary Drucker at SXSW (2017), an annual tech and media conference. He discussed how users had embraced the new gender options, reflected in Tinder facilitating matches for "a quarter of a million transgender users" since the changes were made. Reporting for *Mashable*, Cassie Murdoch (2017a) reminded readers that amid discussions of inclusivity, the campaign was also a business move by Tinder "as they face increasingly strong competition for users from other, more niche – especially LGBTQ-specific – apps." Positive coverage of Tinder's efforts was soon overshadowed when it became apparent that transgender users were still being unfairly reported and banned. That same year, *Vice* featured an article about transgender users' continued experiences of being banned from Tinder without a clear appeals process, with some users feeling that selecting the new gender options made them a target for anti-trans reporting (Tierney, 2017). Their experiences challenged the #AllSwipesAllTypes press release's promise that "No one will ever be banned from Tinder because of their gender."

The issue of trans users being targeted on Tinder reached a new boiling point in 2019 when Tinder opened a technical support account on Twitter that was inundated with account reinstatement requests from trans people. Reports on the deluge featured a tweet that observed, "it's astonishing how every single reply from @TinderSupport is an apology for banning someone for being upfront about being trans" (Parsons, 2019). While Tinder's support account directed these banned users to contact the company through its help page, ongoing complaints attested that Tinder's resources and promised education for its internal team, announced during the #AllSwipesAllTypes campaign, had not successfully changed moderation processes to rectify situations in which trans users were unfairly flagged. In November, Tinder's (2019a) newsroom published a post admitting that despite the expanded gender options, "Trans people continue to be reported at higher rates by cisgender members simply for being who they are." It outlined that Tinder was improving its processes by providing greater support to users, redirecting unwarranted reports to its escalations team, and introducing "in-app warnings" that appeared for reported users instead of banning them outright – something that would enable trans people to stay on the platform even if unfair reporting continued. While details about how these new processes worked were not shared, Tinder doubled down on not allowing users to "filter out" trans people's profiles in the browse screen and stated, "We stand by that decision." In doing so, however, the app also did not provide trans people with the agency to choose whether to be visible to cisgender users. This contrasts with, for example, OkCupid's (n.d.) filter that allows LGBTQ+ users to choose not to be seen by straight users.

Instead, Tinder focused on efforts outside of the app's design, concurrently announcing in the November press release the company's new Tinder Inclusivity YouTube series, which featured videos of trans, non-binary, bisexual, and asexual users talking about their dating experiences. Such an approach insists that trans people convince others of their humanity without truly addressing how gender norms are rigidly baked into apps (Bivens and Haimson, 2016). Information and communication studies scholars Caitlin MacLeod and Victoria McArthur (2019) underscore that Tinder's gender options remain centered on the functional categorization of profiles rather than supporting diverse gender identity presentations. They surmise that, even with the updated gender options, Tinder's "failure to incorporate a nuanced understanding of gender into the app at a deeper level means that users continue to be gendered in potentially unintentional and undesired ways by contexts of their profile's presentation" (p. 836). Hence, the enduring rigidity of these gender options reinforces users' continued assumptions that binary and cisgender self-presentations are the norm, especially if app-sponsored media campaigns do not reach them.

Revisiting this situation after several years, I was surprised to see that Tinder has come a long way in addressing the paucity of in-app updates accompanying its campaigning. Examining Tinder's features in 2025, the gender screen's options of man, woman, or "beyond binary" now expand into further options (e.g., under Man appears Cis Man, Intersex Man, Trans Man, Transmasculine or Not Listed) with quick definitions of these identities. Users can choose multiple gender identities and tailor which ones are shown through the Edit Visibility button at the bottom of the gender screen. Although trans and non-binary users still cannot choose to be omitted from cisgender users' searches, the Discovery settings now allow for filtering users by men, women, beyond binary – a category that includes genderfluid, gender-non-conforming, and intersex users – and everyone. While this still boils gender down to three categories, it loosens the binary with which Tinder functioned for so many years. Match Group has subsequently reaffirmed its commitment to providing these options, declaring that it would not change app features in response to US president Donald Trump's executive order stipulating that male and female are the only genders recognized in America (Parham, 2025). The continued heightened visibility of Tinder's gender options opens the possibility that this greater integration of gender diversity will influence user behaviors and norms, an exception to the earlier campaign and others that followed but lacked meaningful changes to Tinder's design.

The Menprovement Initiative

By 2017, Tinder knew it had a problem with how men treated women on the app. Instagram pages like *Tinder Nightmares* had already been running for years as social media outlets for women to share screenshots of sexist, misogynistic, and threatening messages they received from men (Hess and Flores, 2018). Bumble, having launched in 2014, was increasing in popularity and was frequently compared to Tinder, with media commentary often distinguishing Bumble as the "feminist" dating app (Krichel, 2017). Bumble (2016) followed suit with public callouts of bad behavior and, at one point, published a blog post shaming "Connor," a man who sent sexist messages to his match that upheld stereotypes about women as gold diggers. The statement circulated in the press, alongside screenshots of the messaging conversation in question. Less than a year later, Tinder made its own announcement titled *In Commemoration of National Pig Day* (apparently a real annual celebration in the United States), to call out "Nick" for sending racist and sexist messages when he did not hear back from a female match (Pambakian, 2017). While Bumble's blog post had been witty, Tinder's language took a stronger stance: whereas Connor was "blocked" from Bumble, Nick was "banned for life" from Tinder. Rosette Pambakian, then VP of Communications and Brand for Tinder, wrote about being personally offended by Nick's messages and told him: "Tinder has a zero-tolerance policy on disrespect. No racist rants. No sexist pigs."

The Menprovement Initiative launched later in 2017 toward the end of September and into early October. Tinder unveiled a series of videos, which appear to be intended to bring humor to the topic of gendered interactions on the app. The introduction video – posted to Tinder's (2017) Facebook page at the time of writing but having since been removed from YouTube – opens with pink text across a white screen that reads, "Most men are great," followed by, "And then there are the **douchebags**" (bold in original). After further text, the viewer sees a boardroom of women in "Tinder Worldwide HQ" analyzing the "douchebag situation." As the camera zooms in on charts and visuals, the example of douchebag behavior on the board reads, "He doesn't introduce you to his friends." The women decide to call in someone with "real douchebag experience" and the video cuts to the perspective of a person stepping out of the elevator, who garners deference from men and admiration from women as she makes her way to the boardroom. The short "teaser" version of this video ends before the reveal and we only hear comedian Whitney Cummings's voice announce, "Douchebag expert, at your service," whereas the longer version introduces her more fully and proceeds to discuss various "douchebag" scenarios. Tinder's collaboration with Cummings followed her HBO stand-up comedy show *I'm Your Girlfriend* (2016), in which she joked about relationships, sexuality, and many (bad) dates. Both versions of the video note that it stars actual Tinder employees and the company's press release echoes that "the women of Tinder are on a mission" to call out "douchey behavior."

While *The Menprovement Initiative* was never fully defined, the press release not only announced the videos starring Cummings but also spotlighted a new app feature: Reactions. These are emoji animations, which can be sent when direct messaging a match and they take over the whole screen for a moment to convey a visual message. The initially released Reactions included cartoonish animations that depicted laughing, applauding, giving a strike, rolling eyes, and throwing a martini in the other user's face, among others. The feature integrated the common user practice of sharing reaction GIFs into Tinder's user interface. However, Tinder suggested that its Reactions were specifically for calling out "douchey" behavior, as the press release declared, "It's simple. It's sassy. It's satisfying." With less fanfare, the release also noted that Reactions would be accompanied by updates to Tinder's Community Standards and a simplified reporting process. This last detail was the one that I felt most enthusiastic about, since several of the women I interviewed in previous years had trouble even locating the Report button. It was not, however, a focal aspect of *The Menprovement Initiative*.

Instead, Reactions and their promotional videos took center stage. In the second half of the initiative's full-length introduction video, Cummings and Tinder employees discuss douchey behaviors, such as tipping the bare minimum, being late to a date, documenting every gym session on Instagram, and posting shirtless memes, to which they choose various Reactions that flash over the men's profiles. Only the "advanced douche" scenario includes the kind of unsolicited, sexually presumptive behavior called out on *Tinder Nightmares* and elsewhere, depicting a man sending an opening message with eggplant emoji and a sexual pickup line, for which the drink-in-the-face Reaction is unleashed. Media commentary was quick to point out that Reactions were weak responses to harassment (Davies, 2017). Megan Farokhmanesh (2017), writing for *The Verge*, asserted that in actual scenarios involving abusive behavior, sending one of these animations did not seem to be an effective response: "tossing a cartoon martini onto someone's screen after they ask for nudes or call me a conceited bitch doesn't sound empowering." She observed that Reactions seemed to be turning this kind of behavior into a joke and implied women were still open to talking after receiving offensive messages, since sending a Reaction does not also automatically block the receiver.

Researchers of Tinder tourism Donna James, Jenna Condie, and Garth Lean (2019) mention *The Menprovement Initiative* briefly in their discussion of how women feel they must be responsible for their own safety when using Tinder while traveling. Rather than shifting this responsibility to be equally shared among men and women, they note that Reactions ask women "to respond to men's offensive behaviour with a series of 'wrap on the wrist' GIFs. With such moves, Tinder continues to serve a heteropatriarchal function by trivialising women's safety concerns" (p. 60). This trivialization concerns me as well, since the initiative holds so tightly to the language of "douchebag" – a slang term used colloquially to label someone as being rude or a jerk. Gone is the language of Pambakian's zero-tolerance policy or specifically naming certain behaviors as sexist. Instead, the campaign skirts around addressing the harmful behaviors documented in the studies cited previously: harassment, threats, stalking, and a range of actions under the umbrella of technology-facilitated sexual violence. If the initiative's developers had named the actual issues, the gravity of violent acts and gestures that deny women's sexual consent or attempt to otherwise override their agency may have given them pause to consider whether cartoons and comedic videos would be effective. At the very least, it may have become more apparent that the initiative, with its Reactions, strengthened guidelines, and more straightforward reporting options still placed the labor of stopping this behavior on women's shoulders. Instead of sparking a shift in misogynistic technocultures, I see *The Menprovement Initiative* as still addressing the problem on the individual level, asking women to chip away at it one message at a time, starting with Nick on National Pig Day and having no end in sight.

#representlove: The Interracial Couple Emoji Project

Tinder's National Pig Day post included a statement barring "racist rants" pertaining to the racial slur that Nick called his date. While *The Menprovement Initiative* focused on gender relations, racism experienced through Tinder continued to garner some media attention (e.g., Brown, 2018). In 2018, Tinder finally stepped into the race conversation ... with a focus on emoji. Along with Reddit cofounder Alexis Ohanian and Jennifer 8 Lee, a cofounder of Emojination – an organization that advocates for inclusive emoji – Tinder launched a campaign for the introduction of interracial couple emoji (Tiffany, 2018). The campaign included a video featuring a diverse array of couples with different skin tones and ethnicities (Tinder, 2018). As the video unfolds, items surrounding the couples turn into emoji. Eventually, text flashes across the screen saying, "There's an emoji for everything. Well, almost everything. Isn't it time emoji represented all love?" This question overlies a man and a woman with different skin tones holding hands who turn into an emoji, followed by other emoji-rendered couples of different genders and skin tones. The campaign's website directed people to a Change.org petition and asked them to share it using the hashtag #representlove.

Tinder explained that the petition would go to the Unicode Consortium, the body that creates and governs emoji, along with a technical proposal including the variations of interracial couple emoji, which would become standardized across operating systems and platforms (not just Tinder) if approved. As digital media scholar Kate Miltner (2020) observes, the Unicode Consortium's emoji have been historically homogeneous and included little ethnic or racial representation, with variation in skin tones only introduced in 2015. She reveals a logic of color-blind racism undergirding the creation of the original yellow emoji set that was purportedly "neutral" but reflected whiteness and failed to represent people of color. Miltner notes that despite the increasing diversification of emoji, technology developers continue to center whiteness in their designs and functionality. Although Tinder's petition received more than 50,000 signatures and the Unicode Consortium rolled out 71 variations of "couples of color" (Associated Press, 2019), some ways that emoji continue to center whiteness remained evident in these figures. The new interracial couple emoji followed suit with how skin tones were simply added to existing yellow/white-coded figures that "can be read as phenotypically Caucasian," resulting in all variations having "the same phenotypical features (hair texture, facial features, eye color) as the previously existing base character" (Sweeney and Whaley, 2019). Given these defaults, Tinder's campaign may have been more radical had it also insisted on greater variation of characteristics across the couples (as depicted by the couples in its video, who resemble more detailed Bitmoji) or demanded that the emoji keyboard for couples did not default to the yellow version, requiring users to press and hold the button before being provided with interracial options. Therefore, Tinder's campaign for interracial emoji remained aligned with what scholars Miriam Sweeney and Kelsea Whaley (2019) identify as the Unicode Consortium's appeasement of calls for diversity while avoiding deeper questions about race and representation in relation to emoji.

Another key facet of Tinder's campaign was the app's promotion as a facilitator of interracial relationships. The campaign website featured a graph from an external study indicating an increase in interracial marriages in the United States in 2014, highlighting how this trend coincided with Tinder's rapid adoption in the two years following its 2012 launch. The study's link brings users to Cornell University's arXiv repository for preprint papers, since it appears that the paper has not been published in a peer-reviewed academic journal. Throughout the paper, economics scholars Josue Ortega and Philipp Hergovich build on the field of social network analysis to attain their main goal of creating a "novel theoretical framework to study matching problems under network constraints" (2018, p. 5). In their model, the network constraints include limitations on people's social ties, such as being in a dating pool consisting of one's friends and their contacts, as well as America's history of racial segregation. Much of the paper shows how the authors' network model, represented through numerous formulae, is supported by data demonstrating a correlation between interracial marriages and the adoption of broadband internet between the years 2000 and 2016, which stands in as a proxy for the uptake of "online dating." This detail seems important to me, since people meeting each other online were not subject to the proximity constraints and algorithmic personalization of apps like Tinder. In essence, the study engages with much broader forms of digital intimacy beyond dating apps.

In Hergovich's TEDx (2019) talk about the paper, he discusses how a range of websites and platforms that enable you to "mix and mingle with people you otherwise wouldn't have a chance to encounter" can enhance the diversity of marriages because online platforms enable people to join a "distant global network of friends" and potential partners. Clearly, he is not just talking about Tinder changing relationship configurations. Even so, the study's original paper includes the graph that Tinder showcases in its campaign, depicting increases in the percentage of interracial marriages and noting how these coincided with the creation of Match.com in 1996 and other popular dating platforms in the 2000s. When observing another jump in this percentage reflecting that more than 17 percent of all newlywed couples were interracial, Ortega and Hergovich note, "it is interesting that this increase occurs shortly after the creation of Tinder" (2018, p. 26). To the authors' credit, they appear to recognize that correlational data cannot prove the existence of a causal relationship, noting that other factors may also be responsible for this increase in interracial marriages.

Even so, Tinder's campaign combines this study's findings with those from its own "Global Tinder Survey on Interracial Relationships" to assert the app's role in these changes. According to Tinder's survey data, "a majority of respondents (61%) are very open to the idea of interracial dating/marriage" and "52% of respondents believe interracial couples are not well-represented in today's tech language culture of emojis, GIFs and memes" (Tinder, 2025a). While little information is available about the study's methods, its findings provide the impetus for Tinder to focus on its emoji campaign. However, even taken together, these studies do not – or cannot – specifically prove Tinder has increased the number of interracial marriages. Studies that consider Tinder's specific affordances, such as its matching algorithm and visual focus, continue to find that users tend to seek intra-racial matches (Tanner, 2024) and that Caucasian-looking profiles are perceived as more attractive than the profiles of people from other ethnicities (Ranzini and Rosenbaum, 2020). Lived experiences of racial bias and fetishization as well as white daters' admissions of racial "preference" (Banks et al., 2024; Williams, 2024) also complicate attempts to assert that dating apps simply facilitate interracial dating. It could be that people are succeeding in meeting a diversity of dates *despite* navigating algorithmic sorting in which perceptions of race or ethnicity are implicated or fielding racially biased encounters.

Considering online dating more broadly, Curington, Lundquist, and Lin (2021) discuss data that supports claims that websites and apps help daters to: meet a larger diversity of people than they would offline, overcome barriers to interracial dating for those with existing inclusive preferences, and slowly change the minds of daters with less inclusive partner-seeking tendencies. They explain, however, how this creates a difficult trade-off for daters of color: "They either go online and accept the reality that they may be treated as less than their White friends, or they avoid the demoralizing experience by foregoing a resource that has become critical in forming intimate relationships" (p. 219). By focusing on representation as the key issue of its campaign, Tinder missed the chance to squarely address issues of racism that function through its app. Much like sidestepping sexism through a focus on "douchey" behavior, the emoji campaign gave Tinder two opportunities for self-congratulation – the initial announcement pointing to these positive studies about interracial relationships and later taking credit for the interracial couple emoji – without acknowledging that the context in which users of color may be sharing such emoji remains fraught and potentially dangerous for them. Apryl Williams (2024) recounts how, only two years later, Tinder missed another opportunity to acknowledge how its app "contributes to the unsafety and oppression of Black individuals" (p. 147) when the company issued a statement in support of the Black Lives Matter (BLM) movement, while users with #BLM or protest phrases in their bios were banned. She asserts, "Safety for all, with an anti-racist lens, means making specific plans for users likely to experience sexual racism including racial fetishization and race-based harassment" (p. 148), with these plans including better reporting mechanisms and protections for users. Emoji fall short of this need for more comprehensive protections to address racism facilitated through Tinder.

Surveillance in the name of safety

When it comes to safety, apps and platforms have increasingly turned to technological, rather than cultural, solutions in recent years. In a study of how platforms – including Tinder – frame and perform safety through their Newsroom posts, Rosalie Gillett and her co-authors Zahra Stardust and Jean Burgess (Gillett et al., 2022) found that platforms emphasized techniques for surveillance and identity verification. The authors note that platforms' approaches justified scaling up automation and personal data collection, quoting surveillance scholar Mark Andrejevic's (2019, p. 9) observation that these platforms court the "prospect of total surveillance" which "offers to relieve us of the social burden of having to trust one another at a time when it is becoming harder than ever to do so." Automated policing and 24/7 surveillance systems are appealing in their potential to alleviate the burden of moderation that has been placed upon individuals and to relieve them of the challenge of verifying others' identities. Though, as the previous chapter's discussion of photo verification asserted, just because someone's identity can be triangulated by their data does not necessarily mean that they do not or cannot pose a threat to one's safety. Despite this, Tinder has initiated third-party data-sharing partnerships and automated tools that intensify user surveillance and demand large volumes of data in the name of safety.

With Tinder's (2020b) announcement of a new suite of safety-focused updates, it introduced integration with the "personal safety app" Noonlight for US-based users. As Tinder's (n.d.-i) website explains, this integration allows users to add a badge to their Tinder chats to "let people know you're protected by Noonlight" while allowing the seamless transfer of information about an upcoming date to the Noonlight app. Over on Noonlight's (n.d.) website, the key features of its app are explained, including a prominent button that a user can press when feeling unsafe, which then notifies the police of their exact location. Noonlight's My Timeline feature allows users to add information about their date from Tinder alongside comments. A prompt on the website asks, "See something suspicious? Add a note to your Timeline just to be safe." Users can also populate their "Safety Network" by adding the contact information of their friends, whom the app will help to "trace your steps" if you do not respond to their messages, while also notifying the police. Additionally, Noonlight can connect to Apple Health and provide first responders with supplemental data, such as medical conditions.

For some time, as Apryl Williams (2024) points out, Noonlight was only available on iPhones, which are often more expensive than Android devices. Therefore, displaying a Noonlight badge also doubled as a status symbol, similar to the security agency signs that dot the lawns of mansions in rich neighborhoods. Beyond this class stratification of safety, apps like Noonlight fall into the broader category of rape prevention and safety tools. This genre of apps tends to reinforce the rape culture myth that victims should be responsible for preventing sexual violence by being vigilant, rather than using technology to inhibit or impose consequences for perpetrators (Bivens and Hasinoff, 2018). Further, Noonlight establishes a default connection with the police, who are called not only when users intentionally hold the "panic" button but also in other instances, such as when friend check-ins are not returned. However, the police are not a safe recourse for everyone, especially given the systemic racism and transphobia in law enforcement that can make encounters with officers life-threatening for certain populations (Stanley, 2021). Noonlight's website does not indicate that the safety button can be reprogrammed to easily notify other trusted people or entities.

Tinder's connection to law enforcement and the criminal justice system was further reinforced when it began offering criminal background checks on matches for US-based users. In 2021, Tinder announced a significant financial contribution to the nonprofit organization Garbo, which then began providing background checks to Tinder users in 2022 (Tinder, 2021a, 2022a). While the exact amount of Tinder's investment in Garbo was undisclosed, the *Wall Street Journal* later reported it at US$1.5 million (O'Brien, 2023). Tinder's announcements about this partnership highlighted differences between Garbo and other background check services: Garbo was founded by a woman and survivor of gender-based violence, Kathryn Kosmides, and it was a nonprofit organization. As such, it offered relatively affordable checks at a cost of US$2.50 each plus a processing fee, with the cost of the first two checks covered by Tinder. Most notably, Garbo's checks focused on safety-related information, such as reports of violence or abuse, and – on the advice of racial equity and gender justice groups – excluded from its search results "arrests related to drug possession and traffic violations, which have a disproportionate impact on marginalized groups" (Tinder, 2021a). Even so, media coverage raised questions concerning the reliability of background checks, the propensity for racialized and otherwise marginalized people to have unexplained and decontextualized labels or flags on their records, and the likelihood that these checks could perpetuate the lifelong stigma that many people with criminal charges face (Corrigan, 2021). Kosmides (2023) raised some similar issues concerning access and reliability later in her explanation of why, after about only one-and-a-half years, Garbo was discontinuing its background check app. Alongside these problems, she stated, "Over the last few years, we have faced a lack of support and real initiative from online platforms, continuous harassment and threats by bad actors on these platforms, and the prolific issues across the justice systems including [that] access to proper local, state and federal government records is deteriorating by the day." Possibly linked to her laments about platforms, the *Wall Street Journal* noted disagreements between Garbo and Tinder concerning how the checks worked (O'Brien, 2023). Tinder reportedly wanted to develop a system in which users with clear background checks received a badge while Garbo underscored that such badges would give a false impression of safety amid the underreporting of sexual violence and incompleteness of background checks.

When the news broke about Garbo and Tinder breaking up, a spokesperson from Match Group remarked that they were in conversation with "alternate providers" (O'Brien, 2023). As of 2025, Tinder's (n.d.-j) website indicates that it offers background checks through a partnership with BrightCheck, still providing an in-app button that will bring them directly to a third-party background check app and covering the cost of users' first two searches. Beyond these similarities, however, BrightCheck has some significant differences from Garbo. The service offers three types of paid background checks: an anti-catfish check that highlights its focus on marital status, promising to "identify if a person is registered as married to help avoid a toxic situation"; a criminal check that includes offenses such as "drug trafficking" without discussing any of the under- or overreporting issues that Garbo highlighted; and a social check that retrieves all the social media accounts associated with someone's email address or phone number (BrightCheckPro, Inc., 2024a). Counter to users' practices of slowly sharing social media accounts and adding each other as a trust-building activity (Broeker, 2023), this check claims to help individuals immediately identify if others are scammers or bots with new social media accounts and, again, to see if a person's social media says they are married. While a date who lies about being married could be deceptive in other ways, it warrants noting that the risks associated with dating someone who is married and has yet to disclose this information are different from the risks of dating someone who has yet to disclose a history of abusive or violent behavior, though both are used as rationale for running a background check.

Whereas Garbo functioned as a nonprofit organization, BrightCheck appears to have a multipronged revenue strategy. While each check, regardless of the type, costs only US$1.99, BrightCheck appeals to platforms as a pivotal safety tool. Their aim at creating partnerships with tech companies is laid stark in BrightCheck's downloadable offering entitled "A guide to making trust & safety a revenue generator for online platforms." In this framing, providing safety is not a civic duty or moral imperative for platforms but rather a factor associated with revenue, as the guide's download page cautions platform owners, "Don't let scammers cost you more" (BrightCheckPro, Inc., 2024c). While the main BrightCheck website explains the app for users seeking to run background checks, the BrightCheckPro website explains options for platforms and other businesses to forge partnerships. It includes the "prepaid checks" option being offered by Tinder, noting that this is a way to "let your customers know how much you value their trust and safety" (BrightCheckPro, Inc., 2024b). This website also mentions a suite of features offered to platforms, such as providing real-time, large-scale means through which platforms can regularly run checks on all their users and identify "risk scores" for individuals, though the exact risks posed by users with a high score are not defined. Revisiting this company in 2026, BrightCheck (2026a) appears to have consolidated its web presence, now describing its service as a "unified intelligence layer for digital trust" useful to a range of consumer platforms, financial services, and e-commerce businesses. It centers dating platforms when describing its offerings (BrightCheck, 2026b), noting that its services for verifying user identities and detecting suspicious behavior can "enhance user confidence, increase retention, and foster a safer, more genuine dating experience."

While the extent to which Tinder will further integrate with BrightCheck to access other services is unclear, Scott Bright, CEO of BrightCheck, mentioned an expansion of the company's partnership with Match Group during an interview at the 2024 Global Dating Insights conference in New York. He noted that BrightCheck was integrating more AI solutions even as fraudsters were increasingly using AI for nefarious purposes, describing the current landscape as "an AI arms race between us and the bad guys" (Global Dating Insights, 2024a). Kathryn Kosmides from Garbo gave an interview at the same conference, noting that, in decommissioning the background check portion of their operation, they were focused on "what's having a real impact versus profit motivations," moving toward campaigns about how users can protect themselves and solutions "beyond public records" (Global Dating Insights, 2024b). Despite Garbo's move away from using this form of data, in choosing to integrate BrightCheck, Tinder appears to have reinforced its investment in background checks that rely on public and criminal records, as well as AI tools for making meaning out of this data.

Returning to Tinder's (2020b) earlier announcement about new safety features, this update also included the "Does This Bother You?" prompt. Tinder explains that this functionality, which takes effect when direct messaging with a match, "is powered by machine learning and aided by the Tinder community" to detect if an offensive message has been sent. If Tinder's automated scanning flags a message as being inappropriate, the receiving user will see this question pop up along with a button for quickly unmatching the sender. A year later, this feature was paired with "Are You Sure (AYS)?" – a prompt asking the individual writing a message if they really want to hit Send. Tinder (2021b) stated that people who encountered the "AYS?" prompt were "less likely to be reported for inappropriate messages over the next month" while those who received the "Does This Bother You?" prompt were "more empowered to report bad behavior," as evidenced by the increased frequency of users reporting inappropriate messages on the app. However, scholars point out that it is difficult to know the effectiveness of these features without independently evaluating them – that is, without relying on Tinder's own data – and that their effectiveness is called into question by the opacity of what happens after the report is made and whether harassing users are dealt with effectively (O'Gorman et al., 2024). Investigative reporting has found that even if accounts on Match Group dating apps are reported for sexual assault and subsequently banned, it remains relatively easy for the same user to rejoin the same app or move to another of the company's apps, including Tinder (Dugdale and Harjani, 2025). While a prompt may help one user avoid harassment by quickly unmatching someone, it leaves the harasser free to match and initiate potentially harmful conversations with others. If recipients are so "bothered" (note that the prompt does not ask users, "Does this make you feel unsafe?") that they report the user, there is still no guarantee that taking action will either prevent a perpetrator's return to the app or initiate a meaningful reconciliation process if the user has been unfairly reported.

These message filters traffic in volumes of "big data" that, despite its size, may still be misinterpreted. Although Tinder notes that the tools are trained on content that members have reported in the past, machine learning and AI technologies often have trouble understanding the context of conversations, user emotion or sarcasm, or specific cultural or subcultural references. As a result, Tinder might insert these prompts within conversations meant to convey flirtatious jokes or build comradery through shared vocabulary that could be misunderstood by outsiders as offensive. Automated content moderation can also lead individuals to self-censor or abstain from discussing complex and politically contentious topics (Gorwa et al., 2020). Given that direct messaging with a match is the first opportunity to judge their character and values, artificial nudges toward self-censorship may obscure users' evaluations of each other. This means that if a match really is rude or threatening, one might not find out until the in-person date when technological mechanisms are no longer mediating the conversation. Further, automated interventions rely on sifting through a large volume of user data and monitoring interactions in real time. Tinder's (n.d.-k) Privacy FAQs note that it complies with laws applicable in the European Economic Area and the United Kingdom by asking users in those regions for consent to filter their messages, which includes using "interactions between users to evaluate, train and improve our automated tools." Since this data use does not (presently) require consent in the United States and other countries beyond agreement to Tinder's Terms of Use, these users are unlikely to have the chance to reflect on whether they are comfortable with their one-on-one messages, which are often presumed to be private, being collected and reused as training data.

The technological solutions discussed in this section, from new Tinder features to integration with third-party services, appear to reflect significant interventions over the years and yet they may still miss the mark in terms of addressing hurdles to establishing safety on and through dating apps. These technical solutions still largely place the labor of self-protection on users: Noonlight asks them to stay vigilant and press the panic button if needed, whereas background check services let users play detective with others' data, while "Does This Bother You?" is another reporting mechanism. Across these tools, users are pitted against each other on an individual level, protecting themselves from collective problems like racism and sexism one interaction at a time. These arrangements also carry the heightened potential for victim-blaming when tools are rolled out as safety solutions and the impetus is placed on individuals to implement them, even if they would rather not due to concerns about privacy, transparency, fairness, and flaws in justice systems (e.g., fallible criminal records, unsafe police interactions).

In the bigger picture, this reduction of safety to an individual risk that people are responsible for managing themselves through technology and recourse to law enforcement is characteristic of societies organized by carceral logic, as the spreading out of carceral forms of justice across communication and social arrangements (Coyle and Nagel, 2022; Lane and Ramirez, 2024). Within such justice systems, surveillance is seen as the means by which people are kept safe, as mutual surveillance – watching and always being watched – is considered a deterrent to transgressive behavior, especially when something suspicious triggers the authorities or invokes the legal system, such as Noonlight's direct line to police or BrightCheck's reliance on criminal records. However, in studying dating apps, Zahra Stardust, Rosalie Gillett, and Kath Albury (2023) assert, "Where so-called safety features involve increased surveillance and techno-carceral solutionism, there is potential to make users *less* safe – particularly for app users who are marginalised or stigmatised on the basis of race, sexuality, gender, health status, employment or disability" (p. 274). For instance, when people are over-targeted for policing because of their identity, and therefore more likely to show up in background checks, surveillance does not increase their safety. Additionally, when users continue to be unsure of whether reporting those who have carried out abusive and violent behavior actually incurs consequences, the endless compilation of data and relentless churn of AI tools do little to aid individuals in feeling empowered to protect themselves.

Conclusion: Patchy safety approaches

This chapter has considered the range of approaches that Tinder has taken in relation to safety, from campaigns that aim to shift attitudes to features and third-party services promoted as safety mechanisms and technologies. While they have changed over time, these approaches still reflect patchwork platform governance in several ways. First, they represent ad hoc responses to external pressures, such as comparisons to competitor apps in the media or users collectively calling out unfair treatment. Tinder's more recent safety features were also unveiled in the wake of negative reporting about the app's potential risks and calls for government regulation. Match Group has pointed to Tinder's updates in response to US elected representatives raising fears over the app's lack of safety (O'Brien, 2023) and asserted on its website that it supports a range of platform safety legislation (Match Group, Inc., 2025a). When implemented reactively, the resulting campaigns, features, and partnerships do not reflect a comprehensive plan of action but rather constitute isolated efforts that leave certain risks and harms unaddressed.

This lack of cohesion in safety efforts is a central quality of patchwork platform governance. It leads to an uneven focus on changing user behavior or introducing technological fixes but fails to do both at once, which is truly needed when tending to sociotechnical systems that are determined by culture (aka, people) and technology together. Tinder's campaigns came close to addressing the collective nature of harms circulating through its app, noting that certain users felt less safe, more targeted, and underrepresented. But their promotional materials, media products (e.g., videos, spin-off websites presenting in-house surveys, etc.) and minor design changes fell short of addressing the real problems posed by toxic technocultures that perpetuate cisnormativity, misogyny, and racism. They failed to draw attention to the severity of these problems, did not instill meaningful consequences for users enacting harm, and provided minimal supports and lines of communication for users experiencing these harms. Attention to the people side of the issue, namely, the degree of harm, was lacking alongside effective technical changes, such as a full redesign of how elements like gender or race are considered (or not) in the classification and algorithmic sorting of profiles. On the other hand, Tinder's more recent focus on the technological side of safety seems to elide social and cultural inequities that make these new features effective for some users and potentially dangerous for others. They do not consider how third-party apps that connect directly with police, criminal background checks, and automated mechanisms that compile and interpret data through constant surveillance miss the bigger context within which some people's identities, data, and circumstances unfairly flag them as risky in carceral systems reliant on dataveillance.

The actions and mechanisms discussed throughout this chapter shed light on why women and others experiencing harm on Tinder may be reluctant to report it. More than a lack of transparency over the efficacy of reporting, many of the safety solutions posed – from throwing an animated drink in a harasser's face to following an AI prompt to unmatch someone – invoke few to no consequences in harmful situations. Further, campaigns and features that invoke frequently targeted user groups to testify to their humanity, respond playfully to sexual aggression, address sexual racism through inclusive emoji, intensely surveil each other, and hand over copious amounts of data are also asking these populations to anticipate and brace for harmful behavior. In doing so, this behavior is normalized and doing nothing becomes the most logical and least laborious response, as well as a form of self-protection if one can never be truly sure that a reported user is gone for good.

Of course, while these users may appear to be *doing nothing* in terms of not following Tinder's prescribed routes of action, individuals carry out much "safety work" (Gillett, 2023). Their self-protective actions often fly under the radar, beginning with subtle evaluations of others' authenticity – discussed in the previous chapter – and continue by developing a keen eye for red flags in potentially violent users' profiles, choosing to meet in public spaces, and leaving Tinder altogether if necessary. In geopolitical contexts where women are particularly stigmatized for being on the app, such as in China, they take extra precautions to manage their personal information (Wu and Liu, 2024). In other locations where the threat of gender-based violence is high, such as in urban spaces in Turkey, women preplan escape routes from dates and enlist social networks to be on call through multiple mechanisms, from live location sharing with family members' phones to AirTags shared with specific friends, which give them greater control and certainty over contacts' responsiveness than relying solely on Tinder's built-in features (Gurcan and Ustenel, 2023). Nevertheless, these actions are difficult for Tinder to track, whereas the measures Match Group has taken allow it to amass more user data while demonstrating that it is taking action in the name of safety. After all, Tinder also stands to profit from the engagement, data, and subscriptions of harm-inducing users that it fails to eliminate – Massanari (2015) reminds us that toxic technocultures are lucrative – while companies like BrightCheck also point to how safety becomes an investment deal.

Chapter 4

Making love make money: Business strategies in the app economy

"Dating apps are in their flop era," declared a headline in the online women's magazine *Bustle* in January 2024. Next to a GIF depicting giant-sized cartoonish phones displaying Tinder, Hinge, and Bumble, which were being consumed in a literal dumpster fire, the byline read, "Millennials are tired, Gen Z is barely interested, and the Tinders and Hinges of the world are scrambling to keep up" (Lindsay, 2024). The article's proclamations were paired with user anecdotes reflecting on disenchantment with dating apps alongside studies indicating that Gen Z users were less likely than previous generations to hop on dating apps. It also cited Match Group's 40 percent drop in stock price over 2023, reflecting a decline in paying users on the conglomerate's most popular apps, including Tinder (Jacob, 2023).

These early signs of a downturn in dating app use gained momentum into 2024 as evidence of shifting trends solidified. Ofcom (2024), the United Kingdom's communication services regulator, reported the declining use of many dating apps, noting specifically that Tinder's UK reach declined by 5 percent between May 2023 and May 2024, seeing nearly 600,000 fewer visits to its app and web version. Match Group's (2024a) year-end financial report showed no signs of its stock recovering and noted, "In the past two years, Tinder has experienced a decline in user growth, with plans to return to growth through product initiatives that focus on the female experience and younger users." The company's nod toward young people was unsurprising given the slowing of dating apps' uptake among this demographic, while mention of the "female experience" reads to me as reference to women's disengagement due to their disproportionately intensive experiences of harassment, sexism, and misogyny (discussed in the previous chapter). Media coverage specific to this recent ebb in dating app use also highlighted reports of women feeling more "burnt out" on dating apps than men (Prendergast, 2024), perhaps belying the labor of fielding gender-based inequity and violence.

The timing of this shift has been significant: dating apps fared surprisingly well during the COVID-19 pandemic's lockdowns as users turned to technology to combat loneliness. Tinder even reported that its user engagement increased by 11 percent in 2020 (Tinder, 2020d). But as physical spaces reopened, I noticed an increasing number of in-person dating events and speed-dating nights, reflecting commentary that young people were fatigued not just by dating apps but by their computers and time spent online more generally (Xie, 2024). Coupled with the rising digital backlash through which people have increasingly become wary of the mechanisms built into apps and platforms that prioritize profits over user well-being (Albris et al., 2024), public discourse – especially among young people – has emphasized logging off, engaging face-to-face, and *touching grass*. Merriam-Webster (2025) describes the viral phrase "touch grass" as associated with participating "in normal activities in the real world especially as opposed to online experiences and interactions." This sentiment has extended to dating apps, sometimes perpetuating a false nostalgia about the good old days of offline dating that imagines a panacea of safety, consent, and romance (Albury, 2025), re-entrenching perceptions – discussed in chapter 2 – that non-digital dating is more authentic than any spark initiated through dating apps.

While I was writing this book, people often conveyed concern over my time commitment to such a seemingly fleeting topic: dating apps, aren't they over? Isn't Tinder so 2010s? I have frequently been asked if Tinder will still exist by the time this book is published. My quick answer reflects this book's main premise: it does not matter whether Tinder goes the way of the dinosaur. It was a major catalyst for an era of digitally mediated dating, and the intertwinement of digital technologies and media with our intimate lives will not cease anytime soon. The endurance of digitally mediated intimacy is evidenced by the number of news stories documenting people's transition from dating apps to social media (e.g., sliding into someone's Instagram DMs [direct messages]), exercise apps – "We met on Strava" (Borovinsky, 2023), and even Google Docs as digital tools to facilitate dating and sex lives (Goode, 2022). The longer answer, specific to the question of dating apps' continued financial viability, is reflected in this chapter, as it demonstrates how Tinder represents not just a set of technological arrangements but also financial strategies and economic relationships. It is a for-profit entity reflecting the interests of its owners and shareholders, positioned within an economic ecology among other technology companies deployed amid an always-updating, permanently beta ethos (Neff and Stark, 2004). As such, Tinder and its parent company, Match Group, are always changing and adapting. Tinder's business strategy attests to agility and exploration as it has simultaneously shaped and responded to the digital dating market. At the same time, it is only one app with which Match Group hedges its bets within a growing international market. As such, I am willing to wager that even if Tinder is eventually phased out as an aged or overburdened brand, what Match and a handful of other large players have shaped into the genre of "dating apps" has staying power into the future.

This chapter analyzes Tinder from a political-economic perspective, identifying how revenue generation, monetary flows, and business and marketing strategies have shaped the app and users' relationship with it. In doing so, I take up a political economy of communication and media lens (Mosco, 2009; Wasko, 2014), which approaches Tinder as a commodity in itself – an app that can be owned and marketed – as well as a media distributor and intermediary as it circulates and shapes user media (i.e., profiles, messages) and commercial advertising while producing its own promotional materials. Political economy of communication is concerned with power relations that shape the production, distribution, and consumption of communication and media, paying attention to historical changes in these arrangements (Mosco, 2009). This approach often applies a critical lens to examine the outcomes of these relations and their impacts relating to equity, justice, and the public good (Golding and Murdock, 1991). Scholars have bridged divides across political economy and cultural studies to acknowledge that economic factors shape culture (Fenton, 2007), while STS scholars also recognize the impact of economic influences on technological development (Birch, 2013).

Political economy has become a central concern in the study of platforms. While early platformization involved the process of platforms forming the internet's dominant technological and economic infrastructures (Helmond, 2015), this process has extended much further over the past decade. Platformization now encompasses the permeation of platforms' infrastructures, economic processes, and governmental frameworks across "different economic sectors and spheres of life," intensely shaping sociocultural practices and economic relations that span online and offline realms (Poell et al., 2019, p. 1). Platform companies mediate economic relationships through multisided markets, brokering deals with advertisers, bringing end users into contact with ads and service providers, and often generating revenue from users' relationship to the platform, whether directly through subscriptions or indirectly through engagement and data generation (Poell et al., 2021). On dating apps, the intimate data that users generate – in relation to the app and in interaction with others – flows through these markets, holding potential value for app owners and advertisers. As mobile media scholars Rowan Wilken, Jean Burgess, and Kath Albury observe, "A political economy approach thus usefully directs our attention to what the business structures, revenue models, and cross-platform and other data-sharing arrangements are that make dating apps so lucrative" (2019, p. 16). This kind of analysis also yields a sense of how Tinder's business strategy impacts users, as it entrenches the app's approaches to authenticity and safety (and other dynamics already discussed) into the company's operating model.

This chapter explores Tinder's role in commercializing and generating markets in relation to dating activity through areas that have long been of concern to political economists: *consolidation*, as the extension and entrenchment of corporate influence; *incorporation*, through corporate strategies that structure user behavior; and *globalization*, in the extension of business strategies to an international marketplace (Murdock and Wasko, 2007). While dating and sexual activity have long been subject to commercialization and marketization, and dating apps form only recent phases of the matchmaking industry's longer legacy, Tinder's rise to prominence and positioning as the powerhouse of a dominant dating app corporation provides new insights into strategies in the digital dating market. The following sections first illustrate Tinder's consolidation through its business development and positioning in relation to the handful of other corporate entities that populate the economic landscape of dating apps. Then I discuss incorporation in terms of how Tinder generates revenue as well as the company's social engagement strategies more broadly, since engagement produces data for conversion into value in the platform economy. Lastly, I consider Tinder's global reach through a brief mapping of its international marketing strategies, noting how it participates in the perpetuation of Westernized dating and sexual discourses across geographies while also tailoring a great deal of its media to localized cultural references, especially in large markets like Brazil and Southeast

Asia. Overall, this chapter exposes the agility of Tinder and Match Group's financial strategies while laying bare how certain profit-making approaches allow for, and underscore, the issues about which users are feeling fatigued.

Consolidation: Corporate technology with start-up vibes

Early reporting on Tinder's formation framed the app company just like any other Silicon Valley start-up. Interviews profiled some of the cofounders, most often Sean Rad, Justin Mateen, and Jonathan Badeen, as three guys who united over a bright idea about how to pick up girls. This idea came to fruition in an LA-based start-up incubator called Hatch Labs, which incentivized the development of new business ideas through hackathon-style sprints in which the best pitches received seed money (Barron, 2022). The founders pitched an idea for an app that only connected users after they expressed mutual interest. In this early development process, the app's name had not yet been fully decided, with some reports discussing it as Matchbox (Soper, 2015) while another outlet notes that Rad wanted to call the app Tender but Whitney Wolfe Herd suggested switching the *e* to an *i*, proposing Tinder as the name that stuck (Barron, 2022).

This lighthearted start-up story of spontaneous innovation elides the intensive corporate involvement in Tinder's development, growth, and how it has been sustained over time. Hatch Labs was a joint venture between the mobile development firm Xtreme Labs and the media holding company IAC Inc. (formerly InterActiveCorp) (van Grove, 2014). IAC invested heavily in online assets in the 2000s, acquiring a diverse array of properties, from travel to restaurant recommendation websites and numerous dating websites, such as Plenty of Fish and OkCupid (Wilken et al., 2019). Not only did the company have a default stake in Tinder due to its investment in the incubator – any ideas initiated there became "the exclusive property" of Hatch (Barron, 2022) – it was logical for IAC to become the app's main investor as a seamless expansion of its prominent role in the digital matchmaking industry. This is how Tinder – a fresh, mobile app – became part of a corporation that included one of the longest-running dating websites, Match.com, which originally launched in 1995. Match.com formed the basis for IAC's online dating conglomerate Match Group, which was eventually spun off in 2015 as a publicly listed company in which IAC remains the controlling shareholder.

Operating within IAC provided Tinder with security but also led to power struggles among its leadership. In a 2014 interview, Rad – as Tinder's founding CEO – recognized IAC's support while alluding to the possibility of expanding Tinder's financial efficacy: "We are in a fortunate position that we have internal sources of funding ... We don't need to raise outside capital, but it's something we think about often" (Lawler, 2014). Shortly after, the venture capital firm Benchmark took up a small equity stake in Tinder. Rather than representing a financial commitment, Benchmark's investment consisted of the time and expertise of one of its partners, Matt Cohler, a former executive at Facebook and LinkedIn with a track record of successful investments in upcoming tech companies, such as Uber and Twitter in their greener eras (Swisher, 2014). Cohler became part of Tinder's board and Rad referred to him as a mentor who would help the company grow.

Cohler's addition was shortly followed by IAC's decision to replace Rad as CEO with Chris Payne, a former eBay executive, following the Wolfe Herd sexual harassment lawsuit (Grow, 2014). This would become just one phase in an ongoing struggle between IAC's leadership and Tinder's cofounders, as Rad was reinstated as CEO in 2015 (Bertoni, 2015) only to step down in 2016. Rad then assumed a behind-the-scenes chairman role related to Tinder's investments as Greg Blatt, Match Group's CEO, momentarily doubled as Tinder's CEO

(Wagner, 2016). Blatt was replaced in 2017 by Elie Seidman, former CEO of OkCupid (also part of Match Group), who was succeeded in 2020 by Jim Lanzone, an executive-in-residence at Benchmark (Spangler, 2020). From 2006 to 2008, Lanzone had been CEO of Ask.com, a web property owned by IAC. At the time of his departure from Ask.com, Barry Diller – IAC's CEO – said of Lanzone, "He is a superb executive and leader and I'm hopeful we can be associated in the future" (Schwartz, 2008). Although this hope was later fulfilled, Lanzone stepped down as Tinder's CEO in 2021 to pursue a new role at Yahoo! while Tinder appointed its first female CEO, Renate Nyborg, a former general manager at the mental health app Headspace. Although Nyborg won multiple awards, including a 2022 award in Comparably's category of "Best CEOs for Diversity" along with Tinder placing amid their Best Places to Work (Tinder, 2022b), she left after less than a year at the same time as Tinder reported a 20 percent drop in its share price (Sweney, 2022). Match Group chief executive Bernard Kim then oversaw Tinder until promoting Faye Iosotaluno to CEO in 2024 from her position as Tinder's Chief Operating Officer, nodding to her depth of experience having worked at Match Group since 2017 (Mehta, 2024). Iosotaluno announced in 2025 that she was stepping down to pursue her personal ambitions (including elevating new and diverse voices in tech development), with Match Group's CEO Spencer Rascoff (appointed earlier in 2025) stepping in to lead Tinder indefinitely (Davis, 2025; Iosotaluno, 2025). This leadership lineage demonstrates that, apart from Rad, IAC and Match Group have largely determined who steered the company based on familiar faces and experience within the conglomerate.

Since Tinder's consolidation under Match Group, the app has been a source of revenue and contention. The Securities and Exchange Commission's (SEC) filing for Match Group's initial public offering (IPO) in 2015 boasted that Tinder was the most downloaded mobile dating app in North America for a period that year and, in September alone, Tinder users swiped on an average of 1.4 billion profiles per day. Despite Rad's inflation of user metrics in a press interview (Gorman, 2015), the IPO was considered a success, with trading opening at US$12 per share and surging to US$14.74 at the close of the session (Balakrishnan, 2015). Later in 2017, when Tinder's original founders and staff were able to exercise their stock options, Tinder was valued at $3 billion and they were paid around $600 million (BBC, 2021). However, in 2018, the founders sued IAC and Match Group, alleging that the corporate leadership had prompted the banks to under-value Tinder, contributing to a valuation much lower than the $13 billion these founders believed the app to be worth (Hart, 2021). Match Group settled the lawsuit for $441 million (much less than the $2 billion in damages sought by the app founders) at the end of 2021.

Even amid these struggles, Match Group, Inc.'s (2025b) Investor Relations webpage still centers the app, telling investors that by the end of 2024, Tinder remained number one in downloads and was the highest-grossing "lifestyle app" worldwide. Match Group, Inc.'s (2024) "Business Overview" depicts Tinder as a mainstay of the company's business strategy, flanked only by Hinge in its "largest brands" category alongside numerous "evergreen" apps – Match, OkCupid, Plenty of Fish, and Meetic – and "emerging" apps launched from 2015 onward, such as BLK for "Black singles" and The League for "highly ambitious, career-oriented singles." Match Group has increasingly sought to corner niche dating markets, since buying up the popular Muslim dating app Salams and the lesbian-forward queer dating app Her (Global Dating Insights, 2025b, 2025c). In addition to these groupings, the Business Overview includes an "MG Asia" category featuring Pairs – "a leading dating app in Japan" – and two livestreaming apps, Azar and Hakuna. Zooming out, it gives a breakdown of first-quarter direct revenue across Match Group's properties that depicts Tinder's $481 million in revenue as the foundation upon which the other apps sit, with Hinge bringing in $124 million, MG Asia apps $71 million, and all "evergreen and emerging" apps combined $169 million. It is no wonder, then, that when Tinder's paid subscription rates and overall revenue fell following the pandemic, investment firms with a stake in Match Group pushed the company to focus on refreshing Tinder's business strategy (Reuters, 2025).

Match Group's acquisitions and investments belie horizontal and vertical expansion of its influence across the matchmaking landscape. In addition to its acquisition of niche dating apps, in 2011 Match Group invested in Zhenai – a major internet and telephone matchmaking service in China – and, in 2014, it contributed to a seed round for Three Day Rule, a US-based service that pairs singles through a personal (human) matchmaker (Crunchbase, n.d.-a). Match Group's more recent investments in Noonlight, the security app that allows daters to easily alert authorities if they feel unsafe, and the background check service Garbo also respond to intensified pressure to respond to negative press about dating app risks, discussed previously, to sustain the properties it already owns. In turn, Tinder's acquisitions reflect aims to refine or diversify the app's functionalities, such as through the 2015 acquisition of Tappy, an ephemeral messenger app with similarities to Snapchat, and the 2017 acquisition of the contacts app Humin (Crook, 2015b; Butcher and Russell, 2016). Tech news reported on each case as an "aqui-hire" intended to increase Tinder's range of technical functionality as well as human capital, such as by adding employee teams and, in the case of Humin, opening a new office in San Francisco.

On the investments side, Tinder contributed seed funding in 2016 to a (now-defunct) social networking and friendship app aimed at women, Hey! VINA. Tinder's (2016f) newsroom announcement about the investment declared, "Tinder supports sisterhood," while linking to the app's webpage, which asserted, "Hey! VINA is the Tinder for (girl) friends!" (Hey! Vina, n.d.). Shortly after this investment, Tinder announced the development of Swipe Ventures, led by Rad after his second replacement as CEO, as an arm of the company dedicated to growing "Tinder's reach through acquisitions, investment opportunities, and development of new businesses – with a focus on the dating and broader social spaces" (Tinder, 2016g). While Swipe Ventures has received little press since, Tinder has focused subsequent acquisitions on digital video capabilities by acquiring Wheel, an app for sharing mobile videos, and quietly investing in Ozone, an AI video-editing tool (Crunchbase, n.d.-b). These investments indicate a turn toward hosting and generating more video content while orienting Tinder closer to its promise of integrating AI into the dating experience (Stacey, 2024).

Tinder's investment in Hey! VINA as an app focused on female friendship and forays into promoting Tinder for a range of uses strike me as potential efforts to keep up with the app's longtime rival, Bumble. Following Whitney Wolfe Herd's departure from Tinder, she launched her own dating app premised on women *making the first move*, with the chat function requiring women to send the first message in a heterosexual match, enveloped in promotion focused on female empowerment (Alter/Austin, 2021). Bumble offers two additional modes alongside its dating default: BFF (Bumble For Friends) as a social networking service and Bizz for professional networking. Despite Bumble's promotion as a female-led start-up, Wolfe Herd formed a partnership in 2014 with Andrey Andreev, the Russian founder of Badoo – a massive dating website launched in 2006 and popular in Europe and South America. Andreev went on to invest in Bumble, with Badoo claiming a majority owner stake of 79 percent, allowing Bumble to scale – like Tinder – "without needing to seek outside capital," the company has stated (O'Hear, 2016). Alongside Badoo, Andreev consolidated his dating app investments under a company named MagicLab, his stake in which he later sold to the American investment firm Blackstone in 2019. This firm appointed Wolfe Herd as MagicLab's CEO amid the company's valuation at $3 billion (Lunden, 2019). She renamed it Bumble, Inc., which held a successful IPO in 2021, though its closing market cap of $7.7 billion on the first day of trading paled in comparison to Match Group's market cap of $45.5 billion at the time (Bursztynsky, 2021). Even so, Bumble Inc.'s consolidation of rival dating apps (e.g., Fruitz, a popular app in Europe that allows people to playfully display their desires through fruit metaphors, acquired in 2022) gives it similar capability to Match Group in terms of being able to market specific apps to different audiences and experiment with various functionalities across properties. Bumble's brief investment in Chappy, a gay dating app, enabled the company to see if focusing on this demographic would be successful – porting Bumble's discourse about empowerment to the app (Tepper, 2016) – before exiting the crowded landscape of gay dating. Unlike Match Group's sustained expansion into niche dating technologies, Bumble Inc. has redirected LGBTQ+ users to Bumble as an app committed to "fighting all kinds of inequality" (Megarry, 2020). In light of falling revenue, Bumble Inc. has also since announced that it would discontinue Fruitz and another previously acquired app, Official, to focus on Bumble and Badoo as its core businesses (Forristal, 2025). Bumble Inc.'s return to amassing users on its most popular apps therefore differs from Match Group's persistence in spreading across dating populations and communities.

Despite Bumble's profits historically trailing Tinder's, Match Group has sought to purchase and litigate this rival. Match Group's unsuccessful bid to purchase Bumble for $450 million in 2017 was followed by a 2018 lawsuit in which it accused Bumble of being a "Tinder-clone" infringing on Tinder's patented design (Safronova, 2018). In turn, Bumble retaliated with a lawsuit against Match Group for damages to its reputation. Both companies finally agreed to settle all litigation between them in 2020, though with settlement details remaining undisclosed (Match Group, 2020).

By tracing Tinder's development under Match Group as well as Match Group's business strategies, it is possible to see how Match Group is consolidating the digital dating industry and beyond. It is doing so by purchasing dating apps catering to niche groups and different geographical regions while expanding to in-person matchmaking and social technologies, such as its livestreaming apps. By incorporating enhanced photo and video functionalities, Tinder also expands to blur the lines between dating and social connection. As rival corporations, such as Bumble Inc., follow suit, the digital dating industry becomes fractured between two large players that have consolidated the majority of revenue-generating dating app properties under their banners (Curry, 2025b). As a result, smaller, independent dating apps suffer from fewer resources for promoting and sustaining their technologies. When they are bought up, they become subject to hierarchical governance – as seen in Match Group's sway over Tinder's leadership – and may become homogenized as their owners deploy similar marketing strategies and functionalities across apps, reflected in the swipe's integration across Match Group apps like OkCupid, even when that app's original design logic was largely driven by long-form profiles and quizzes.

In this way, media conglomerates like Match Group or Bumble Inc. hold horizontal power across the dating app sector within a broader ecology of apps and platforms. They are, however, still subject to the influence of major intermediary platforms, such as Facebook and Google, which deploy and govern much of the digital infrastructure that sectoral apps rely on (van Dijck, 2021). As mentioned in chapter 2, Tinder relies on Amazon Web Services for storing user data, especially sensitive facial geometry data, meaning that Tinder users are subject to Amazon's data-handling practices and policies. Further, apps downloaded through the Apple and Google Play stores must conform to these corporations' policies and design requirements. Match Group came up against the Google Play store's restrictions when it sought to include payment options in its apps, which would circumvent Google Play's payment system and its associated fees (Hatmaker, 2022). Match Group initiated an antitrust lawsuit against Google, accusing the Google Play store's policies of harming competition through requirements for developers to use Google's proprietary payment channels (Fung, 2023). While Match Group settled the lawsuit after Google conceded, its in-app payment channels are still subject to Google's fees, although at a somewhat lower percentage. This clash with Google, owned by Alphabet, a company that dominates massive digital infrastructures in the realms of search, advertising, and increasingly AI, belies how even large conglomerates like Match Group are still subject to hierarchies of vertical integration across the digital ecosystem (van Dijck, 2021). While Match Group exercises considerable influence over the digital dating industry, massive platform intermediaries have a tremendous say in how apps in this sector function.

Incorporation: How does Tinder make money?

Incorporation involves the strategies through which a company becomes and remains financially sustainable over time. These strategies are designed to position an app like Tinder to generate profit while also structuring users' relationship to the app around exchange in the form of money, data, and time. Like other new technology companies reliant on investment for their initial financial capacity, Tinder did not launch with revenue generation strategies in place. These would come much later after the free app gained popularity, shifting instead to a "freemium" model with paid options and advertiser partnerships in 2015. It is possible to conceive of Tinder's business model as involving three aspects essential to making money in this industry: user payments, advertiser partnerships and campaigns, and modes of fostering user engagement that enable the compilation of a vast database of users and their intimate data.

Subscriptions and in-app purchases

Tinder's unveiling of its first subscription plan, Tinder Plus, heralded massive changes to the app (Crook, 2015c). This original plan provided access to new but paywalled features, including Rewind – the ability to return to a profile that one has discarded – and Passport, which allows users to bypass the distance constraint of 160 km to search for matches worldwide. It also allowed subscribers to browse advertising-free once ads became part of the app, enabling a cleaner and more user-friendly experience. Shortly following Tinder Plus's launch, the company made an additional change that would render the subscription even more appealing: the imposition of a swipe limit for everyone but paying users. In a Newsroom post entitled "Keeping Tinder real," Tinder (2015c) explained the impetus for this change: "to encourage people who right swipe like crazy to be thoughtful in their swiping, we've introduced an algorithm that intelligently limits the number of likes a user can make in a consecutive 12-hour period." While presuming that "most of our users will never even encounter this limit," those bumping up against it could now purchase Tinder Plus. The post's focus on curbing "excessive right swiping" came at a time when Tinder was under pressure to remove spambots programmed to right-swipe on all users (Paul, 2014). While Tinder remained vague about the cap on free swipes, even noting that in some situations the algorithmic calculation was individualized, many users complained about hitting their limit shortly after the change (Cook, 2015). Conjectures on the Tinder subreddit as to the exact limit have circulated numbers spanning from 25 to 100 daily likes per free user along with the hypothesis that female users are provided with more likes than male users

(Gospodyn, 2021). Despite backlash, Tinder retained the swipe limit as a key constraint on nonpaying users.

At the time of writing, Tinder offers three subscription tiers, continuing Plus but adding Gold and Platinum (Tinder, 2025b). Along with the original Plus perks, users at this base subscription level can "Go incognito," hiding their profile from others' searches while retaining the ability to swipe on users, being visible only to those they have liked. Gold and Platinum subscriptions include everything available to Tinder Plus users but add multiple features:

- Super Like – a vertical swipe functionality that enables the paying user to be prioritized in the "super-liked" user's Discovery search and indicates to this potential match that they have been super-liked;
- Boost – increases the paying user's profile visibility to those nearby for 30 minutes;
- The ability to see who "Likes You," which displays those who have right-swiped on a paying user in a grid interface; and,
- Daily lists of curated profiles, called "Top Picks," tailored to the user based on their profile information and past swiping behavior. Free accounts receive one Top Pick suggestion per day while paid users receive multiple suggestions.

Additionally, Platinum subscribers can message other users prior to matching with them; have their right swipes designated as "Priority Likes," a designation that "helps to make sure your Likes and Super Likes are seen faster by a potential match, before the Likes of non-subscribers" (Tinder, n.d.-l); and review the likes they have sent in the past seven days. A mysterious subscription option was announced in 2023 as Tinder Select: a tier that requires users to apply, or receive an exclusive invitation, and pay US$499 per month (Vasani, 2023). Select's announcement appeared to position Tinder in competition with more exclusive or elite apps, such as Raya or The League, which impose particular criteria on users and include vetting processes. A note on Tinder's website in 2025 states, however, that this membership tier is in the process of being "retired" (Tinder, n.d.-m), indicating that it may not be serving the company's revenue aims as anticipated.

Outside of subscriptions, Tinder offers some premium features *à la carte* through individual purchases. Users can pay for Super Likes or Boosts, and Tinder has even been testing a Super Boost feature for purchase *on top* of subscription packages that renders one's profile extra visible (more visible than with the plain Boost) during Tinder's busiest times (Tinder, n.d.-n). In 2021, Tinder introduced an in-app currency, Tinder Coins, to make these purchases more seamless and as a reward for sustained activity on the app but announced in 2022 that the currency's viability was being re-examined (Serrano, 2022). Regardless of whether users are purchasing coins, spending their money directly on extra features, or considering signing up for subscriptions, Tinder's free version prompts users toward paying through color-coded paywalls around premium features and frequent pop-ups advertising subscription deals. The pricing for subscription plans and individual purchases has varied across time and geographical location. With Tinder Plus's rollout, the company garnered controversy over charging a lower rate for users under age 30, which a spokesperson rationalized as due to younger people's constrained budgets (akin to a student discount), but others – including a California appeals court – deemed as discriminatory against older users (Doubek, 2018). While Tinder has moved away from age-geared pricing since settling an age discrimination lawsuit (D. Lee, 2019), standard prices are not listed on Tinder's website. In 2024, my app showed monthly subscription rates "starting at" Can$9.99 for Tinder Plus, Can$39.99 for Gold, and Can$52.99 for Platinum (though checking in halfway through 2025, I was offered a discount reducing Platinum to Can$19.99 per month, making this more extensive plan cheaper than Gold for an unknown period). Tinder's ability to set the price according to demand and other data it may have on users reflects the powerful differential pricing enabled in data-driven markets. Such markets allow technology corporations, whether dating apps or ticketing services like Ticketmaster, to circumvent standard pricing with algorithmically derived and always fluctuating valuations of their services.

Whether through subscriptions or one-off advantages (with paid features like Boost akin to an algorithmic cheat code), these payments do more than unlock features; they rearrange the rules of the (Tinder) game completely. Features that enable one to see that another user has liked them, such as Super Like and Likes You, do away with Tinder's double opt-in premise. They hold the potential to sway users toward liking those whom they may not notice otherwise, or to swipe right on others simply because they have already shown interest, though some users perceive Super Liking as desperate or creepy, thus having the opposite effect (Thompson, 2017). Features such as Boost, Super Boost, Top Picks, and Priority Likes manipulate Tinder's algorithmic presentation of users in the Discovery feed. While this may not seem to be an issue given that Tinder's algorithmic ranking is opaque and these features augment users' agency over their profile circulation, increased visibility for some users means decreased visibility for others. Further, this visibility is purchased rather than based on (however contrived) indicators of compatibility.

While the inequity these perks allow may just be dismissed as capitalism's default arrangements in which the wealthy have access to greater privileges, premium features that enable differential access to safety mechanisms concern me the most. For instance, if Tinder's requirement for two users to right-swipe on each other before unlocking the ability to interact allows users to vet each other prior to initiating contact, the Platinum ability to send messages without matching first overrides this boundary. Since the ability to pay for a high-priced membership is not an indication of one's character, Platinum members may harass other users through this functionality, especially if they feel entitled to other users' attention in exchange for their monthly subscriber fee. In contrast, a feature like incognito mode could improve users' safety by affording greater privacy through a hidden profile. While it may be easy to dismiss the need for such a feature, associating it with the cheating spouse who wants to swipe without being caught by their partner, there are multiple scenarios when differential visibility can be protective: for instance, when LGBTQ+ people are in a geographical region with predominantly homophobic politics, when someone wishes to avoid an abusive ex who is also on the app, or in more mundane scenarios to prevent colleagues or others from viewing one's dating desires. Even so, as a paid feature, users are prompted to exchange cash for greater privacy while others can pay to override boundaries that otherwise enable distancing from unwanted suitors and prevent nonconsensual contact. Such arrangements illustrate when app business models brush up against governance policies and structures, sometimes in ways that erode existing regulatory designs or safety mechanisms.

Advertising

Tinder's first in-app advertisement debuted in April 2015 with a video promoting the beer company Budweiser's #Whatever, USA campaign (Crook, 2015d). The campaign involved a contest that users could enter to win a trip to a random location in America where Bud Light would build a party town and invite celebrities. The ad showed up as an auto-playing video appearing on a profile card in the Discovery screen, which users could left-swipe away, right-swipe to "like," or hit an "Enter Now" button to learn more about the contest. While experimenting with different-length videos, Tinder made it clear that swipe data would be provided to advertisers as valuable information about their campaign and product, as Tinder's then-VP of Advertising Brian Norgard (founder of Tappy, Tinder's first acquisition) reflected: "If you think about the way Tinder works, with 'like' and 'pass', we have a really amazing signal for advertisers" (Crook, 2015d). That signal being their response to a clear call to action: swiping, rather than the passive viewing that occurs with pre-roll and webpage ads. Sometimes consumers were also courted by ads through the appeal of data, such as when – in that same year – Tinder partnered with the razor company Gillette for an experiment to see whether clean-shaven men receive more likes, dubbed the "Shave Test." Tinder recruited college-age male users in the United States to analyze their profiles and track their swipes, finding (unsurprisingly, given who was footing the bill) that "well-groomed guys got 74% of the right swipes" (Schaffer, n.d.). Not only did Gillette report this statistic and other findings in their promotional materials as proof that shaving was attractive; the "experiment" received free publicity through coverage in various media outlets by virtue of the media buzz that Tinder attracts (e.g., Luecke, 2015). Although such campaigns are sparing on details about how samples of Tinder users differ from the general population, they reflect Tinder's ability to leverage data in multiple ways: in-app as a reflection of user interest, which can be used to tailor ads even further, and outside the app as a point of interest and publicity – though only if Tinder is perceived as reflecting real trends regarding desire and attraction.

Tinder's advertising channels have formalized over time into three main routes that bring advertisers, brands, products, and services into contact with app users. First, Tinder has a track record of developing elaborate partnerships with specific clients. In the app's early days of advertising, these partnerships were especially geared toward popular culture and youthful interests. For instance, pop star Jason Derulo appeared in users' Discovery feeds and those who swiped right on his profile received a YouTube link to his new music video (McIntyre, 2015). Another 2015 campaign involved a partnership with Calvin Klein, comprising in-app as well as print and billboard ads depicting fashion models in sensual embraces overlaid with fictional steamy text message conversations displaying remarks such as, "Hahah a light threesome never hurt anyone ☺ ☺ ☺" (Hypebeast, 2015). With a different tenor, another of Tinder's early advertising partnerships with the gaming company Bethesda promoted their mobile game Fallout Shelter by circulating profiles for its animated characters in Tinder that, upon matching, directed users to a download link for the game (Makuch, 2015). As Tinder and its users have matured, more recent brand partnerships have involved other companies in the tech ecosystem and targeted different elements of life, such as a partnership with Lyft enabling users to gift rides to their matches to facilitate their arrival at a date location (Lyons, 2021) and a collaboration with the meal kit delivery service Hello Fresh offering a special "Date Night Delights" recipe series (Tinder, 2023a). These partnerships have been smoothed into Tinder's ethos as an app for hooking up or dating, with Calvin Klein tapping into the potential for casual and spontaneous sexual encounters at a time when the business was oscillating between hook-up promotion and swiping for true love. In contrast, the Hello Fresh campaign suggests that "cuffing season" (a time, generally during colder months, when people are looking to settle into longer relationships) is followed by "forking season," a period when the relationship becomes even more serious, marked by home cooking and stay-in dinners. It is also, apparently, enhanced through a limited-edition collection of "Forking Seasonings" available for $14.99 while supplies last.

Early ad campaigns enabled Tinder to experiment with different formats that now comprise the range of offerings available through Match Group's direct marketing sales. The conglomerate's marketing arm, Match Media Group, offers advertisers the chance to distribute their materials across its portfolio of apps (Match Group Americas, LLC, n.d.). Despite this range, four of the six ad products on offer are specific to Tinder. They include a branded profile card with which users can match to "reveal brand custom messaging and drive downstream actions," such as the linked content that became available after matching in the Jason Derulo or Fallout Shelter campaigns. There is also a Tinder quiz that prompts users to swipe on their preferred answers. Other offers include the "Tinder native video card" as the video version of the branded profile card and a display card that takes users to a linked page with just one click (or tap) rather than requiring them to match with the card first. Each product is designed to work with Tinder's display of profile "cards" in the Discovery screen, coinciding with Rad's original vision that advertising would be most effective "when people are in the mindset of discovery" (Crook, 2015d). This choice leaves Tinder's messaging, explore, and profile screens free of advertising save for Tinder's attempts to sell subscriptions. Match Media Group invites advertisers with a budget of $25K+ to get in contact about running a campaign, offering to collaborate to develop "the optimal media mix to drive measurable results" and noting that tailored campaigns involving social media, in-person events, and custom content solutions are available. These tailored options have become a mainstay of contemporary brands, who seek to implement immersive brand activations as highly engaging experiences for potential customers that also garner algorithmic visibility across social media (Carah and Angus, 2018).

Tinder's third marketing channel has involved a turn toward programmatic advertising, as an automated, data-driven process of delivering personalized ads in real time (Busch, 2016). In 2017, Tinder partnered with Facebook (now Meta) to leverage its Audience Network advertising platform through which ads could be purchased and served in the Tinder app (Stewart, 2017). When then-CEO Greg Blatt announced the partnership on an investor call, he was unsure of how many additional ads this would infuse into Tinder but he noted that the current inventory from direct sales was "so small" while Facebook would provide "the ability to hit any ad load we want," since the Audience Network promises to connect apps with "millions" of advertisers (Meta, 2025c). However, reporting on the partnership also noted that advertisers who did not want their content to appear on a dating app could opt out through Meta's advertising platform, reflecting that Tinder's brand may not align with every advertiser's aims or values. These hesitations appear to work both ways, as the Match Group Advertising Policy notes that it may prohibit certain categories of content flowing through programmatic ad networks (Match Group Americas, LLC, 2025). While programmatic advertising provides new opportunities for, and a higher volume of, targeted advertising on Tinder, it ties Tinder more intricately to infrastructural platforms like Meta and Google. Further, the increased speed and automated processes associated with programmatic marketing present challenges in terms of smoothing ads into Tinder's aim to associate this content with the app's focus on relationships and love. Beyond business concerns, programmatic advertising also leverages user data, targeting users according to datafied and algorithmically profiled identities that may not always seamlessly map on to how users see themselves (Cheney-Lippold, 2017). All these factors make programmatic advertising a lucrative and scalable solution for the mature era of Tinder's advertising endeavors, yet present unwieldy complications for user experiences and the company's vision.

Generating intimate data

Of course, personal data is only generated through users being present on the app, engaging with it and other users. In a digital landscape of network effects, where the use of a platform is rendered more valuable to the company and others when there is a large network present, users are only likely to join and remain on Tinder if a volume of other people are also on the app. Further, users are necessary to drive in-app sales, subscriptions, and advertiser interest. This is why dating app companies become involved in fostering, engaging, and sustaining data cultures (Albury et al., 2017), which arise from the convergence of user practices, datafication processes, and infrastructures, rendering relational intentions, desires, interactions, and outcomes into data. To attract users and their data, Tinder has engaged in a range of activities meant to promote its app, which have shifted over time and in relation to whether their purpose is to draw new users or maintain existing engagement.

Although nearly a decade apart, Tinder's debut visual campaign, #ITSTARTSHERE, directed by Kaz Firpo (2023), and its more recent 2023 campaign, It Starts With a Swipe™, share more than similar titles, they both attempt to counteract cynical attitudes toward dating apps. I recall being captivated by the first ad, which Tinder uploaded to Vimeo in 2014, as part of its target millennial audience. As I have written previously (Duguay, 2017), the ad's dreamy music overlying nostalgically grainy beach and urban scenes appealed to an early 2010s aesthetic reflective of Instagram filters and the rising popularity of big-city dramas like *Girls* (2012–17). It featured potential users seemingly in their twenties and gave post-racial nods to "diversity" by including racially ambiguous lead actors with a range of supporting friends. The video cuts from a woman and a man spending time on their hobbies and doing their own thing to matching on Tinder and meeting for a romantic rooftop date. Their depiction as normal yet ideal suitors meeting with relative ease and a sense of safety defied panic about desperate swipers and dangerous internet strangers.

In contrast, the It Starts With a Swipe™ campaign contends with years of digital dating disenchantment. It reframes Tinder for Gen Z, who have already experienced

– or at least heard of – the problems with dating apps: ghosting, shallowness, danger, heteronormativity, homogeneity. This is evident in one batch of campaign videos that include the formulaic tagline, “It sucks to be wrong about [e.g., the spice level of the food on your date], but it’s great to be wrong about Tinder.” This statement implies that young daters are wrong when they assume that connection cannot be sparked through Tinder. The app’s aged reputation is further counteracted by the campaign enlisting French mixed-media photographer Pol Kurucz, who self-describes as exploring “human eccentricity by challenging social, gender and aesthetic norms” (Kurucz, n.d.). His style has imbued Tinder’s billboard images and videos with bright colors – often hot pink – and a combination of scenes wherein “modern day fairytales” meet the “electrified dating journey” (Tinder, 2023b) (e.g., floating beds, oversized toothbrushes). The ads also feature same-sex and gender-ambiguous couples as part of a racially diverse cast. Along with “wrong about” scenarios, the campaign includes “meet cute” videos (described in chapter 1) that demonstrate how texting with matches can drum up romance at the level of a modern-day romcom. The campaign’s static images tap into Gen Z sentiments and phrases, such as one that shows two people kissing on a merry-go-round surrounded by the words “Realizing you’re not dead inside.” The campaign won Effie awards in recognition of its marketing effectiveness and was credited for a slight increase in Tinder’s 2023 earnings (Sanchez, 2023). Both campaigns’ unbridled attempts at authentically channeling youthful trends and aesthetics gamble, though, on being seen as trying too hard and therefore risk selling out (Banet-Weiser, 2012). Given this risk and the limited circulation of conventional ads – one must encounter them in an increasingly fragmented online environment or by chance in person – Tinder has also turned to the cult of personality to put its messages in front of fans and into algorithmic feeds.

Since the early Jason Derulo ads, Tinder has frequently associated its brand with celebrities. From James Blunt being blunt about how users could improve their profiles (Murdoch, 2017b) to Megan Thee Stallion promoting the Put Yourself Out There contest in which users could win US$10,000 for making a profile that is "unapologetic and authentic," mimicking the star who "made it to the top by being herself" (Tinder, 2020e), Tinder has worked with celebrities to bolster its visibility and appeal to fans. However, with influencer marketing becoming a central way that individuals are exposed to products (Hund, 2023), Tinder has also invested in partnerships with prominent social media personalities. For instance, in 2025 Tinder enlisted TikTok influencers to create content about their dating lives under the hashtag #theconnectionexperience (Flynn, 2025). The hashtag campaign included Madi Webb, a TikToker with 2.6 million followers at the time, whose videos fall into the "get ready with me" genre as she speaks to the camera while doing her makeup or bedtime skincare routine. In Webb's six-episode #theconnectionexperience saga (madibwebb, 2024), she tearfully discusses horrible past dates (arranged without an app) before bringing viewers into a saucy Tinder love story as it unfolds. As someone who dates men and women, Webb explains early on that it is difficult for her to know when women are interested in more than being friends. Then she matches with a woman on Tinder, dishes about their three-hour first date, and includes a video from a hotel room in Las Vegas where she invited the woman to accompany her on a business trip. Viewers following this rapidly escalating romance get a peek at the woman's side profile and hear her voice, but the date's identity is left a mystery. This video's reality-TV-like magnetism is followed by one of Webb's more conventional daily routine videos to help unpack the excitement. She explains how hopeful she is about this new relationship and rounds off the series by declaring, "Oh my god, I can't believe I met her on Tinder, that's so crazy!" Her surprise reinforces Tinder's efforts to dispel notions that the app precludes positive and meaningful relationship experiences.

Over the course of these short TikToks, Webb subtly highlights Tinder's features and draws. She explains Tinder's recently introduced Matchmaker feature, in which users can let friends and family swipe on their behalf, shouts out Tinder's "identity verification safety measures and whatnot" (adding that she's also preserving her safety with "pepper spray in the bag – we're good!"), and manages to ask her newfound love, "What made you give me a Super Like on Tinder?" Despite these feature name drops and captions tagging Tinder's TikTok account alongside #ad, the videos give the sense of letting viewers into Webb's actual dating life. Congruent with how influencers balance performances of authenticity with branding and revenue generation (Cunningham and Craig, 2017), Webb's straightforward introduction of the partnership in the first video, the integration of Tinder into her regular genre format, her affective intensity (e.g., crying, showing embarrassment or joy), and the shot featuring her mystery date that allows viewers to feel as though they are being let behind the scenes, all make this series feel like a real Tinder success story.

Once potential Tinderers have logged in and become regular users, in-app mechanisms are designed to retain and bolster their engagement. A feature like Matchmaker works to stave off swipe fatigue by shifting the work of narrowing options to trusted acquaintances. Tinder has also developed notifications and in-app experiences meant to draw users to their phones. In 2019, it launched Swipe Night as an interactive, real-time story experience in which users choose between options to unfold the plot and chat with each other about their choices at the end. Employing actors, script writers, and "Drake's go-to music video director" Karena Evans (Tinder, 2019b), Swipe Night's two seasons spanned seven immersive episodes. What Tinder's then-CEO Jim Lanzone called a "social entertainment experience" (Tinder, 2021c) was so popular that it won Tinder the Entertainment Grand Prix at the 2021 Cannes Lions Festival for the company's creativity, with Tinder reporting that more than 20 million users participated in the first edition (Tinder, 2021d). Hoping to spark ongoing conversations beyond these single events, Tinder (2021e) introduced Vibes, a functionality that allows users to answer questions about everything "from personality traits to pop culture" and see others' answers on their profiles for a limited period. The app also pushes notifications to users when there is a Swipe Surge, as a temporary spike in activity during which there are more active users with whom to match.

Tinder's retention and engagement efforts have extended to in-person environments. The app's Festival Mode bridges modalities, as it enables users to match with others who are going to the same music festival up to a month in advance (Perez, 2022). Tinder's more recent efforts to support in-person events appeal to those resisting online dating, especially after the pandemic's digital isolation, such as through the 2023 Single Summer Series intended to bridge "the gap between online and offline dating" (Tinder, 2023c). Announced in partnership with the founder of the Chaotic Singles Party, Cassidy Davis, whose events were premised on bringing a random match from a dating app to a party, Tinder's sponsored events offered advance tickets to users and encouraged them to, specifically, bring someone they met on Tinder. Rather than simply attending a singles' party, encouraging people to match on Tinder first ensures that, even if these individuals never use the app again, Tinder has collected their data – individually and in connection with at least one other user.

In this way, Tinder serves as a massive database of daters, one from which other users can choose but one that is also amassed for the purpose of tailoring the app's algorithmic curation and advertising. Data infrastructure scholars Esther Weltevrede and Fieke Jansen (2019) assert that what populates this database amounts to "intimate data" that not only accumulate as lively and habitual data from users' everyday lives but also foster close relationships between Tinder and third-party advertisers and platforms, as well as users and third parties when their ads and recommendations are fed back into users' habits. Through an investigation of Tinder's network connections and data packet transfer processes, they illustrate seamless data flows that connect Tinder with the Facebook and Google advertising ecosystems. With media studies scholar Anthony Burton, Weltevrede underscores that Tinder's intensive processes of datafication prioritize revenue generation potential, as swiping (left or right) on an advertisement invokes much more back-end activity in the app (e.g., banner loading, analytics processing, interaction tracking) than when a match is formed (Weltevrede and Burton, forthcoming). They argue not only that Tinder responds to current user actions but that the app's data processing preempts future actions according to logics of engagement and monetization by registering the user's data as desire (for people and products). As such, Tinder is just as much a technology for datafication as it is for dating, since it translates user engagement, fostered through campaigns, sponsored events, and celebrity and influencer endorsements, into intimate data that solidifies the app within sophisticated online advertising ecosystems.

Globalization

While Tinder use spans many countries worldwide, the app's spread, uptake, and daily negotiation across locales have not been seamless. Communication scholars Jason Vincent Cabañes and Cecilia Uy-Tioco (2022) identify how mobile media has given rise to "glocal intimacies" through which local and global cultures intertwine. They identify three dimensions as central to the formation of glocal intimacies, which include digital access, contextual localities, and sociotechnical dynamics. In this final section of the chapter, I consider Tinder in light of these dimensions and how they have shaped its globalization.

There exist both technological and geopolitical barriers to accessing Tinder. In 2017, when Tinder rolled out its desktop version, Tinder Online, it framed this option as serving those in "emerging markets" who lack sufficient phone storage for the app or whose data plans may not be enough for Tinder's image-heavy feed (Crook, 2017). Tinder Online was first made available in Argentina, Brazil, Colombia, Indonesia, Italy, Mexico, the Philippines, and Sweden before expanding to other locations. A couple of years later, Tinder also introduced a Lite version of its app with reduced storage needs and data usage. The company identified this option as essential to reaching users in Southeast Asia, where internet access may be variable and data plans are expensive (Perez, 2019). In contrast, daters in China find that international apps can become unreliable not due to technical issues but because their use is limited or banned as part of the country's "Great Firewall" of surveillance and censorship efforts (Wu and Trottier, 2021). With Tinder's earlier login functionality requiring a Facebook account, Chinese users reported needing a VPN to first sign up to Facebook and then join the dating app. While VPNs became unnecessary after Tinder began allowing users to login with their phone numbers, users still sometimes found the app was slow on local networks and difficult to find in Chinese app stores. Given these challenges, digital media scholars Shangwei Wu and Daniel Trottier (2021) observe that users of international, as opposed to local, dating apps in China tend to comprise smaller, privileged groups who reflect somewhat exclusory "bubbles of cosmopolitanism" (p. 10). Geopolitical developments can also shift access, reflected in Match Group's decision to restrict access to its apps in Russia after President Vladimir Putin's decision to invade Ukraine (though Match Group was much slower than other corporations to take this action) (Race, 2023). These issues of access shape not only how many users are on Tinder worldwide but also *who* is on Tinder, since access to technological infrastructure is often shaped by several intersecting factors, such as class and gender, while geopolitical tensions may affect entire nations.

Considerations pertaining to contextual localities have to do with whether and how mobile media and their associated practices are considered local and how well (or not) people receive global interventions into the local (Cabañes and Uy-Tioco, 2022). Given Tinder's association with sexual encounters and relationships, its integration into local contexts has often been affected by how these pursuits are perceived and their associated gender roles or biases. Despite Tinder's uptake in Turkey, for example, there is still a risk that women using the app will be seen as shameful, reflected in local dating jargon, *Tinder'a düşmek,* which means "to slide into Tinder" or "falling for Tinder" and is used to shame women for being on the app (Cöbek and Ergin, 2021). Researcher Vishnupriya Das (2019) explains how the shifting commercialization of femininity in India has given rise to the figure of the "New Indian Woman," similar to figures of a *new woman* across South and Southeast Asia, who "embodies a global lifestyle but sticks to Indian values" (p. 130). With India's dating app market saturated by numerous domestic and international apps, Tinder has struggled to connect with this image and negotiate these contradictory gender expectations. In 2016, Tinder released a television ad in which Indian parents showed acceptance of their daughter's use of the app, which failed to please both those attached to more traditional matrimonial matchmaking and more progressive users, who scoffed at the implication that parental approval was needed (Parthasarathi and Agarwal, 2023). Yet, Tinder's more recent marketing campaigns in India have since leaned into emphasizing women's empowerment, freedom of choice when it comes to dating, and how the app can protect women's safety (Morris and Dobson, 2023). This approach applies postfeminist and neoliberal feminist discourses from Western markets, which media scholars Samuel Morris and Amy Dobson observe as central to the way that "Tinder positions itself as a key tool in the building of gender equality and 'modernity' for India" (2023, p. 4281). However, international companies also face backlash when seen as being guilty of cultural imperialism or the Americanization of culture, which may inadvertently fortify local apps' targeted appeals, such as India's TrulyMadly – a main Tinder rival – being able to assert its "Indianness" despite sharing some similarities with Tinder in design and framing (Das, 2019).

These localized initiatives are reflective of how Tinder's international marketing has combined a more general brand image and broad messaging with regionally tailored strategies. A section of Tinder's website houses newsrooms for 16 countries, which host press releases and announcements about new features or campaigns. When digital media researcher Alex Chartrand and I began examining the posts shared through each newsroom, we expected to find much of the same content simply translated into different languages. Our assumption was premised on past research showing that online dating services largely do not align their marketing with country-specific cultural values (Paul et al., 2022) as well as our experience of often receiving the same messaging in Canada that Tinder circulates in the United States. To interrogate our assumptions, we collected posts from these newsrooms for approximately a year and a half (January 2024–July 2025), examining a total of 459 posts. Of these, 270 were indeed similar in their topics and often relayed the same information with only small changes or amendments catering to specific countries. Such homogeneous posts were often circulated when Tinder introduced a new feature. For instance, the 2025 launch of the Double Date feature (a resurrection of Tinder Social, which allows pairs of users to swipe on each other), was announced widely across newsrooms with similar stories and only small deviations across posts, such as different models in the Japanese images promoting the feature from the models appearing across several other stores (e.g., France, Germany, Spain, Sweden). We also found that some posts and topics were recurrent across smaller regions or groupings of countries, such as Australia, Canada, the United Kingdom, and the United States (6), as well as a grouping of posts across Australia, India, Japan, Korea, and Thailand (11), and certain posts recurred across European countries (France, Germany, Italy, the Netherlands, Spain, Sweden) and the United Kingdom (15). However, 156 posts in our sample could be classified as local content with themes and media that did not appear anywhere else, reflecting Tinder's efforts to tailor its marketing to specific countries or regions.

The volume and sophistication of this tailored media differed between newsrooms. Brazil's newsroom contained 47 posts over this duration, followed closely by France (46) and Germany (44), with these newsrooms containing many more posts than Canada (12) or Sweden (10), which had the fewest. Brazil's newsroom included many posts highlighting local media collaborations, such as the *Match o Papo* podcast (Tinder, 2024f), featuring Brazilian actress and model Clara Moneke interviewing guests about their flirtations and gossip. Several posts also drew attention to the collaboration *Tinder Apresenta: MTV Beija Sapo* (Tinder Presents: MTV Kiss the Frog), a revival of a mid-2000s Brazilian game show in which a contestant (the prince or princess) must choose one of three participants dressed as frogs to kiss at the end of the episode (Tinder, 2024g). While this version of the show features participants' Tinder profiles as a key means for introducing and scrutinizing them, it also harnesses nostalgia associated with the original series.

Tinder's multipronged marketing efforts, involving local brand partnerships and targeted media strategies, have also been documented in Southeast Asia (Lim, 2022). We noticed efforts to target countries in this market with the numerous posts to the Thailand newsroom (37), reflected in – for instance – a partnership with the Bangkok-based pet clothing company Clawset to promote pet lovers turning to Tinder to connect with each other (Tinder, 2024h). Tinder's announcement of this partnership provides local "insights" from Thai users' data, noting a 12 percent increase in Thai women mentioning dogs on the app over the past year. Tinder's media production expands more broadly to Southeast Asia in its YouTube channel dedicated to the region, where it hosts talk shows in Vietnamese, fictional narratives in Indonesian, and a reality series starring daters in the Philippines, among commercials and other content. At the time of writing, I found more than ten country- or region-specific Tinder YouTube channels, though some of these – like Tinder Sweden or Tinder Denmark – only hosted a handful of ads translated into national languages. These channels were a stark contrast to the Brazilian or Indian channels, which overflowed with custom content.

While there are limitations to our comparison of newsroom content (for instance, we did not investigate whether Tinder deleted posts over the duration that we studied), Tinder's localized marketing strategies defy simplistic assumptions that Match Group seeks to sell Tinder globally through a singular approach. While Tinder capitalizes on the transnational expansion of gendered discourses relating to dating empowerment and shifting attitudes toward casual sex (Morris and Dobson, 2023), the company appears to adjust the app's promotion and messaging for specific markets. However, aside from the Lite version, Tinder's interface, features, and functionality remain the same wherever it is made available and tend to carry certain meanings and implications with them. Cabañes and Uy-Tioco (2022) observe that technological affordances become enveloped in local social intimacies, giving rise to particular sociotechnical dynamics that interweave the global and local. Research in Manila showed that while Filipino women viewed Filipino men on

Tinder as lacking cosmopolitanism, they used the app to find foreigners whom they considered to have more globalized sensibilities (Cabañes and Collantes, 2020). While Tinder sparked exciting new relationships for these women, such dating practices were still weighed down by local conservative views opposing relationships with Westerners. Since such arrangements were only available to middle-class women with mobile media access, they also tended to reinforce class divisions in the city. The app's association with casual sex and its rapid swipe functionality opened the door for users to experience sexism, bias, racism, and discrimination associated with one's nationality. The women in Manila spoke of fielding sexual harassment and deflecting racist, classist slurs from Western men. Racist bias similarly circulated among men seeking men on Tinder in China, as users observed that white individuals were idealized while Chinese users were stereotyped as being submissive (Wu and Trottier, 2021). Research comparing Tinder use across Mexico City, Mexico and Madrid, Spain also highlights how Tinder's dominant stigmatization due to its association with casual sex combined with varying local attitudes toward sexual diversity and family-oriented values (Cardoso-González, 2019). This difference in attitudes led to users in Madrid viewing the app as slightly less associated with security risks and violence than users in Mexico, whose experiences of Tinder were shaped by more conservative and religious ideologies. While Tinder provides an interface between the global and the local, its use and associated experiences are shaped by local sociocultural attitudes as well as meanings and associations attached to its affordances, which travel across geographies.

Conclusion

This chapter has explored different ways that Tinder, and its parent company, Match Group, have contributed to the marketization of encounters (sexual, romantic, or otherwise) between people. Match Group has consolidated a large proportion of the dating app industry under its umbrella, developing apps for broad markets (e.g., Hinge) alongside niche apps that can be cross-promoted according to shifting trends or desires. This horizontal expansion makes Match Group a dominant player in this industry and contributes to the longevity of its business, even if individual apps become seen as stale or passé. However, this dominance is dependent on massive technology companies that supply the digital infrastructures integrated into Match Group apps and upon which they rely (e.g., Apple's app store, Amazon Web Services, Meta's single sign-on, and Google and Facebook ad ecosystems). While this interdependence can present challenges for Match Group, such as Meta's introduction of Facebook Dating that coaxes some users to remain within the confines of its platform for matchmaking services, Match Group's volume and variation of dating app properties render it versatile in the markets it already saturates. Meanwhile, its international marketing efforts appear to be serious about reaching new, large populations of potential daters through tailored infrastructures for augmented access and campaigns rooted in localized cultural references as well as celebrity and media cultures. Such campaigns tap into globalized sentiments relating to dating, neoliberal feminism, and sexuality while toeing the line of traditional and local conventions relating to intimacy.

Tinder's business strategy, however, is not always in the best interest of users. The development of premium pricing tiers forces users to pay for a better app experience: one without advertising or constant prompts to upgrade, with no swipe limit, and with the promise of greater algorithmic visibility (or, alternatively, without the threat of algorithmic invisibility). Certain paid privileges enable the circumvention of protective design mechanisms, allowing subscribers to bypass the need for others to opt into interacting with them. However, this element of protection, which provides users with choice (consent, really) concerning whether to be contacted is fundamental, considering the previous chapter's discussion of how sexual harassment, the hurling of racial slurs, violent threats, and other dangerous speech start on the app, making it a risky space for many individuals. Given that associations between Tinder and casual sex – along with the baggage of stigma, inequitable gender relations, and racism – travel with the app globally, and that these associations combine with technological affordances that can facilitate the app's use for potentially harmful behavior, users across the world become subject to these risks as Tinder is marketed more widely.

With the increasing marketization of our intimate lives, there is also the opportunity for resistance (Murdock and Wasko, 2007). Individuals may cringe when an influencer drops "Super Like" into a video and scroll to the next TikTok. They might decide to stay at home instead of attending a Tinder-sponsored party. Entire communities may opt for a locally developed dating app that they determine is better catered to what they are looking for. Even so, Match Group's dominance and Tinder's multipronged marketing strategy introduce friction to resistance: users who refuse to subscribe endure constant reminders of how their search for love may be successful if they shell out a bit of money while those who switch from Tinder to another app are likely to end up on a Match Group property. Although these other dating apps may present different features or interfaces, Match Group has integrated the ubiquitous swipe and other popular features across them, giving rise to similar interfaces with few of the issues that users experience through Tinder addressed by these options. Given these circumstances, logging off, deleting, and disengaging are also forms of resistance. It is possible that dating apps' "flop era" may be the accumulated outcome of users deciding they no longer want to participate in this marketplace of dating, giving rise to a form of dispersed yet collective resistance to these technologies and how they configure our intimate lives.

Conclusion: Striking a match

Early in 2024, Match Group – Tinder's parent company – announced it was now "in a relationship" with OpenAI, creator of the popular generative AI tool ChatGPT (2024b). The press release, which stated that it was written by ChatGPT and edited by Match Group's Corporate Communications Team, announced how the partnership included Match Group obtaining over 1,000 ChatGPT Enterprise licenses that would enable the company to imbue AI technologies into multiple aspects of its work, from communications to coding, and throughout its app properties. The press release included direct quotes from ChatGPT, as though the tool were sentient, exclaiming, "I'm thrilled that Match Group matched with me." The press release also foreshadowed, "Match Group and OpenAI are just getting started on this romantic tech journey." Two key announcements since this moment stand out to me as signaling Match Group's centering of technological solutions as the way forward for this app.

Fast-forward to April 2025: Tinder launches an in-app, AI chat experience titled *The Game Game*. Following on the heels of stand-alone apps, such as Rizz and Ari, which offer AI-powered virtual dating coaches, *The Game Game* places users in fictional scenarios with AI characters whom they must woo into agreeing to a date. Launched in the United States on April Fool's Day, Tinder released the game with the caveat that it was designed to be over-the-top for fun and to help users practice their flirting. As some users observed on the Tinder subreddit that the game was buggy and they thought it was simply a joke (Spiritual-Station267, 2025), introducing the game lightheartedly may have been strategic in allowing OpenAI to test out its Real-Time API, a breakthrough in AI voice conversations that allows the tool to respond to human speech more seamlessly and without as much delay as previous technologies (Barr, 2025). Spencer Rascoff, who had been appointed as Match Group's CEO for only a couple of months at the time, showed off one of the game scenarios in a video posted to his Instagram, chatting with Myla, a fictional 32-year-old nurse, in a cooking workshop (spencerrascoff, 2025). As she quips about the smell of fresh herbs mixed with spice, he slides in the line, "You're a little bit spicey, you know?" and points appear on the screen rewarding his flirtatiousness. Each scenario comes with a time limit within which users must accumulate enough points to fill up three flame icons in the corner of the screen, after which they have the best chance of success when asking the AI character on a date. Tips appear after each scenario to highlight what the user could have done differently. After hitting the limit of five scenarios, users are returned to Tinder's Discovery screen to implement what they have learned.

By the end of that same month, Match Group featured in yet another press release, this one hosted on the website of World, an initiative cofounded by OpenAI's CEO Sam Altman. The announcement described a partnership in which Match Group would pilot the use of one of World's tools – World ID – for identity and age verification of users, starting with those located in Japan (World, 2025a). While the reason for this starting location was not stated, Japan has fostered the uptake of digital forms of identity, such as by releasing a digital identification app that integrates information from the nationally issued "My Number Card" for use with online verification services, such as for online banking and age verification for alcohol sales (Government of Japan, n.d.). World ID is a service that provides what its originators call "proof of human" by using a biometric data verification process that "proves you are a unique human" (World,

2025b). This service is different from Tinder's other identity verification mechanisms, such as those that compare one's profile to government-issued ID or even the automated photo verification service discussed in chapter 2 that compares one's profile photos to a real-time selfie or video. Instead, World has developed a hardware device called an Orb, which takes photos of a user's face and eyes and transforms them into encrypted data. Imaging one's eye is particularly important, as the World (2025c) website explains that this information is turned into an iris code as a "compact numeric representation of an individual's unique iris texture" that "serves as a digital stand-in for the iris." The iris code is used to verify an individual as a unique human, thus unlocking a World ID that can be accessed through World's app and used as identification in third-party apps, such as Tinder.

In the keynote presentation announcing that World's identity and cryptocurrency services were now available in the United States, which includes Match Group CEO Rascoff announcing the company's new partnership, AI is invoked as both a problem and a solution (World, 2025d). Alex Blania, another cofounder of World and the CEO of Tools for Humanity – the company developing World – appears alongside Sam Altman (who holds a chairman role at Tools for Humanity) as they discuss how AI has made it increasingly difficult to tell apart real people from artificial agents, such as ChatGPT or bots. The company's Chief Device Officer, Rich Heley, takes the stage to explain how the Orb solves this problem, since it runs "sophisticated AI models, using a number of visible light and infrared sensors, to determine humanness." AI technology, therefore, is what determines one's difference from an AI agent.

World ships Orbs to operators, such as café owners, who make them accessible in different geographical locations to those nearby who come to have their irises scanned. In 2025, Japan had 89 Orb locations listed on the World website while the United States only had 12 sites. Operators and those who sign up for World ID through this process receive Worldcoin tokens, a cryptocurrency that was not functioning in the United States (where Tools for Humanity is headquartered) until April 2025 when its partnership with Match Group as well as payment services like Stripe and Visa was announced. This financial incentive has drawn scrutiny for its potential to attract users who may not fully understand the implications of providing their biometric data (Chafkin, 2023). Even so, World ID holds potential for Tinder, which is the only app showcased in Match Group's partnership announcement, to continue what it has long chased through other forms of verification: showing user profiles that "represent real people seeking real connections" (World, 2025a). Being "real" once again stands in for being authentic as the partnership announcement highlights how the dating app use case is just one step toward realizing a "more authentic internet" entirely.

These two developments strike me as holding similarities and contradictions. They both appear to be aimed at addressing Tinder's mounting problem of user disengagement, which the previous chapter described as an urgent threat to Match Group's revenue. This disengagement can be linked to the stabilization of Tinder's meaning (outlined in chapter 1) around dating app melancholia that views such apps as sad and interactions through them as shallow, frivolous, or hopeless in leaving users endlessly looking for love but never finding it. I have mentioned how Tinder's most recent ad campaigns even try to overtly counter this stabilization, telling users they're *wrong* about Tinder. But the melancholia is merely a symptom of deeper issues: design mechanisms and behavioral standards linked to establishing authenticity, which render users who cannot conform to them into targets for rejection; the circulation of gendered double standards, forms of racial discrimination, and cisheteronormativity that normalize aggressive and sexually entitled advances toward women, sexual racism and fetishization, and targeted reporting of transgender users; and a business strategy that constantly prompts users toward engagement and paying for premium features, some of which override Tinder's premise of matching as a means for consenting to interaction. As I have stressed, Tinder is not the cause of longstanding sociocultural issues, such as misogyny and racism, but its design, governance, business model, and framing sometimes facilitate and exacerbate them.

Match Group's AI developments can be seen as interventions or solutions to such issues. *The Game Game* holds the potential to teach users when their flirting crosses a line. For instance, Tinder has included sponsored partnerships with male influencers, such as Twitch streamer Austin from *The Austin Show* (2025), presumably to reach men who could brush up on their etiquette. The in-game tips provided after a user completes a scenario are themed around sparking connection as much as instilling respect into conversations, such as, "Balance persistence with respecting conversational flow," a tip that dissuades interrupting others or bombarding them with comments or demands. While *The Game Game* takes a lighthearted approach to shifting user behavior, the World ID initiative is more serious, with this technology discussed as being essential for humanity. Similar to Tinder's past verification mechanisms, the connection between identification and authenticity is linked to an understanding of authenticity as safety.

But the logic underlying these interventions is also resonant of the flaws in other attempts to address complex technocultural problems, which I have drawn attention to throughout this book. Bias, discrimination, and violence do not take place simply because people do not know better. The rampant misogyny that women experience through Tinder is not a byproduct of men incorrectly thinking that overriding women's boundaries is an effective form of flirtation. If it were, *The Menprovement Initiative*'s reaction GIFs may have been a sufficient wake-up call. Rather, violent and oppressive behavior involves one person exerting power over another, generally not because of ignorance but because structural and systemic aspects of society provide them with the privilege to do so while rewarding this behavior, and they have learned there are few consequences.

Similarly, identifying someone as human is not sufficient for deterring them from committing harmful acts: humans often hurt humans. Despite the wealth of evidence that online identity verification does not necessarily make people safer and can, in fact, make some individuals less safe through threats to their privacy (Kennedy et al., 2016; Rösner and Krämer, 2016), identity-related solutions remain the mainstay of attempts to preserve safety in digital spaces. Biometric data and iris codes are not sufficient for proving one's humanity if we understand this term to mean not only biological characteristics but also interpersonal qualities associated with humaneness, such as compassion. Ultimately, these interventions are guilty of technological solutionism (Morozov, 2013), relying on technology – especially internet-centered and digital technologies – to solve all of humanity's difficult problems. Technological solutionism is insufficient when addressing problems that stem as much from sociocultural structures and systems as they do from technological decisions.

Beyond this insufficiency, some technologically driven solutions can give rise to further problems and potential harms. Critics of AI's rapid and often unregulated uptake have pointed out how this technology often repeats biases and oppressive practices of the past (Apprich et al., 2018; Benjamin, 2019). Looking more closely at screenshots from *The Game Game*, even as it attempts to invoke new behaviors, illustrated figures of women in the fictional scenarios are often petite and feminine, with some characters seemingly sexualized: multiple YouTube demonstrations show a scenario with an android-like female character who does not appear to be wearing clothes while her laptop obscures her chest (Emlovz, 2025; Wingman Plus, 2025). With such imagery also likely to be AI-generated and riddled with recurrent problems of visual AI tools sexualizing women's bodies (Lamensch, 2023), its inclusion in the game's context reinforces the notion that women who conform to beauty ideals are the ones who deserve respect. In terms of World ID, I have previously noted research showing that biometric technologies work better for some individuals and not others (Buolamwini, 2023). This data can also be misused by a number of actors, from the potential for law enforcement to unfairly profile individuals (Joseph, 2025) to the actually occurring fraudulent sale of World IDs to those in jurisdictions where the technology is not accessible but who wish to access its services (Chafkin, 2023).

Given the lack of regulation concerning AI technologies, the rapid ways that technology companies are outpacing governments' ability to enforce user protections, and the environmental cost of AI infrastructures, there have been calls – sincere or not – from within industry for slowing down AI development (Mohammad et al., 2023). Alongside these calls are strong scholarly warnings of the harm that may occur if development proceeds in its current direction (Gebru and Torres, 2024; Hogan, 2024). At the least, slowing down is warranted, given the blurriness of what people even mean when they speak of AI, which is invoked when referring to a range of tangible (e.g., generative tools, predictive and machine-learning programs) and more metaphorical and all-encompassing uses (Elish and boyd, 2018; Suchman, 2023). AI is often spoken about as a new frontier or in similar colonial language (such as World's "Pioneer Grant"), mimicking earlier characterizations of "homesteading" on the early internet (Wyatt, 2021). Such mind-sets assume the colonization of *terra nullius* – that there is no one already present and nothing already in place – when AI interventions like the ones described above elide what people are already doing on dating apps. As I asserted in earlier chapters, Tinder users have layered and specific practices of determining whether a match is who they say they are and they put in considerable "safety work" as steps for protecting themselves on and off the app (Broeker, 2023; Gillett, 2023). *The Game Game* does not appear to teach or spread these practices and World ID may ask users to accept a verified checkmark over other indications of trustworthiness.

In any case, Tinder's back-to-back AI innovations seem to lead us down a circular spiral. *The Game Game* aims to teach people what it is like to be human – to make real connections – by learning from AI. On the other hand, World AI aims to draw a stark differentiation between AI and humans, assuring those handing over their biometric data that there is a very real distinction. Not only does the aspiration for dating app users to be as flawless as AI and as real as humans burden them with the responsibility to solve Tinder's problems, but providing AI tools to train them toward this comportment also presents a false solution, since socio-technical issues cannot be solely addressed at the individual level. While it may be tempting to throw one's hands up and call for burning it all down (or, to at least let AI burn itself out before its environmental impacts accelerate the climate crisis that is burning up our planet), I am not yet done with thinking about how digital intimacy could be preserved, and even enjoyable, in this era of platformization. However, my solutions are certainly not AI-inspired quick fixes, as I emphasize balancing technological change with socio-cultural shifts. In this concluding chapter, I raise different ways of thinking about people and digitally mediated dating, centered on human rights and relational perspectives that guard against the rampant technological solutionism of our current AI moment by asserting that technology alone will never provide answers to the complexity of digital intimacy.

What if Tinder could be fun again?

When I re-downloaded Tinder in 2024 for this book project, I was surprised at just how transactional the interface had become. I was already familiar with the app's central swipe functionality, having added my voice to critiques of it as rapid, binary, and focused on visual appearances (David and Cambre, 2016; Duguay, 2018). As chapter 1 delved into, the swipe has been the crux of widespread criticism about Tinder's complicity in dating apps' rendering of courtship into nothing more than a market in which users are commodities or entrepreneurs selling themselves (Bandinelli and Gandini, 2022; Nickenig, 2024). An art installation called "Tender – It's how people meat" (figure 3) presents a visceral representation of these arrangements by depicting a piece of meat affixed to a rotating lever above a smartphone with the Tinder app open. As the artists Matei Szabo, Cors Brinkman, Marcello Gómez Maureira, and Jeroen van Oorschot describe it, "A piece of pork tenderloin swipes every picture of a potential date to the right, aiming to find a soul mate" (van Oorschot, 2015). Such an artwork can be read as a multileveled critique of how people become objectified as pieces of meat through Tinder's swipe, how the app constructs a meat market that reduces love and sex to a thoughtless transaction, and that there is no need to be a human to match with others, since the tenderloin is sufficient for carrying out the swipe gesture. Given the swipe's affordances and its interpretation within heterosexual culture's gendered courtship games, Tinder has benefited from how its technology has rationalized intimacy, while needing to mitigate melancholic associations between swiping and cold, sad, objectification.

Even so, as Tinder's business model has matured over the past decade, there is now much more to the app that makes it feel like a marketplace. As described in chapter 4, its screens are littered with prompts to subscribe, accrue coins, or outrightly purchase features that promise greater success in matching. The market logic underlying Tinder and similarly designed apps, as well as the integration of these apps into platformized markets, is now at the forefront and screams that one simply needs to buy more to get more: invest in

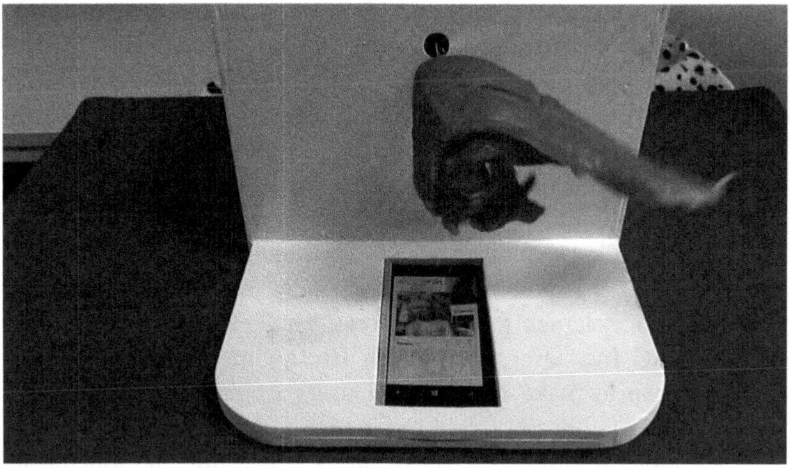

Figure 3. A still image from the recording of Tender, which was so popular that I first encountered it ambiently online as a looping GIF in the mid-2010s. With permission of the artists: Matei Szabo, Cors Brinkman, Marcello Gómez Maureira, and Jeroen van Oorschot.

your (potential) matches. Users found the swipe's uncertainty and excitement fun in Tinder's early years and have since developed ways to overcome the app's transactional arrangements, such as by moving conversations elsewhere and signaling the kinds of intimate relationships they want, from hook-ups to romantic relationships and everything in between. But the current experience of being bombarded with ads, pressured to buy visibility in the form of premium features, and having little recourse against toxic behavior results in an experience that is often not fun – dangerous at worst or lackluster at best for many users.

Blogger, journalist, and activist Cory Doctorow (2025) points to the widespread worsening of people's experiences with platforms and apps, indicating that I am not just imagining this shift. He describes how many dominant platforms have undergone a process of "enshittification" involving four phases: (1) Being good to users, which is often facilitated through having sufficient investment capital to offer services for free and results in the network effect of forming a solid user base that makes a platform difficult to leave; (2) Treating users worse to make the platform better for business customers; (3) Treating business customers worse by clawing back value for themselves; (4) Becoming "a giant pile of shit" (p. 10) because users and business customers are locked into an ecosystem geared toward extracting value from them.

While Doctorow's term is admittedly "funny and naughty" (p. 3), it is possible to look at Tinder over the long term and notice elements of this process. Tinder's development under IAC Inc. (eventually Match Group) meant that it did not have to make money from users immediately. It provided them with an ad-free experience for more than two years, amassing a critical user population, before introducing its first subscription tier. When that happened, it also imposed a swipe limit, which spurred users toward paying and allowed official advertisers to occupy eyeballs while being able to crack down on rogue ad campaigns and off-label uses. Once it started accommodating business customers, Tinder built several brand, celebrity, and influencer partnerships over the years. The app's popularity was appealing and propelled their notoriety, especially when alignment could be mustered between personalities, products, and Tinder's ethos, such as through a carefully crafted razor campaign associating shaving with sexiness or "get ready with me" TikToks that showcase beauty products as essential to preparing for steamy dates. Attracting users, commercializing, and appealing to business customers covers the first two phases.

But Tinder pulled the "enshittification lever" (Doctorow, 2025, p. 332) on users and business customers to complete the process over the years. As Doctorow points out, this lever is easy to "twiddle" because platforms can change multiple aspects of their technological and economic relationships with users and customers without their control. We can see this in Tinder's variable pricing for subscription plans, its adjustments to the algorithmic curation of profiles that leave users guessing how to become visible, and its increasing demands for user data, justified through safety measures and resulting in a lucrative database of identifiable consumers. On the business side, twiddling looks not only like brands paying high prices for visibility and having to rely on Tinder's official channels for access to users and valuable metrics, given the app's closed API, but increasingly like initially valued partnerships being discarded for an endless supply of programmatic advertising via Meta or Google. Doctorow points out how the programmatic ad tech ecosystem ramps up value for these infrastructural platforms but often leaves business customers unsure as to whether their ads are actually being seen. For users, programmatic advertising means no more carefully crafted brand activations to ensure that the spray of products and services does not encroach on intimacy-seeking.

Since Doctorow's concept of enshittification is broad enough to apply to a range of platforms, from Uber to Amazon, he engages mainly with shifts to the technological, regulatory, and economic landscape that allowed for this process to become widespread. I agree with him that the loss of open APIs and interoperability, for instance, contributes to this situation: the ability to make a third-party app that overcomes the issue of algorithmic invisibility (e.g., instantiated in apps that once connected to Tinder to provide a grid view of nearby users but that no longer work) could render Boost and a number of premium features obsolete and empower users in their swiping. Regulation could facilitate greater competition among technology companies, perhaps addressing the consolidation of the world's most popular dating apps under two massive and still growing conglomerates (Match Group and Bumble Inc.) to provide users with greater choice and raise the standards for dating app experiences. These are important and significant avenues for change. However, this broad framing does not address a platform or app's specific cultures of use nor the sociocultural values and practices amid which certain apps are embedded.

Conditions that render some Tinder users' experiences less fun are as much about these developments in the tech landscape as they are about society's sexual and dating cultures as well as practices and understandings of digital intimacy forged among Tinder users. With the resurgence of conservative and traditional values in many contexts, from the widespread social media circulation of "tradwife" content to the popularity of marriage-focused television shows like *Love Is Blind* (2020–present), the ongoing and often intensified stigmatization of casual sex and sexual pleasure more broadly shapes gender relations and dating experiences. Further, spikes in anti-trans political movements, ongoing racism, and intensive political polarization are making everyday life unbearable for many groups of people (Butler, 2024; Klein, 2024). In efforts to understand recent political formations and their intensity, author and activist Naomi Klein (2024) points to how capitalism, or whatever it has morphed into (see Doctorow's discussion of technocapitalism giving rise to technofeudalism), squeezes citizens and gives rise to inequalities that leave people blaming each other and hurling hatred instead of addressing systemic issues. These political economic developments and people's responses to them are driving individuals further apart, accentuating divides across difference without allowing for change or escape from a broken system. While fixing all of this is clearly beyond the scope of a book about a dating app, it lends perspective to the kinds of values, principles, and relational logics we might want to consider when rethinking dating apps' designs, policies, and role in our lives and societies. The problem is not that Tinder cannot be fun for *anyone* in its present iteration but rather that it is not fun – it's shitty, or enshittified – for a lot of people a lot of the time for reasons that warrant sociocultural shifts alongside, and intersecting with, changes to our technologies, regulation, and economic systems.

The right to play and pleasure

Even if it can feel as though we are individual people swiping on other individual profiles, Tinder is a social app. For many of us, it is embedded within our everyday lives in which safety, well-being, and enjoyment are experiences co-created with others. As I illustrated in chapter 3, safety is a collective endeavor and one that serves as the foundation for connecting with others and finding enjoyment through dating apps. Scholars have begun thinking about safety, and facets of what it means to participate online, in light of human rights approaches to digital citizenship. At the core of these approaches lies the United Nations' (1948) Universal Declaration of Human Rights and its foundational stipulation that "All human beings are born free and equal in dignity and rights." This core stipulation can orient how we call for rights – including the right to security and to be free of discrimination – to be embedded within and upheld through our technologies. Importantly, scholars working with this framework are thinking not only about rights to be free from forms of harm but also rights to participation. Advancements in thinking about the right to digital forms of play as well as the right to sexual expression strike me as particularly relevant to Tinder.

Since Tinder was designed as a game, and there are game-like elements about courtship, it makes sense to ponder what safe and fun gameplay could look like on a dating app. Would it be possible to ditch the unspoken rules that uphold gendered double standards? Can we reconfigure the game's design in ways less conducive to such rules and norms? Games studies scholars have long asserted the importance of play. In his book aptly titled *Play Matters*, Miguel Sicart (2017) declares: "To play is to be in the world. Playing is a form of understanding what surrounds us and who we are, and a way of engaging with others. Play is a mode of being human" (p. 1). Play, perhaps more so than the texture of one's iris, is a significant indicator of human life. Yet, Sicart reminds us that play can at times be dangerous and unenjoyable. This is evident in the ways that sexism, misogyny, racism, and other forms of oppression are enacted through and within video games, and I have often found such parallels between the struggles and stakes of platform studies and (digital) game studies. Within gaming, these issues similarly stem from a combination of sociocultural and technological factors, such as the way that historical processes of digital inequality have given rise to a "dominant default able-bodied, anglophone, cis-het, white technomasculine culture of gaming" (Apperley and Gray, 2020, p. 41). As such, scholars call for changes regarding representation in and surrounding video games, changes to game rules and governance in multiplayer social games, and efforts to shift gaming cultures toward greater inclusivity (Shaw, 2017; Blamey, 2019). Thus, games studies points to the need for change at multiple levels when it comes to these difficult problems.

Scholars across games studies and digital media studies who are taking seriously the importance of play are increasingly turning toward arguments concerning children's rights. These scholars are fighting against knee-jerk reactions to risks that children encounter online that lead adults and authorities to propose banning technologies from their lives. Instead, they argue that safe, exploratory, and engaging digital play is important for young people's social participation (Livingstone and O'Neill, 2014). Their approach also highlights how developers of play spaces, such as online game creators and owners, often target young people as consumers in ways that compromise their safety or enjoyment as these corporations capitalize upon and commercialize play (Grimes, 2021). This is an issue that may garner a great deal of rage when considering children, whom we have long tried to shelter from a barrage of advertisements and persuasive marketing tactics. But it also ties into chapter 4's revelation that several of Tinder's paid features enable overriding built-in protections (e.g., mutual swiping required for interaction) and chapter 3's details about how user data (biometric and otherwise) are mandatorily traded for the promise of safety.

In considering how to create a digital world that respects children's rights while they engage in play, Angela Colvert, Kruakae Pothong, and Sonia Livingstone write that "there are many intersecting and overlapping factors that shape possibilities for play, realised through particular combinations of social-cultural factors (people), material-functional factors (products) and spatial-contextual factors (places)" (2024, p. 4). They explain that these factors interact on multiple levels: the micro level of individual experiences and interpretations, the meso level of relationships and interactions, and the macro level of public and private sector policies and practices. A change in any factor at any level affects possibilities for play. For instance, within the realm of "products," a change in a platform's design can then affect relations in the realm of "people," from how individual users feel about their ability to express themselves to the broader social norms enacted through that platform. These insights about how to make platforms safer for children also hold the potential to make them safer for all of us. While my thinking about Tinder is squarely within the realm of its use by adults, rights-based frameworks can apply if we also recognize that adults have a right to play, and such frameworks point us to considering changes across a range of factors and levels instead of looking to a singular feature, policy, or campaign to remedy large-scale barriers to digital participation.

While play can encompass a broad range of activities, users have found Tinder to be fun and playful for the spontaneity and flirtatiousness of the swipe, the suspense of matching and, ultimately, the potential of connecting over mutual desire. However, in chapter 1, I outlined how the "fun" of Tinder can quickly devolve into an ego-boosting game based on looks and complicated, gendered expectations within heterosexual cultures of casual sex. What might it look like if the game of Tinder was associated with unlocking pleasure and enjoyment, not avoiding sexual stigma and shame? Sexuality scholars call for us to think about sexuality and intimacy as rights within citizenship, again asserting the need not only for the right to protection from harm in these realms but also for the right to sexual participation and intimate expression (Plummer, 2003; Richardson, 2018). As these ideas have been taken up more widely, there have been calls across public health and sex education to integrate pleasure into resources and programming, especially since programs that focus only on risk, danger, and negative outcomes tend to be less effective in spurring people toward respectful and safer sexual conduct (Hirst, 2013; Ford et al., 2019).

Media studies scholars similarly highlight the need for platforms and the range of actors surrounding them (e.g., regulatory bodies, parents, schools) to recognize the role that digital technologies can have in sexual development and expression that is pleasurable (and not always dangerous) (Albury, 2016; Paasonen et al., 2019). For instance, research shows dating apps can be part of teens' sexual development (Albury and Byron, 2018) while platforms that permit a range of sexual expression can be conducive to adults' identity development, social connections, and sense of belonging (Tiidenberg and van der Nagel, 2020; Sundén et al., 2026). However, platforms that stamp out sexuality through moderation practices offer little agency and few mechanisms of consent for participating in such activities (Spišák et al., 2021). As such, people are denied digital sexual citizenship when they are not given the freedom to negotiate their sexuality amid the entanglements of people, technologies, and institutions that converge in our everyday use of apps and platforms (Albury, 2016). It is imaginable that by the time one signs up for Tinder, undergoes identity verification through biometric or legal processes, exerts considerable effort discerning algorithmic recommendations from one's actual preferences to find a match, and negotiates content filters in messaging screens that may miss the context for flirtatiousness, there is little pleasure left if this is what it takes to make a connection. Many of Tinder's interventions in the name of safety are focused on making potentially harmful behaviors more difficult to deploy, which is only half the work if we consider that pleasurable consensual conduct could also be facilitated.

Focusing on risk and avoiding danger misses how users and app developers can co-create an environment for pleasure. Such an environment is only possible through the recognition of pleasure as integral to sexual rights. The Global Advisory Board for Sexual Health and Wellbeing (GABSHW) (2020), a group of academics, activists, healthcare professionals, and other experts, stipulates the necessary preconditions and foundations for pleasure:

> Self-determination, consent, safety, privacy, confidence and the ability to communicate and negotiate sexual relations are key enabling factors for pleasure to contribute to sexual health and well-being. Sexual pleasure should be exercised within the context of sexual rights, particularly the rights to equality and non-discrimination, autonomy and bodily integrity, the right to the highest attainable standard of health and freedom of expression.

These factors are part of the GABSHW's working definition of sexual pleasure, which builds on the World Health Organization's (n.d.) recognition of sexual rights as constituted by the application of existing human rights to sexuality and sexual health. The defense and preservation of human rights goes beyond what Tinder or any one company can do through its technology. However, all apps, platforms, and means through which humans forge connection are inherently implicated in the negotiation of rights. Imagine how the conditions for intimacy that dating apps invoke could change if the GABSHW's preconditions and foundations for pleasure shaped app policies, terms, and technical designs.

So far, I have emphasized sexual rights and the recognition of pleasure in relation to sexuality because sex and its stigmatization play a large role in the rights-infringing dynamics facilitated through Tinder. But if we take seriously the importance of pleasure, establishing a technological landscape that is fun for myriad reasons, such as the possibility of discovering something or someone new, then an app environment in which human rights are recognized and upheld – throughout technological, economic, and governance-related layers of this technology – is also conducive to these forms of pleasure. By combining these frameworks surrounding play and pleasure, it becomes apparent that an inroad to reframing Tinder and dating apps as fun – regaining the playfulness and pleasure of digitally mediated dating – involves considering how this technology and its sociocultural arrangements can foster human rights. This is especially important, since rights are a precursor to citizenship and those who face barriers to digital citizenship are pushed out of and excluded from some of the most important public spheres in our society. Apryl Williams (2024) drives this home when she discusses how the entrenchment of racism on dating apps can serve as a form of eugenics that affects not only this generation of people who are *on* the apps but also the next generation in terms of who will go on to form relationships and grow families. These frameworks in favor of establishing and defending digital rights point us toward thinking about the necessity of change at multiple levels to facilitate play and pleasure.

From rights to relationality

While rights-based arguments build from existing frameworks and invoke familiar language that is increasingly being taken up by regulators and platform companies alike (e.g., Meta's Oversight Board purports to uphold global human rights standards), they do not always evoke change (Duguay, 2024). Human rights frameworks are often premised on access to citizenship within neoliberal capitalism and therefore advance toward an ultimate goal of aligning individuals as consumer-citizens within this socioeconomic and political system. This is evident in instances when LGBTQ+ struggles for rights, such as the right to recognition of queer relationships and freedom from labor discrimination, also entrench queer people further in normative structures of capitalism, such as through an impetus to participate in marriage and nuclear family formations or the false empowerment of commercial participation (e.g., buying "live laugh lesbian" T-shirts from a company that later pulls them under anti-LGBTQ+ political pressure). While small changes can be effected within these structures, shifting the possibilities of rights and freedoms incrementally for some people at some times, neoliberal capitalism as an overarching socioeconomic and political arrangement depends on hierarchies and uneven distributions of power, which take the shape of oppressions discussed throughout this book as they play out on Tinder: misogyny, racism, cisheteronormativity, and others. Therefore, arguing for rights that afford freedom in this context means gaining the freedom to be a consumer-citizen within the modes of citizenship that fit into this system.

This conundrum necessitates modes of thinking that discard, circumvent, or consider avenues outside of our existing systems. Colombian-American anthropologist Arturo Escobar (2018) provides another view of these issues and proposes a new way of thinking about design – the design not only of technologies but also of social worlds – that leads us elsewhere. He draws on feminist and cultural studies perspectives to describe the interlinking of capitalism with patriarchy throughout industrialization and post-industrialization, which entrenches hierarchies and separates people from each other and other life forms. These hierarchical structures and systems orient people toward value-producing forms of labor and modes of living, globally implemented through exploitation and extraction imposed by imperialistic and colonial regimes. Escobar envisions a fork in the trajectory of this development. One path leads toward the increasingly prominent Silicon Valley-born dream of humans surpassing the constraints of biology through technology. This fantasy is "loaded with the promise of unlimited growth, novelty, power, adventure, and wealth (as if these were the ultimate criteria of a good life), albeit at the cost of alienating us ever more from our participation in the life of Earth" (p. 221), as these promises require environmental destruction and the exploitation of people and other living beings for their realization. Processes of enshittification bent on unlimited growth, with increasing anticipation that AI will supercharge this growth, to yield greater wealth for platform shareholders at the cost of users and their privacy, autonomy, and ability to function in a digital society, are clearly attempts to make this fantasy a reality. In the other direction, Escobar sees the possibility of "the re/creation of worlds based on the horizontal relation with all forms of life, respecting the human embeddedness in the natural world" (p. 17). This direction holds the possibility of preserving and enhancing people's lives while transitioning away from social, political, and economic designs that are destructive. But it is only possible if we overcome what separates us (from people, other living beings, and the Earth) – a proposition that strikes me as relevant for rethinking dating apps as technologies aspiring to facilitate meaningful connections.

This latter direction orients us toward relationality, as a way of understanding the world and everything in it as interconnected. This perspective has oriented my analysis to the relationship between users and Tinder throughout this book, paying attention to how features, interfaces, devices, and other material objects shape interactions and user choices while also keeping in mind higher-level influences, such as governance approaches and business strategies. Escobar highlights that alongside attention to materiality in design and related disciplines, Indigenous worldviews have enhanced his understanding of relationality, as he often draws on perspectives from Indigenous people in Latin America. In turn, I have learned a great deal about relationality from Indigenous scholars in Canada and North America more broadly whose perspectives can be put in dialogue with Escobar's invocations. Michi Saagiig Nishnaabeg writer Leanne Betasamosake Simpson discusses capitalism as being intertwined with colonialism: "Colonialism and capitalism are based on extracting and assimilating. The alternative to extractivism is deep reciprocity. It's respect, it's relationship, it's responsibility, and it's local" (2017, p. 75). Speaking out about extractivism as continued colonial theft of Indigenous people's land, such as through Canada's ongoing oil and gas pipeline projects, she points to reciprocity as a different approach to being in relationship with others and all of creation, one that is based on responsible giving and taking. This concept of reciprocity is also central in the stories Potawatomi botanist Robin Wall Kimmerer (2013) tells about how humans have a role to play in the responsible stewardship of different kinds of life on Earth. Professor of Geography Michif-settler Max Liboiron defines responsibility as "the obligation to enact good relations" (2021, p. 24), referring to people's relationship to each other and the land. They underscore that not all relations are the same, nor do they carry the same obligations – these obligations depend on specific relationships to particular people and places.

I see these discussions of relationality as building on calls for change in sociotechnical arrangements, and providing greater contour to them beyond human rights arguments alone. Asserting that people have the right to play and pleasure, and should have the freedom to connect and be treated with respect on dating apps without experiencing discrimination, bias, or violence, is important. It is legible within current regulatory and policy contexts wherein rights-based arguments are recognized and can be used to call for some protections or incremental changes. But assertions of freedom based on rights-related arguments also come with the baggage of neoliberal capitalism that affords rights to individual consumer-citizens based on their conformity and productiveness within existing systems. Relational perspectives instead consider how we can circumvent, surpass, or discard those systems to consider the how and why of change – how and why anyone would, could, or should treat others with inherent value, dignity, and respect. This impetus for change comes from the realization that we are all already connected and in relationship with each other, since we are alive and sharing this Earth. Thus, this call for change is grounded in the need for reciprocity and people's existing obligation toward responsible action, premised on the understanding that safety, happiness, thriving, and life more broadly are only realizable through upholding our collective responsibilities to each other. Liboiron (2021) connects responsibility with the potential for change, stating: "Orientations, which come out of obligations, mean that you are facing a particular direction with a specific horizon of possible action before you. Orientations are the condition of possibility for some futures and not others" (p. 155). By recognizing our obligations to others, it points us toward a different future from one in which we are stuck flirting with AI or lowering the bar for matching to a verified iris texture. Instead, it enables us to develop technological arrangements that facilitate tapping into our interdependence with others and connecting further from this premise.

Co-creating playful and pleasurable digitally mediated dating

Even amid these frameworks and perspectives, I cannot pinpoint steps and prescriptions for creating a perfect dating app. It probably does not, and cannot, exist because certain technologies work well for specific people in certain contexts but never for everyone. Similarly, Liboiron (2021) warns us that there needs to be specificity when it comes to our obligations, as individuals are obligated to specific people and land in different ways. If one opens up a dating app and has no sense of specificity – no idea who these strangers are – then it is difficult to feel obligated to preserve a fun and enjoyable experience for them. Similarly, if technology developers are designing for people like themselves, then the app will work best for those types of people; if they attempt to design for "everyone" or contexts they know little about, they can indeed create something only marginally useful at best and severely dangerous at worst. Escobar's (2018) reenvisioning of design hinges on this notion of embracing difference and scaffolding connections across it as he conceptualizes – drawing from Zapatista activists' thinking and feminist calls for solidarity – designing for the pluriverse, "a world where many worlds fit" (p. xvi). This kind of design stems from local communities and their needs; it is creative in bridging worlds and co-creating new worlds that are habitable for a range of people. As such, designing for the pluriverse avoids the assimilation of colonialism and capitalism that Simpson (2017) warns against. As Escobar argues that autonomy is the key to designing these new worlds, it reminds me of why I am hesitant to fully jettison rights-based arguments: I see in the defense of rights, especially people's right *to* participation, the assertion of a right to exercise agency and autonomy in relation to the digital, something that we are enmeshed in daily. With agency alongside key qualities of designing for relationality that Escobar (2018) emphasizes – creativity, autonomy, and specificity – I want to end by contrasting the following scenarios of digital intimacy with the enshittified conditions of Tinder that I described earlier.

When I think about instances of digital intimacy that may afford pluriversal connections, I recall scenes from studies spanning decades of technologies. A striking one is ethnographer Shelley Correll's (1995) description of a 1990s bulletin board service (BBS), the *Lesbian Cafe*, through which women gathered to co-create a flirtatious text-based fantasy of meeting in a bar. Correll observes, "By posting notes stating that they are ordering drinks, placing wagers over the pool table, and holding intimate conversations next to the fire, a common sense of reality is created on which future interactions can build" (pp. 279–80). Though this creative expression may sound quaint compared to today's immersive video games, the women used the BBS's bare-bones interface to playfully build a common context and interact in ways conducive to intimate sharing, forming friendships, and even occasionally planning to meet up across geographies for the possibility of dating.

In contrast to earlier, geographically untethered technologies, mobile media technologies open the possibility of grounding creative uses and practices in local places to share desires and worlds with others. I was again struck by an example of this, mentioned only briefly in Mowlabocus's (2010) examination of gay men's interfacing with digital technologies in the 2000s, in which men used the early Bluetooth functionality in mobile phones to cruise each other on trains or subway lines. Such interactions leverage both transportation (as a technology) and digital technology during daily commuting, combining "the quotidian *and* the erotic, offering a site of potential sexual adventure" that escapes the mundanity of labor flows (p. 191). Men discussed how Bluetooth features were free and enabled straightforward connection, which – of course – needed to be negotiated to ascertain others' intentions and the viability of continuing this interaction following the commute, with safety fostered through previously established cultural mores of nondigital cruising as well as the privacy afforded by personal, mobile communication. Bluetooth exchanges could be short, flexible, and ephemeral – they could "come into being only to 'melt' away and be re-formed in different places" (p. 194). Building on this, I am reminded of research into how the expansion of mobile technologies, and dating apps among them, enables a co-presence among LGBTQ+ people that allows them to know that they are not uniformly embedded in a heteronormative environment but that people like them exist nearby too (Blackwell et al., 2015; Tang, 2017). In this way, flexible mobile technologies open digital and geographical spaces of commonality through which people can form connections.

Further, the geographical affordances of mobile apps can anchor world-sharing and world-making practices in ways specific to places and communities. In a study of sexual platforms, the Swedish kink app Darkside facilitates a woman encountering someone else's diaries about secret play sessions at a local grocery store (Sundén et al., 2022). Reading these stories, which have been shared with the app community, then enables her to better understand and express her desires. The study's authors underscore that sexual platforms' embeddedness in local contexts and their contrast with mainstream platforms' aversion to sexuality enable such encounters: "While connecting people and bringing them close, our platforms also afford a way of playing with and at a distance – as there can be safety to distance – in relation to which specifically regional geographic imaginaries create their own sense of proximity, cultural intelligibility, and belonging" (p. 435). People can join these apps and have shared experiences with others through a locally grounded sense of commonality – imagined or not – that can facilitate self-exploration and sexual connection, with the possibility of fostering a shared sense of obligation, respecting others because you know them in a way.

None of these configurations of digital intimate technologies and users across the 1990s, 2000s, and 2020s is utopic. Patrons of the *Lesbian Cafe* had to develop in-group symbols for sexual references, a precursor to today's algospeak, to avoid having their flirtatious messages removed by the BBS's central moderators. Being able to contact someone else through Bluetooth can be intrusive, and Mowlabocus also discusses how, without settings and/or regulatory expectations for limiting its use, this feature can and does facilitate the nonconsensual receipt of sexual and potentially harmful content. Sexual expression on platforms such as Darkside was not immune to normative expectations surrounding gender and sexuality as well as associations between national belonging and whiteness in the Swedish context. Despite these challenges, I wish to draw attention to some similarities across these scenarios that resonate with the frameworks and approaches to change I have been discussing. First, each held room for technology users to enact agency, autonomy, and creativity on some level. With early and new technologies, such as BBS and Bluetooth, functionalities were basic compared to today's apps and platforms but this allowed people to develop a new range of uses for them. On more sophisticated platforms, such as Darkside, the option to share a variety of content, including stories and diary entries, enables a range of self-expression beyond a profile photo or short biography. It is also worth noting that while reduced or different approaches to governance open possibilities for risk, they also put risk management more squarely in the hands of users. For instance, the *Lesbian Cafe* patrons developed practices to deal with "bashers" who entered the chatroom to insult them, banding together to ignore and counter these individuals in ways that strengthened solidarity among these women. Similarly, less user activity was channeled toward profit-making through these technologies, as BBSs were often free, eventually Bluetooth came as standard in mobile phones, and Darkside is a nonprofit platform.

Secondly, these scenes illustrate localized, community-specific instances of connection, with the latter two also being embedded within a particular geographic space. The localized quality of such an interaction enables people to function within a specific context, whether spoken or unspoken. Among lesbians on the BBS and gay men on the train, the unspoken fiber of connection is a shared queer identity through which one can anticipate at least some semblance of friendliness or solidarity while the Swedes on Darkside imagine a degree of national familiarity. Even if these relations and their implied obligations do not always hold, as is increasingly the case with the current global context of political polarization, they provide a sense of common ground upon which to forge connection. In their reimagining of approaches to platform governance, media studies scholars Amy Hasinoff and Nathan Schneider (2022) argue for the integration of transformative justice models that are context-sensitive, incorporate a range of flexible and diverse tools for responding to harm, and foster accountability through community-developed norms. I agree with them that the massive scale with which platforms and popular apps, such as Tinder, carry out governance is not sustainable. The automated and one-size-fits-all approaches these massive platforms take cannot be attuned to facilitating connection in ways that are specific, localized, and imbued with sufficient care to enable people to interact across difference without these differences triggering dominating or violent behavior. However, as Match Group acquires more apps, including those initially developed by and for specific communities or identity niches, I do not see the industry moving to foster technologies that are context-specific or that are governed through a user community's self-determination. To do so, large entities would need to find ways to distribute the authority and management (and, potentially, revenue) of apps back to their user communities to safeguard against their homogenization. A more robust safeguard might be finding ways to dissolve and prevent monopolization across the industry, as mentioned earlier, and provide resources to communities to run their own apps.

Lastly, and most importantly, these scenes provide glimpses of world-sharing and collective world-making. A cozy lesbian bar is fabricated by women otherwise situated in places without any lesbian-specific venues and, for some, the inability to be out as lesbian in public. Two people riding the train separately suddenly have their afternoons converge. A grocery chain dating back to the 1930s has the dominant association of grocery shopping with reproductive labor that sustains normative family formations disrupted and subverted through a shared kink fantasy. For people who have found friendships, intimate encounters, romantic relationships, friends-with-benefits, and a variety of connections with others through Tinder, this app has also facilitated a sort of world-sharing and even world-making when all sorts of relationships emerge. But I am not convinced that the dominant assemblage of what dating apps have become, which has been heavily influenced by Tinder's popularity, is most conducive to this world-making. Flexible design, small-scale governance that grants autonomy to localized users, and creative ways to enact agency that are not co-opted by transactional interfaces channeling user energy toward revenue generation all strike me as changes that could render this technology more conducive to sparking meaningful connections among people. In short, a dating app that is fun – playful and pleasurable – will provide these foundations that enable people to recognize and realize their relational interdependence as they encounter each other. Though if such qualities cannot be worked into what we presently call dating apps, or if such a model is not sustainable in a revenue-generating digital matchmaking industry, people are sure to discover and appropriate other technologies for digital intimacy, just as they have done in the past and will do so into the future.

References

ABC News. (2014) Hot or not's co-founders: Where are they now? https://abcnews.go.com/Business/founders-hot-today/story?id=23901082

Abidin, C. (2016) "Aren't these just young, rich women doing vain things online?": Influencer selfies as subversive frivolity, *Social Media + Society*, 2(2), 1–17.

Abidin, C. (2017) #familygoals: Family influencers, calibrated amateurism, and justifying young digital labor. *Social Media + Society*, 3(2), 1–15.

Abidin, C. (2018) *Internet celebrity*. Emerald.

Abidin, C. (2023) What I talk about when I talk about authenticity: An auto-bibliographic inquiry. In Heřmanová, M., Skey, M., and Thurnell-Read, T. (eds.) *Cultures of authenticity*. Emerald, pp. 209–14.

Ahmed, S. (2006) *Queer phenomenology: Orientations, objects, others*. Duke University Press.

Albris, K., et al. (2024) Introduction: The digital backlash. In Albris, K. et al. (eds.) *The digital backlash and the paradoxes of disconnection*. Nordicom, pp. 11–22.

Albury, K. (2016) Politics of sexting revisited. In McCosker, A., Vivienne, S., and Johns, A. (eds.) *Negotiating digital citizenship: Control, contest and culture*. Rowman & Littlefield, pp. 213–30.

Albury, K. (2017) Heterosexual casual sex: From free love to Tinder. In Smith, C., Attwood, F., and McNair, B. (eds.) *The Routledge companion to media, sex and sexuality*. Routledge, pp. 81–90.

Albury, K. (2025) Disaffection with mobile dating apps: Reflections on nostalgia, safety and social change. In Goggin, G. and Hjorth, L. (eds.) *The Routledge companion to mobile media*, 2nd ed. Routledge.

Albury, K. and Byron, P. (2018) Taking off the risk goggles: Exploring the intersection of young people's sexual and digital citizenship in sexual health promotion. In Aggleton, P. et al. (eds.) *Youth, sexuality and sexual citizenship*. Routledge, pp. 168–83.

Albury, K., et al. (2017) Data cultures of mobile dating and hook-up

apps: Emerging issues for critical social science research, *Big Data & Society*, 4(2), 1–11.
Albury, K., et al. (2019) Safety, risk and wellbeing on dating apps: Final report. Swinburne University of Technology. https://doi.org/10.25916/5dd324c1b33bb
Albury, K., et al. (2020) Dating apps as public health 'problems': Cautionary tales and vernacular pedagogies in news media. *Health Sociology Review*, 29(3), 232–48.
Albury, K., et al. (2021) Not your unicorn: Trans dating app users' negotiations of personal safety and sexual health. *Health Sociology Review*, 30, 72–86.
Alhabash, S. and Ma, M. (2017) A tale of four platforms: Motivations and uses of Facebook, Twitter, Instagram, and Snapchat among college students? *Social Media + Society*, 3(1), 1–13.
Alter/Austin, C. (2021) How Whitney Wolfe Herd turned a vision of a better Internet into a billion-dollar brand. *TIME*. https://time.com/5947727/whitney-wolfe-herd-bumble/
Anderson, T.L. (2005) Relationships among Internet attitudes, Internet use, romantic beliefs, and perceptions of online romantic relationships. *Cyberpsychology & Behaviour*, 8, 521–31.
Andrejevic, M. (2019). Automating surveillance. *Surveillance & Society*, 17(1–2), 7–13.
Andy Tyler Photography. (2013) The Tinder launch party @ Cirque Le Soir, London. https://andytylerphotography.co.uk/blog/2013/11/27/the-tinder-launch-party-cirque-le-soir-london
Angel, K. (2021) *Tomorrow sex will be good again: Women and desire in the age of consent*. Verso.
Apperley, T.H. and Gray, K.L. (2020) Digital divides and structural inequalities: Exploring the technomasculine culture of gaming. In Kowert, R. and Quandt, T. (eds.) *The video game debate 2: Revisiting the physical, social, and psychological effects of video games*. Routledge, pp. 41–52.
Apprich, C., et al. (2018) *Pattern discrimination*. University of Minnesota Press.
Archrival. (n.d.) Tinder U brand ambassadors. *Archrival Opportunities*. https://opportunities.archrival.com/program/14/tinder-u-ambassadors/5383076
Are, C. and Briggs, P. (2023) The emotional and financial impact of de-platforming on creators at the margins. *Social Media + Society*, 9(1), 1–12.
Associated Press. (2019) New interracial couple emoji mark victory for partners of color. *The Guardian*, 9 March. https://www.theguardian

.com/technology/2019/mar/08/new-interracial-couple-emoji-tinder
AustinShow. (2025) AustinShow on TikTok. *TikTok*. https://www.tiktok.com/@austinshow/video/7487049175645900074?q=tinder%20game%20game&t=1752674496836
Balakrishnan, A. (2015) Tinder parent Match ends up 22% in trading debut. *CNBC*. https://www.cnbc.com/2015/11/19/match-ipo.html
Bandinelli, C. (2022) Dating apps: Towards post-romantic love in digital societies. *International Journal of Cultural Policy*, 28(7), 905–19.
Bandinelli, C. and Gandini, A. (2022) Dating apps: The uncertainty of marketised love. *Cultural Sociology*, 16(3), 423–41.
Banet-Weiser, S. (2012) *Authentic™: The politics of ambivalence in a brand culture*. New York University Press.
Banet-Weiser, S. (2018) *Empowered: Popular feminism and popular misogyny*. Duke University Press.
Banks, J., et al. (2024) From the auction block to the Tinder swipe: Black women's experiences with fetishization on dating apps. *New Media & Society*, 27(7), 4228–45.
Bans, L. (2015) I spent a week on Tinder ... As a strawberry milkshake. *GQ*. https://www.gq.com/story/tinder-female-milkshake
Barlow, J.P. (2019) A declaration of the independence of cyberspace. *Duke Law & Technology Review*, 18(1–2), 5–7.
Barr, K. (2025) The problem isn't Tinder's new AI but the dating apps themselves. *Gizmodo*. https://gizmodo.com/the-problem-isnt-tinders-new-ai-but-the-dating-apps-themselves-2000583553
Barron, J. (2022) A Tinder revenge story. *Intelligencer*. https://nymag.com/intelligencer/2022/01/tinder-sean-rad-barry-diller.html
Bayer, J.B., et al. (2016) Sharing the small moments: Ephemeral social interaction on Snapchat. *Information, Communication & Society*, 19(7), 956–77.
Baym, N.K. (2015) *Personal connections in the digital age*, 2nd ed. Polity Press.
BBC. (2015) Tinder fights STD ad campaign in US. https://www.bbc.com/news/technology-34390795
BBC. (2020) Pakistan blocks Tinder and Grindr for "immoral content." https://www.bbc.com/news/technology-53977780
BBC. (2021) Match settles legal fight with Tinder founders for $441m. https://www.bbc.com/news/business-59497392
Beauman, F. (2011) *Shapely ankle preferr'd: A history of the lonely hearts ad*. Chatto & Windus.
Belmonte, L. (2020) A provincial health minister's Tinder and Grindr

warning is going viral. *Narcity*. https://www.narcity.com/news/ca/nl/john-haggie-warning-people-about-using-tinder-and-grindr-is-going-viral

Benedict, T.J. (2022) The computer got it wrong: Facial recognition technology and establishing probable cause to arrest. *Washington and Lee Law Review*, 79(2), 849–98.

Benjamin, R. (2019) *Race after technology: Abolitionist tools for the New Jim Code*. Polity.

Bergström, M. (2021) *The new laws of love: Online dating and the privatization of intimacy*. Polity.

Berkowitz, D., et al. (2021) Tinder: A game with gendered rules and consequences. *Social Currents*, 8(5), 491–509.

Berlant, L. (1998) Intimacy: A special issue. *Critical Inquiry*, 24(2), 281–8.

Bertoni, S. (2015) Tinder CEO Sean Rad: From boss, booted, and back. *Forbes*. https://www.forbes.com/sites/stevenbertoni/2015/10/09/tinder-ceo-sean-rad-from-boss-booted-and-back/

Birch, K. (2013) The political economy of technoscience: An emerging research agenda. *Spontaneous Generations*, 7(1), 49–61.

Bishop, S. (2023) Influencer creep: How artists strategically navigate the platformisation of art worlds. *New Media & Society*, 27(4), 2109–26.

Bivens, R. and Haimson, O.L. (2016) Baking gender into social media design: How platforms shape categories for users and advertisers. *Social Media + Society*, 2(4), 1–12.

Bivens, R. and Hasinoff, A.A. (2018) Rape: Is there an app for that? An empirical analysis of the features of anti-rape apps. *Information, Communication & Society*, 21(8), 1050–67.

Blackwell, C., Birnholtz, J., and Abbott, C. (2015) Seeing and being seen: Co-situation and impression formation using Grindr, a location-aware gay dating app. *New Media & Society*, 17(7), 1117–36.

Blakk, F. (2018) SWIPE RIGHT. *YouTube*. https://youtu.be/Bl3dNa4CzKM?si=ckM-fH6ByjhZzH6r

Blamey, C. (2019) "Mute, report, block": Dissonance in moderating Overwatch. *Proceedings of DiGRA 2019 Conference: Game, play and the emerging ludo-mix*, August 6–10, Kyoto, Japan.

Bogle, K.A. (2008) *Hooking up: Sex, dating, and relationships on campus*. New York University Press.

Book, I. (n.d.) Artistic projects. https://www.iannabook.com/artistic-projects.html

Borovinsky, K. (2023) Is Strava the new dating app? *Elle*. https://www.elle.com/beauty/health-fitness/a45676230/strava-running-app-explained/

Bosker, B. (2013) Here's one of the college kids helping Tinder take over campuses. *Huffington Post.* https://www.huffpost.com/entry/tinder-app-college-kids_n_3530585

boyd, d. (2012) White flight in networked publics? How race and class shaped American teen engagement with MySpace and Facebook. In Nakamura, L. and Chow-White, P.A. (eds.) *Race after the Internet.* Taylor & Francis, pp. 203–22.

boyd, d. (2014) *It's complicated: The social lives of networked teens.* Yale University Press.

Breslouer, L. (2015) What being a cupcake on Tinder taught me about dating. *Thrillist.* https://www.thrillist.com/eat/nation/being-a-cupcake-on-tinder

BrightCheck, Inc. (2026a) BrightCheck. https://www.brightcheck.com/

BrightCheck, Inc. (2026b) Industries. https://www.brightcheck.com/industries#social-community-platforms

BrightCheckPro, Inc. (2024a) PrePaid checks. https://web.archive.org/web/20241014140753/https://brightcheckpro.com/pre-paid-checks/

BrightCheckPro, Inc. (2024b) BrightCheck Pro. https://web.archive.org/web/20240609142605/https://www.brightcheckpro.com/

BrightCheckPro, Inc. (2024c) A guide to making trust & safety a revenue generator for online platforms. https://web.archive.org/web/20241014142422/https://brightcheckpro.com/white-papers/

Brock, A. (2020) *Distributed Blackness: African American cybercultures.* New York University Press.

Broeker, F. (2023) "We went from the anonymity of the internet into my private WhatsApp": Rituals of transition among dating app users in Berlin. *New Media & Society*, 25(10), 2551–71.

Brown, A. (2018) "Least desirable"? How racial discrimination plays out in online dating. *NPR.* https://www.npr.org/2018/01/09/575352051/least-desirable-how-racial-discrimination-plays-out-in-online-dating

Bucher, T. (2021) *Facebook.* Polity.

Bucher, T. and Helmond, A. (2017) The affordances of social media platforms. In Burgess, J., Poell, T., and Marwick, A. (eds.) *The Sage handbook of social media.* Sage, pp. 233–53.

Bumble (2016) An open letter to Connor. *Bumble Buzz.* https://bumble.com/the-buzz/an-open-letter-to-connor

Buolamwini, J. (2023) *Unmasking AI: My mission to protect what is human in a world of machines.* Random House.

Burgess, J. (2017) Convergence. In Ouellette, L. and Gray, J. (eds.) *Keywords for media studies.* New York University Press, pp. 47–9.

Burgess, J. and Baym, N.K. (2020) *Twitter: A biography*. New York University Press.

Bursztynsky, J. (2021) Bumble stock closes up 63% after soaring in market debut. *CNBC*. https://www.cnbc.com/2021/02/11/bumble-ipo-bmbl-starts-trading-on-nasdaq.html

Busch, O. (2016) The programmatic advertising principle. In Busch, O. (ed.) *Programmatic advertising: The successful transformation to automated, data-driven marketing in real-time*. Springer, pp. 3–15.

Butcher, M. and Russell, J. (2016) Tinder acquihires Humin to go beyond dating, and get an SF office too. *TechCrunch*. https://techcrunch.com/2016/03/29/tinder-acquires-humin-as-it-broadens-out-from-dating-creates-sf-office/

Butler, J. (2024) *Who's afraid of gender?* Knopf Canada.

Cabañes, J.V.A. and Collantes, C.F. (2020) Dating apps as digital flyovers: Mobile media and global intimacies in a postcolonial city. In Cabañes, J.V.A. and Uy-Tioco, C.S. (eds.) *Mobile media and social intimacies in Asia: Reconfiguring local ties and enacting global relationships*. Springer, pp. 97–114.

Cabañes, J.V.A. and Uy-Tioco, C.S. (2022) Glocal intimacies: Theorizing mobile media and intimate relationships. *Communication, Culture and Critique*, 15(4), 463–70.

Campbell, J.E. (2004) *Getting it on online: Cyberspace, gay male sexuality, and embodied identity*. Routledge.

Caplan, R. (2024) A working history of the verified internet: Part 3 – The celebrity wars. *Data & Society*. https://datasociety.net/points/a-working-history-of-the-verified-internet-3/

Carah, N. and Angus, D. (2018) Algorithmic brand culture: Participatory labour, machine learning and branding on social media. *Media, Culture and Society*, 40(2), 178–94.

Cardoso-González, R.A. (2019) Connected emotions on Tinder: The development of social skills and a digital self among users from Mexico City and Madrid. In Fox, B. (ed.) *Emotions and loneliness in a networked society*. Springer, pp. 87–111.

Carlson, B. (2020) Love and hate at the cultural interface: Indigenous Australians and dating apps. *Journal of Sociology*, 56(2), 133–50.

Carpenter, C.J. and McEwan, B. (2016) The players of micro-dating: Individual and gender differences in goal orientations toward micro-dating apps. *First Monday*, 21(5). https://doi.org/10.5210/fm.v21i5.6187

Carr, A. (2016) I found out my secret internal Tinder rating and now I wish I hadn't. *Fast Company*. https://www.fastcompany.com/3054871/whats-your-tinder-score-inside-the-apps-internal-ranking-system

Cassell, J. and Cramer, M. (2008) High tech or high risk: Moral panics about girls online. In McPherson, T. (ed.) *Digital youth, innovation and the unexpected.* MIT Press,. pp. 53–76.
Cassidy, E. (2018) *Gay men, identity and social media: A culture of participatory reluctance.* Routledge.
Cavallero, J. (2021) As a disabled person, dating apps were already tough. Then I failed Tinder's verification test. *Washington Post.* https://www.washingtonpost.com/gender-identity/as-a-disabled-person-dating-apps-were-already-tough-then-i-failed-tinders-verification-test/
Chafkin, M. (2023) Don't scan your eyeballs for Worldcoin's magic beans. *Bloomberg.* https://www.bloomberg.com/news/newsletters/2023-08-07/what-s-the-purpose-of-worldcoin-orb-eye-scanning-crypto-token-project
Chan, L.S. (2021) *The politics of dating apps: Gender, sexuality, and emergent publics in urban China.* MIT Press.
Cheney-Lippold, J. (2017) *We are data: Algorithms and the making of our digital selves.* New York University Press.
Cho, A. (2017) Default publicness: Queer youth of color, social media, and being outed by the machine. *New Media & Society,* 20(9), 3183–200.
Christensen, M.A. (2021) "Tindersluts" and "Tinderellas": Examining the digital affordances shaping the (hetero)sexual scripts of young womxn on Tinder. *Sociological Perspectives,* 64(3), 432–49.
Chun, W.H.K. (2024) *Discriminating data: Correlation, neighborhoods, and the new politics of recognition.* MIT Press.
Clarke-Billings, L. (2016) What do Tinder's 37 new gender identity options mean? *Newsweek.* https://www.newsweek.com/what-do-tinders-37-new-gender-identity-options-mean-522679
Clayton, N. (2002) SCOT: Does it answer? *Technology and Culture,* 43(2), 351–60.
Cöbek, G. and Ergin, M. (2021) Swipe me if you can: Cultural and gendered uses of Tinder in Turkey. *International Journal of Social and Humanities Sciences,* 5(3), 11–38.
Cohen, S. (1972) *Folk devils and moral panics.* Paladin.
Collins, P.H. (2022) *Black feminist thought: Knowledge, consciousness, and the politics of empowerment.* Routledge.
Colvert, A., Pothong, K., and Livingstone, S. (2024) Playful by design: Embedding children's rights into the digital world. *ACM Games: Research and Practice,* 2(2), 1–10.
Comunello, F., Parisi, L., and Ieracitano, F. (2021) Negotiating gender scripts in mobile dating apps: Between affordances, usage norms and practices. *Information, Communication & Society,* 24(8), 1140–56.

Cook, J. (2015) Tinder's paid subscription service could ruin everything that made the app great. *Business Insider*. https://www.businessinsider.com/tinder-plus-being-tested-in-europe-2015-2
Correll, S. (1995) The ethnography of an electronic bar: The lesbian cafe. *Journal of Contemporary Ethnography*, 24(3), 270–98.
Corrigan, H. (2021) Tinder's plan for criminal record checks raises fears of "lifelong punishment." *The Guardian*, April 13. https://www.theguardian.com/technology/2021/apr/13/tinder-plan-criminal-record-checks
Couch, D. and Liamputtong, P. (2007) Online dating and mating: Perceptions of risk and health among online users. *Health, Risk & Society*, 9(3), 275–94.
CounselorWriter. (2022) Did anyone do phone dating in the '90s? *r/datingoverforty, Reddit*. https://www.reddit.com/r/datingoverforty/comments/ncqyd8/did_anyone_do_phone_dating_in_the_90s/
Coyle, M. and Nagel, M. (2022) Introduction: Penal abolition as a challenge to carceral logic. In Coyle, M.J. and Nagel, M. (eds.) *Contesting carceral logic: Towards abolitionist futures*. Routledge, pp. 24–37.
Crawford, K. and Gillespie, T. (2016) What is a flag for? Social media reporting tools and the vocabulary of complaint. *New Media & Society*, 18(3), 410–28.
Crook, J. (2014) The story of Whitney Wolfe vs. Tinder. *TechCrunch*. https://techcrunch.com/2014/07/09/whitney-wolfe-vs-tinder/
Crook, J. (2015a) Tinder ditches moments. *TechCrunch*. https://techcrunch.com/2015/11/12/tinder-ditches-moments/
Crook, J. (2015b) Tinder acquires ephemeral messenger Tappy. *TechCrunch*. https://techcrunch.com/2015/01/12/tinder-acquires-ephemeral-messenger-tappy/
Crook, J. (2015c) Tinder Plus will launch on Monday. *TechCrunch*. https://techcrunch.com/2015/02/28/tinder-plus-will-launch-on-monday/
Crook, J. (2015d) Tinder's first advertisement is one big experiment. *TechCrunch*. http://techcrunch.com/2015/04/03/tinders-first-advertisement-is-one-big-experiment/#.ou7tvpz:O85t
Crook, J. (2017) Tinder Online is a new web version of the dating app. *TechCrunch*. https://techcrunch.com/2017/03/28/tinder-unveils-web-version-of-the-app-called-tinder-online/
Crunchbase. (n.d.-a) Match Group funding rounds. https://www.crunchbase.com/discover/funding_rounds/field/organizations/num_investments/match-group
Crunchbase. (n.d.-b) Tinder funding rounds. Crunchbase. https://www

.crunchbase.com/discover/funding_rounds/field/organizations/num_investments/tinder

Cunningham, S. and Craig, D. (2017) Being "really real" on YouTube: Authenticity, community and brand culture in social media entertainment. *Media International Australia*, 164(1), 71–81.

Curington, C.V., Lundquist, J.H., and Lin, K.-H. (2021) *The dating divide: Race and desire in the era of online romance*. University of California Press.

Curry, D. (2025a) Tinder revenue and usage statistics (2026). *Business of Apps*. https://www.businessofapps.com/data/tinder-statistics/

Curry, D. (2025b) Dating app revenue and usage statistics. *Business of Apps*. https://www.businessofapps.com/data/dating-app-market/

Dame-Griff, A. (2023) *The two revolutions: A history of the transgender internet*. New York University Press.

Daroya, E. (2018) "Not into chopsticks or curries": Erotic capital and the physic life of racism on Grindr. In Riggs, D.W. (ed.) *The psychic life of racism in gay men's communities*. Lexington Books, pp. 125–41.

Das, V. (2019) Dating applications, intimacy, and cosmopolitan desire in India. In Punathambekar, A. and Mohan, S. (eds.) *Global digital cultures: Perspectives from South Asia*. University of Michigan Press.

David, G. and Cambre, C. (2016) Screened intimacies: Tinder and the swipe logic. *Social Media + Society*, 2(3). https://doi.org/10.1177/2056305116641976

Davies, H.J. (2017) Does Tinder's Menprovement initiative do enough to protect women? *The Guardian*, October 9. https://www.theguardian.com/lifeandstyle/2017/oct/09/tinder-menprovement-protect-women-dating

Davis, D-M. (2025) Tinder CEO to step down in July. *TechCrunch*, May 22. https://techcrunch.com/2025/05/22/tinder-ceo-to-step-down-in-july/

Deaux, K. and Hanna, R. (1984) Courtship in the personals column: The influence of gender and sexual orientation. *Sex Roles*, 11, 363–75.

DeSantis, A.D. (2007) *Inside Greek U.: Fraternities, sororities, and the pursuit of pleasure, power, and prestige*. University Press of Kentucky.

Dias, V. (2016) Tinder and Grindr add new health safety sections to help users find STD test sites. *WNWO*. https://nbc24.com/news/local/tinder-and-grindr-add-new-health-safety-sections-to-help-users-find-std-test-sites

Dixon, S. (2025) Tinder – statistics & facts. *Statista*. https://www.statista.com/topics/10082/tinder/

Dobson, A.S. (2015) *Postfeminst digital cultures: Femininity, social media, and self-representation*. Palgrave Macmillan.

Doctorow, C. (2025) *Enshittification: Why everything suddenly got worse and what to do about it.* MCD Books.

Doubek, J. (2018) "We swipe left" on Tinder's "discriminatory" pricing, court says. *NPR.* https://www.npr.org/sections/thetwo-way/2018/02/01/582351802/we-swipe-left-on-tinder-s-discriminatory-pricing-court-says

Dry_Conversation7090. (2022) What's with all the "add me on Snapchat." *r/Tinder, Reddit.* https://www.reddit.com/r/Tinder/comments/x7z01a/whats_with_all_the_add_me_on_snapchat/

Duffy, B. (2017) *(Not) Getting paid to do what you love: Gender, social media, and aspirational work.* Yale University Press.

Dugdale, E.E. and Harjani, H. (2025) Rape under wraps: How Tinder, Hinge and their corporate owner chose profits over safety. *The Guardian,* February 13. https://www.theguardian.com/us-news/2025/feb/13/tinder-hinge-match-investigation

Duggan, L. (2002) The new homonormativity: The sexual politics of neoliberalism. In Castronovo, R. and Nelson, D.D. (eds.) *Materializing democracy: Toward a revitalized culture politics.* Duke University Press, pp. 175–94.

Duguay, S. (2017) Dressing up Tinderella: Interrogating authenticity claims on the mobile dating app Tinder. *Information, Communication & Society,* 20(3), 351–67.

Duguay, S. (2018) Swiped: A focal gesture and contested app visions. In Morris, J.W. and Murray, S. (eds.) *Appified: Culture in the age of apps.* University of Michigan Press, pp. 127–35.

Duguay, S. (2019) "There's no one new around you": Queer women's experiences of scarcity in geospatial partner-seeking on Tinder. In Nash, C.J. and Gorman-Murray, A. (eds.) *The geographies of digital sexuality.* Palgrave Macmillan, pp. 93–114.

Duguay, S. (2020) You can't use this app for that: Exploring off-label use through an investigation of Tinder. *The Information Society,* 36(1), 30–42.

Duguay, S. (2022) *Personal but not private: Queer women, sexuality, and identity modulation on digital platforms.* Oxford University Press.

Duguay, S. (2024) Queer women and digital platforms: Identity modulation for digital sexual citizenship (and beyond?). In Aggleton, P. et al. (eds.) *Routledge handbook on sexuality, gender, health and rights,* 2nd ed. Routledge.

Duguay, S., Burgess, J., and Light, B. (2017) Mobile dating and hookup app culture. In Messaris, P. and Humphreys, L. (eds.) *Digital media: Transformations in human communication,* 2nd ed. Peter Lang, pp. 213–21.

Duguay, S., Burgess, J., and Suzor, N.P. (2018) Queer women's experiences of patchwork platform governance on Tinder, Instagram, and Vine. *Convergence: The International Journal of Research into New Media Technologies*, 26, 237–52.

Duguay, S., Dietzel, C., and Myles, D. (2022) The year of the "virtual date": Reimagining dating app affordances during the COVID-19 pandemic. *New Media and Society*, 26(3), 1384–402.

Edwardes, C. (2015) Tinder? I'm an addict, says hook-up app's co-creator and CEO Sean Rad. *The Standard*. https://www.standard.co.uk/lifestyle/london-life/tinder-i-m-an-addict-says-hookup-apps-cocreator-and-ceo-sean-rad-a3117181.html

Eglash, R. (2004) Appropriating technology: An introduction. In Eglash, R., et al. (eds.) *Appropriating technology: Vernacular science and social power*. University of Minnesota Press, pp. vii–xxi.

Eler, A. and Peyser, E. (2016) Tinderization of feeling. *The New Inquiry*. http://thenewinquiry.com/essays/tinderization-of-feeling/

Elish, M.C. and boyd, d. (2018) Situating methods in the magic of Big Data and AI. *Communication Monographs*, 85(1), 57–80.

Ellis, M. (2019) How to use Tinder without Facebook friends knowing. *MUO*. https://www.makeuseof.com/tag/use-tinder-without-facebook-friends-knowing/

Ellison, N.B., Hancock, J.T., and Toma, C.L. (2011) Profile as promise: A framework for conceptualizing veracity in online dating self-presentations. *New Media & Society*, 14(1), 45–62.

Ellis-Petersen, H. (2015) WLTM Bumble – A dating app where women call the shots. *The Guardian*, April 12. https://www.theguardian.com/technology/2015/apr/12/bumble-dating-app-women-call-shots-whitney-wolfe

Emlovz. (2025) Tinders latest feature: AI flirting game (quick review). *YouTube*. https://youtu.be/iocRI6EnOTo?si=_WzJ2zUCj88wQ7mE

Escobar, A. (2018) *Designs for the pluriverse: Radical interdependence, autonomy, and the making of worlds*. Duke University Press.

Evans, S.K., et al. (2017) Explicating affordances: A conceptual framework for understanding affordances in communication research. *Journal of Computer-Mediated Communication*, 22(1), 35–52.

Fansher, A.K. and Eckinger, S. (2021) Tinder tales: An exploratory study of online dating users and their most interesting stories. *Deviant Behavior*, 42(9), 1194–208.

Farokhmanesh, M. (2017) Tinder's new "reaction" feature is a weak attempt to combat its most horrible male users. *The Verge*. https://www.theverge.com/2017/10/4/16418572/tinder-reactions-men-harassment-dating

Farvid, P. and Aisher, K. (2016) "It's just a lot more casual": Young heterosexual women's experience of using Tinder in New Zealand. *Ada: A Journal of Gender, New Media, and Technology*, 10, 1–18.

Farvid, P., Braun, V., and Rowney, C. (2017) "No girl wants to be called a slut!": Women, heterosexual casual sex and the sexual double standard. *Journal of Gender Studies*, 26(5), 544–60.

Fenton, N. (2007) Bridging the mythical divide: Political economy and cultural studies approaches to the analysis of the media. In Devereux, E. (ed.) *Media studies: Key issues and debates*. Sage, pp. 7–13.

Ferris, L. and Duguay, S. (2019) Tinder's lesbian digital imaginary: Investigating (im)permeable boundaries of sexual identity on a popular dating app. *New Media & Society*, 22(3), 489–506.

Filice, E., et al. (2022) Sexual violence and abuse in online dating: A scoping review. *Aggression and Violent Behavior*, 67, 1–18.

Firpo, K. (2023) Tinder #ITSTARTSHERE. https://firpo.tv/itstartshere

Flynn, K. (2018) Tinder really doesn't like commenting on Bumble's gun photo ban. *Mashable*. https://mashable.com/article/tinder-copies-bumble-bans-guns-profile-photos

Flynn, K. (2025) Tinder taps TikTok influencers to lure Gen Z. *Axios*. https://www.axios.com/2025/01/25/tinder-dating-influencers-tiktok

Ford, J.V., et al. (2019) Why pleasure matters: Its global relevance for sexual health, sexual rights and wellbeing. *International Journal of Sexual Health*, 31(3), 217–30.

Forristal, L. (2025) Bumble sunsets acquired apps, Fruitz and Official, to cut costs. *TechCrunch*, February 19. https://techcrunch.com/2025/02/19/bumble-sunsets-fruitz-and-official-as-it-looks-to-cut-costs/

Foucault, M. (1982) The subject and power. *Critical Inquiry*, 8(4), 777–95.

Fraser, N. (1990) Rethinking the public sphere: A contribution to the critique of actually existing democracy. *Social Text*, 25/26, 56–80.

Fung, B. (2023) Tinder owner Match Group settles antitrust claims against Google's app store. *CNN*. https://www.cnn.com/2023/11/01/tech/tinder-match-group-google-lawsuit

Gabbatt, A. (2015) Popularity of "hookup apps" blamed for surge in sexually transmitted infections. *The Guardian*, May 28. https://www.theguardian.com/us-news/2015/may/28/hookup-apps-stds-tinder-grindr

García-Gómez, A. (2025) Critical femininities: Exploring young women's digital sexual cultures. *Journal of Gender Studies*, 34(7), 1023–36.

Garwood-Cross, L., et al. (2023) The Covid Sex Lives project: Health messaging, hooking up and dating among men who have sex with men during the UK COVID-19 pandemic. University of Salford. https://salford-repository.worktribe.com/output/1640747

Gebru, T. and Torres, É.P. (2024) The TESCREAL bundle: Eugenics and the promise of utopia through artificial general intelligence. *First Monday*, 29(4). https://doi.org/10.5210/fm.v29i4.13636

Getty Images. (2015) 199 Tinder Plus launch party with Jason Derulo and Zedd stock photos, high-res pictures, and images. https://www.gettyimages.ca/photos/tinder-plus-launch-party-with-jason-derulo-and-zedd

Gibbs, J.L., Ellison, N.B., and Lai, C.-H. (2011) First comes love, then comes Google: An investigation of uncertainty reduction strategies and self-disclosure in online dating. *Communication Research*, 38(1), 70–100.

Gibbs, M., et al. (2015) #Funeral and Instagram: Death, social media, and platform vernacular. *Information, Communication & Society*, 18(3), 255–68.

Giddens, A. (1991a) *The consequences of modernity*. Polity.

Giddens, A. (1991b) *Modernity and self-identity: Self and society in the late modern age*. Polity.

Gill, R. (2007) Postfeminist media culture. *European Journal of Cultural Studies*, 10(2), 147–66.

Gillespie, T. (2018) *Custodians of the internet: Platforms, content moderation, and the hidden decisions that shape social media*. Yale University Press.

Gillett, R. (2018) Intimate intrusions online: Studying the normalisation of abuse in dating apps. *Women's Studies International Forum*, 69, 212–19.

Gillett, R. (2023) "This is not a nice safe space": Investigating women's safety work on Tinder. *Feminist Media Studies*, 23(1), 199–215.

Gillett, R., Stardust, Z., and Burgess, J. (2022) Safety for whom? Investigating how platforms frame and perform safety and harm interventions. *Social Media + Society*, 8(4). https://doi.org/10.1177/20563051221144315

GLAAD. (2014) Facebook offers new custom gender field, expands options for transgender users. https://glaad.org/releases/facebook-offers-new-custom-gender-field-expands-options-transgender-users/

Glamour. (2015) I'm a lesbian, so why do straight men keep showing up on my Tinder? https://www.glamour.com/story/im-a-lesbian-so-why-do-straigh

Global Dating Insights. (2024a) Scott Bright of BrightCheck – Live interview at GDI New York 2024. *YouTube.* https://youtu.be/IXeV9vlvJVc?si=jHTkpnBc3-S9fAlK

Global Dating Insights. (2024b) Kathryn Kosmides of Garbo – Live interview at GDI New York 2024. *YouTube.* https://youtu.be/lF9OwQn62yA?si=i642yhKIdr2ANkOz

Global Dating Insights. (2025a) Global dating app revenues top $6 billion, likely primed to grow. https://www.globaldatinginsights.com/featured/global-dating-app-revenues-top-6-billion-likely-primed-to-grow/

Global Dating Insights. (2025b) Match Group acquires Muslim dating app Salams in unannounced deal. https://www.globaldatinginsights.com/featured/match-group-acquires-muslim-dating-app-salams-in-unannounced-deal/

Global Dating Insights. (2025c) HER joins Match Group as dating giants eye queer platforms. https://www.globaldatinginsights.com/featured/her-joins-match-group-as-dating-giants-eye-queer-platforms/

Goffman, E. (1959) *The presentation of self in everyday life.* Doubleday.

Golding, P. and Murdock, G. (1991) Culture, communication, and political economy. In Curran, J. and Gurevitch, M. (eds.) *Mass media and society.* Edward Arnold, pp. 15–32.

Goode, L. (2022) "Date Me" Google docs and the hyper-optimized quest for love. *Wired.* https://www.wired.com/story/date-me-google-docs-and-the-hyper-optimized-quest-for-love/

Gorman, M. (2015) Company distances itself from Tinder CEO Sean Rad after controversial comments. *Newsweek.* https://www.newsweek.com/match-group-distances-itself-tinder-ceo-sean-rad-396235

Gorwa, R., Binns, R., and Katzenbach, C. (2020) Algorithmic content moderation: Technical and political challenges in the automation of platform governance. *Big Data and Society,* 7(1). https://doi.org/10.1177/2053951719897945

Gosine, A. (2007) Brown to blonde at Gay.com: Passing white in queer cyberspace. In O'Riordan, K. and Phillips, D.J. (eds.) *Queer online: Media, technology & sexuality.* Peter Lang, pp. 139–54.

Gospodyn. (2021) How many swipes do each person have? *r/Tinder, Reddit.* https://www.reddit.com/r/Tinder/comments/roj040/how_many_swipes_do_each_person_have/

Government of Japan. (n.d.) Digital identification app. *Digital Agency.* https://services.digital.go.jp/en/auth-and-sign/

Grazian, D. (2003) *Blue Chicago: The search for authenticity in urban blues clubs.* University of Chicago Press.

Griffiths, D.A. and Armstrong, H.L. (2024) "They were talking to an idea they had about me": A qualitative analysis of transgender individuals' experiences using dating apps. *Journal of Sex Research*, 61(1), 119–32.

Grimes, S. (2021) *Digital playgrounds: The hidden politics of children's online play spaces, virtual worlds, and connected games*. University of Toronto Press.

Grow, K. (2014) Tinder co-founder Sean Rad demoted from CEO position. *Rolling Stone*. https://www.rollingstone.com/culture/culture-news/tinder-co-founder-sean-rad-demoted-from-ceo-position-45846/

Gurcan, C. and Ustenel, A.O. (2023) "It's like a gamble, anything could happen": Women and navigating safety and agency in online dating in urban Turkey. *Feminism and Psychology*, 34(1), 151–71.

Hahn, J. (2021) Tinder says 2020 was its busiest year despite COVID pandemic. *People*. https://people.com/human-interest/tinder-says-2020-was-its-busiest-year-despite-pandemic/

Haimson, O.L. and Hoffmann, A.L. (2016) Constructing and enforcing "authentic" identity online: Facebook, real names, and non-normative identities. *First Monday*, 21(6). https://doi.org/10.5210/fm.v21i6.6791

Hall, R. (2024) Are dating apps fuelling addiction? Lawsuit against Tinder, Hinge and Match claims so. *The Guardian*, February 17. https://www.theguardian.com/lifeandstyle/2024/feb/17/are-dating-apps-fuelling-addiction-lawsuit-against-tinder-hinge-and-match-claims-so

Haraway, D. (1988) Situated knowledges: The science question in feminism and the privilege of partial perspective. *Feminist Studies*, 14(3), 575–99.

Haraway, D. (1991) *Simians, cyborgs and women: The reinvention of nature*. Routledge.

Haraway, D. (2016) *Staying with the trouble: Making kin in the Chthulucene*. Duke University Press.

Hart, R. (2021) Match settles Tinder lawsuit for $441 million just before jury handover. *Forbes*. https://www.forbes.com/sites/roberthart/2021/12/01/match-settles-tinder-lawsuit-for-441-million-just-before-jury-handover/

Hasinoff, A.A. and Schneider, N. (2022) From scalability to subsidiarity in addressing online harm. *Social Media + Society*, 8(3). https://doi.org/10.1177/20563051221126041

Hatmaker, T. (2022) Match and Google reach interim compromise over app payments. *TechCrunch*. https://techcrunch.com/2022/05/20/match-google-restraining-order-apps/

Hearn, A. and Banet-Weiser, S. (2020) The beguiling: Glamour in/as platformed cultural production. *Social Media + Society*, 6(1). https://doi.org/10.1177/2056305119898779

Helmond, A. (2015) The platformization of the Web: Making web data platform ready. *Social Media + Society*, 1(2). https://doi.org/10.1177/2056305115603080

Helmond, A. and van der Vlist, F.N. (2019) Social media and platform historiography: Challenges and opportunities. *TMG Journal for Media History*, 22(1), 6–34.

Hess, A. (2014) What I learned from talking to Tinder's Justin Mateen about women. *Slate*. https://slate.com/human-interest/2014/07/tinder-lawsuit-sexual-harassment-and-gender-discrimination-at-tinder-and-in-the-male-dominated-tech-world.html

Hess, A. and Flores, C. (2018) Simply more than swiping left: A critical analysis of toxic masculine performances on Tinder Nightmares. *New Media and Society*, 20(3), 1085–102.

Hey! Vina. (n.d.) Hey! Vina + Tinder. https://www.heyvina.com/tinder

Hicks, M. (2017) The mother of all swipes. *Logic(s) Magazine*, 2. https://logicmag.io/sex/the-mother-of-all-swipes/

Hinchliffe, E. (2022) Gen Z make up more than half of Tinder's users – and they're using the app way differently than millennials do. *Fortune*. https://fortune.com/longform/renate-nyborg-tinder-ceo-interview-gen-z-dating-apps/

Hirst, J. (2013) "It's got to be about enjoying yourself": Young people, sexual pleasure, and sex and relationships education. *Sex Education*, 13(4), 423–36.

Hoffmann, A.L., Proferes, N., and Zimmer, M. (2016) "Making the world more open and connected": Mark Zuckerberg and the discursive construction of Facebook and its users. *New Media & Society*, 20(1) 199–218.

Hogan, B. (2010) The presentation of self in the age of social media: Distinguishing performances and exhibitions online. *Bulletin of Science, Technology & Society*, 30(6), 377–86.

Hogan, B. (2013) Pseudonyms and the rise of the real-name web. In Hartley, J., Burgess, J., and Bruns, A. (eds.) *A companion to new media dynamics*. Wiley-Blackwell, pp. 290–308.

Hogan, M. (2024) The fumes of AI. *Critical AI*, 2(1). https://doi.org/10.1215/2834703X-11205231

Hronis, A. (2024) Dating apps are accused of being "addictive". What makes us keep swiping? *The Conversation*. http://theconversation.com/dating-apps-are-accused-of-being-addictive-what-makes-us-keep-swiping-224068

Hund, E. (2023) *The influencer industry: The quest for authenticity on social media.* Princeton University Press.

Hypebeast. (2015) Calvin Klein uses sexting and Tinder in its latest marketing campaign. *Hypebeast.* https://hypebeast.com/2015/7/calvin-klein-uses-sexting-and-tinder-in-its-latest-marketing-campaign

Iosotaluno, F. (2025) After almost 8 unforgettable years at Match Group and Tinder ... *LinkedIn.* https://www.linkedin.com/posts/faye-iosotaluno_after-almost-8-unforgettable-years-at-match-activity-7331366994530762753-iNPt?utm_source=share&utm_medium=member_desktop&rcm=ACoAAAk7VNEBMksrbK1po1yRaconkFCcXWafoHU

Jacob, D. (2023) Match Group stock tumbles after paying users fall again. *Wall Street Journal.* https://www.wsj.com/livecoverage/fed-meeting-interest-rate-decision-fomc-november-2023/card/match-group-stock-tumbles-after-paying-users-fall-again-qDUPt5pjbw8j7pDlYkPq

James, D., Condie, J., and Lean, G. (2019) Travel, Tinder and gender in digitally mediated tourism encounters. In Nash, C.J. and Gorman-Murray, A. (eds.) *The geographies of digital sexuality.* Springer, pp. 49–68.

Jane, E.A. (2016) *Misogyny online: A short (and brutish) history.* Sage.

Jane, E.A. and Vincent, N.A. (2017) Random rape threat generator. https://unsworks.unsw.edu.au/entities/publication/3a3d5ebb-4ccb-4cef-ac6c-e4916ace7ca8

Johnson, D. (2021) How to log into Tinder, the popular dating app, using a computer or mobile device. *Business Insider.* https://www.businessinsider.com/guides/tech/tinder-login

Joseph, J. (2025) Predicting crime or perpetuating bias? The AI dilemma. *AI & Society*, 40, 2319–21.

Junck, L.D. (2021) *Down the rabbit hole: An ethnography on loving, desiring and Tindering in Cape Town.* Unpublished PhD thesis, University of Cape Town.

Kanthawala, S., et al. (2023) Algorithmic conspirituality: Explicating its emergence, dimensions, and persuasibility. *New Media & Society*, 27(5), 2885–910.

Kaplan, K.A. (2003) Facemash creator survives Ad Board. *The Harvard Crimson.* https://www.thecrimson.com/article/2003/11/19/facemash-creator-survives-ad-board-the/

Kennedy, J., Meese, J., and van der Nagel, E. (2016) Regulation and social practice online. *Continuum: Journal of Media & Cultural Studies*, 30(2), 146–57.

Kim, H., et al. (2024) Exploring multi-faceted motivations and strategies using mobile dating applications: Case study of Tinder users in South Korea. *Proceedings of the ACM on Human–Computer Interaction*, 8(8), 1–14.

Kimmerer, R.W. (2013) *Braiding sweetgrass: Indigenous wisdom, scientific knowledge and the teachings of plants*. Milkweed Editions.

Kirkpatrick, D. (2010) *The Facebook effect: The inside story of the company that is connecting the world*. Simon and Schuster.

Klein, N. (2024) *Doppelganger: A trip into the mirror world*. Vintage Canada.

Kosmides, K. (2023) Evolving with purpose: Our next phase at Garbo. *Garbo*. https://www.garbo.io/blog/next-phase-at-garbo

Kozma, A. (2018) Shame, class, and embodiment in the *Catfish* universe. *Television & New Media*, 19(5), 467–85.

Krichel, S. (2017) We asked women how they act on Bumble vs. Tinder. *Vice*. https://www.vice.com/en/article/we-asked-women-how-they-act-on-bumble-vs-tinder/

Krüger, S. and Spilde, A.C. (2020) Judging books by their covers – Tinder interface, usage and sociocultural implications. *Information, Communication & Society*, 23(10), 1395–410.

Kurucz, P. (n.d.) BLABLA. *Pol Kurucz*. http://www.polkurucz.com/blabla

Lamensch, M. (2023) Generative AI tools are perpetuating harmful gender stereotypes. Centre for International Governance Innovation. https://www.cigionline.org/articles/generative-ai-tools-are-perpetuating-harmful-gender-stereotypes/

Lane, J. and Ramirez, F.A. (2024) Carceral communication: Mass incarceration as communicative phenomenon. *New Media & Society*, 26(2), 674–91.

Laner, M.R. and Kamel, G.W.L. (1978) Media mating I: Newspaper "personals" ads of homosexual men. *Journal of Homosexuality*, 3(2), 149–62.

Lawler, R. (2014) Tinder is raising from Benchmark at a valuation north of $750 million. *TechCrunch*. https://techcrunch.com/2014/09/10/tinder-is-raising-from-benchmark-at-a-valuation-north-of-750-million/

Leaver, T., Highfield, T., and Abidin, C. (2020) *Instagram: Visual social media cultures*. Polity.

Lee, B. (2015) Ex Machina stunt at SXSW has users falling for a robot on Tinder. *The Guardian*, March 16. https://www.theguardian.com/film/2015/mar/16/ex-machina-stunt-sxsw-users-falling-for-robot-tinder

Lee, D. (2019) Tinder settles age discrimination lawsuit with $11.5 million worth of Super Likes. *The Verge*. https://www.theverge.com/2019/1/25/18197575/tinder-plus-age-discrimination-lawsuit-settlement-super-likes

Lee, J. (2021) Talking through race: Two raced women's Tinder stories. *Communication, Culture and Critique*, 14(3), 454–70.

Lee, J. (2019) Mediated superficiality and misogyny through cool on Tinder. *Social Media + Society*, 5(3). https://doi.org/10.1177/2056305119872949

Liboiron, M. (2021) *Pollution is colonialism*. Duke University Press.

Licoppe, C. (2020) Liquidity and attachment in the mobile hookup culture: A comparative study of contrasted interactional patterns in the main uses of Grindr and Tinder. *Journal of Cultural Economy*, 13, 73–90.

Licoppe, C., Riviere, C.A., and Morel, J. (2016) Grindr casual hook-ups as interactional achievements. *New Media & Society*, 18(1), 2540–58.

Lieu, J. (2016) You can match with a sexually transmitted infection on Tinder. *Mashable*. https://mashable.com/article/tinder-sti-fake-profile

Light, B., Burgess, J., and Duguay, S. (2018) The walkthrough method: An approach to the study of apps. *New Media & Society*, 20(3), 881–900.

Lim, J. (2022) Choosing the right love: Online dating platforms and gender inequality in Southeast Asia. In Kim, Y. (ed.) *Media in Asia: Global, digital, gendered and mobile*. Routledge, pp. 211–25.

Lin, K.-H. and Lundquist, J. (2013) Mate selection in cyberspace: The intersection of race, gender, and education. *American Journal of Sociology*, 119(1), 183–215.

Lindsay, K. (2024) Dating apps are in their flop era. *Bustle*. https://www.bustle.com/wellness/dating-apps-have-gotten-worse-hinge-tinder-bumble-gen-z-millennials

Lingel, J. and Golub, A. (2015) In face on Facebook: Brooklyn's drag community and sociotechnical practices of online communication. *Journal of Computer-Mediated Communication*, 20(5), 536–53.

Linne, J.W. (2020) "It's not you, it's Tinder." Gamification, consumption, daily management and performance in dating apps. *Convergencia: Revista de ciencias sociales*, 27, 1–26.

Liu, J. (2020) The carceral feminism of SESTA-FOSTA: Reproducing spaces of exclusion from IRL to URL. In Ramos, R. and Mowlabocus, S. (eds.) *Queer sites in global contexts*. Routledge, pp. 117–32.

Liu, X. (2015) "No fats, femmes, or Asians." *Moral Philosophy and Politics*, 2(2), 255–76.

Livia, A. (2002) Public and clandestine: Gay men's pseudonyms on the French Minitel. *Sexualities*, 5(2), 201–17.

Livingstone, S. and O'Neill, B. (2014) Children's rights online: Challenges, dilemmas and emerging directions. In van der Hof, S., van den Berg, B., and Schermer, B. (eds.) *Minding minor wandering the web: Regulating online child safety*. Springer, pp. 19–38.

Livingstone, S. and Sylwander, K.R. (2025) There is no right age! The search for age-appropriate ways to support children's digital lives and rights. *Journal of Children and Media*, 19(1), 6–12.

Lovelock, M. (2017) Catching a catfish: Constructing the "good" social media user in reality television. *Television & New Media*, 18(3), 203–17.

Luecke, A. (2015) Research says women of Tinder don't like beards. *Esquire*. https://www.esquire.com/style/grooming/a32478/women-on-tinder-dont-like-beards-020514/

Lunden, I. (2012) Updated: Has dating site Badoo found a love match in the form of Hot or Not? *TechCrunch*. https://techcrunch.com/2012/04/02/has-dating-site-badoo-found-a-love-match-in-the-form-of-hotornot/

Lunden, I. (2019) Andrey Andreev sells stake in Bumble owner to Blackstone, Whitney Wolfe Herd now CEO of $3B dating apps business. *TechCrunch*. https://techcrunch.com/2019/11/08/badoos-andrey-andreev-sells-his-stake-in-bumble-to-blackstone-valuing-the-dating-app-at-3b/

Lundquist, J.H. and Curington, C.V. (2019) Love me Tinder, love me sweet. *Contexts*, 18(4), 22–7.

Lyons, K. (2021) Tinder and Lyft partner so you can send your match a ride for an IRL date. *The Verge*. https://www.theverge.com/2021/10/7/22714762/tinder-lyft-partner-match-free-ride

MacKee, F. (2016) Social media in gay London: Tinder as an alternative to hook-up apps. *Social Media + Society*, 2(3). https://doi.org/10.1177/2056305116662186

MacKenzie, D. and Wajcman, J. (1985) *The social shaping of technology*. Open University Press.

Mackinnon, L. (2022) Love, games and gamification: Gambling and gaming as techniques of modern romantic love. *Theory, Culture & Society*, 39(6), 121–37.

MacLeod, C. and McArthur, V. (2019) The construction of gender in dating apps: An interface analysis of Tinder and Bumble. *Feminist Media Studies*, 19(6), 822–40.

madibwebb. (2024) Playlist dating updates (w Tinder). *TikTok*. https://www.tiktok.com/@madibwebb/playlist/Dating%20Updates%20

(w%20Tinder)-7423951480652483371?is_from_webapp=1&sender_device=pc
Makuch, E. (2015) Fallout Shelter ads come to Tinder. *GameSpot.* https://www.gamespot.com/articles/fallout-shelter-ads-come-to-tinder/1100-6429848/
Malik, S. (2020) For some women in Pakistan, banning Tinder means a loss of freedom and connectivity. *Vice.* https://www.vice.com/en/article/for-some-women-in-pakistan-banning-tinder-means-a-loss-of-freedom-and-connectivity/
Marchal, N., et al. (2024) How negative media coverage impacts platform governance: Evidence from Facebook, Twitter, and YouTube. *Political Communication*, 42(2), 215–33.
Markowitz, D.M. and Hancock, J.T. (2018) Deception in mobile dating conversations. *Journal of Communication*, 68(3), 547–69.
Marvin, C. (1988) *When old technologies were new: Thinking about electric communication in the late nineteenth century.* Oxford University Press.
Marwick, A.E. (2015) Instafame: Luxury selfies in the attention economy. *Public Culture*, 27(1), 137–60.
Mason, C.L. (2016) Tinder and humanitarian hook-ups: The erotics of social media racism. *Feminist Media Studies*, 16(5), 822–37.
Massanari, A. (2015) #Gamergate and The Fappening: How Reddit's algorithm, governance, and culture support toxic technocultures. *New Media & Society*, 19(3), 329–46.
Match Group. (2020) Match Group and Bumble settle litigation. *PR Newswire.* https://www.prnewswire.com/news-releases/match-group-and-bumble-settle-litigation-301075424.html
Match Group. (2024a) Report on Form 10-K for the fiscal year ended December 31, 2024. https://s203.q4cdn.com/993464185/files/doc_financials/2024/ar/MTCH-ARS-2025-03-27.pdf
Match Group. (2024b) Match Group teams up with OpenAI to spark a love affair with innovation. *Investor Relations.* https://ir.mtch.com/investor-relations/news-events/news-events/news-details/2024/Match-Group-Teams-Up-with-OpenAI-to-Spark-a-Love-Affair-with-Innovation/default.aspx
Match Group Americas, LLC. (2025) Match Group advertising policy. https://www.matchmediagroup.com/advertisingpolicy
Match Group Americas, LLC. (n.d.) Match Media Group. https://www.matchmediagroup.com
Match Group, Inc. (2024) Business overview: May 2024. https://s203.q4cdn.com/993464185/files/doc_financials/2024/Match-Group-Business-Overview-May-2024-vF.pdf

Match Group, Inc. (2025a) Government relations. https://findahelpline.com/countries/us

Match Group, Inc. (2025b) Investor relations. https://ir.mtch.com/investor-relations/overview/default.aspx

McCosker, A., et al. (2019) Swiping, stealthing and catfishing: Dating apps in the media. Swinburne University of Technology, Melbourne. https://doi.org/10.25916/5d7ed40274311

McCreanor, T., et al. (2024) Alcohol marketing on social media: Young people's exposure, engagement and alcohol-related behaviors. *Addiction Research & Theory*, 33(3), 161–71.

McCulloch, G. (2019) *Because internet: Understanding the new rules of language*. Riverhead Books.

McIntyre, H. (2015) Tinder is getting into the music game, starting with Jason Derulo. *Forbes*. https://www.forbes.com/sites/hughmcintyre/2015/04/02/tinder-is-getting-into-the-music-game-starting-with-jason-derulo/

McNamara, B. (2016) Tinder now has 40 gender options. *Teen Vogue*. https://www.teenvogue.com/story/tinder-update-40-gender-options

McRobbie, A. (2008) *The aftermath of feminism*. Sage.

McVeigh-Schultz, J. and Baym, N.K. (2015) Thinking of you: Vernacular affordance in the context of the microsocial relationship app, Couple. *Social Media + Society*, 1(2). https://doi.org/10.1177/2056305115604649

Megarry, D. (2020) Gay dating app Chappy announces it's closing down this month. *Gay Times*. https://www.gaytimes.com/life/gay-dating-app-chappy-is-closing-down/

Mehta, I. (2024) Match Group promotes Faye Iosotaluno to Tinder CEO. *TechCrunch*. https://techcrunch.com/2024/01/09/match-group-promotes-faye-iosotaluno-to-tinder-ceo/

Merriam-Webster. (2024) Definition of 'meet-cute'. https://www.merriam-webster.com/dictionary/meet-cute

Merriam-Webster. (2025) Definition of 'touch grass'. https://www.merriam-webster.com/dictionary/touch+grass

Meta. (2023) You can now have multiple personal profiles on Facebook. *Facebook Newsroom*. https://about.fb.com/news/2023/09/you-can-now-have-multiple-personal-profiles-on-facebook/

Meta. (2025a) Names allowed on Facebook. Facebook Help Center. https://www.facebook.com/help/229715077154790

Meta. (2025b) Authentic identity representation. Transparency Center. https://transparency.meta.com/policies/community-standards/authentic-identity-representation

Meta. (2025c) Meta audience network. https://www.facebook.com/audiencenetwork/

Miltner, K.M. (2020) "One part politics, one part technology, one part history": Racial representation in the Unicode 7.0 emoji set. *New Media & Society*, 23(3), 515–34.

Mohammad, L., Jarenwattananon, P., and Summers, J. (2023) An open letter signed by tech leaders, researchers proposes delaying AI development. *NPR*. https://www.npr.org/2023/03/29/1166891536/an-open-letter-signed-by-tech-leaders-researchers-proposes-delaying-ai-developme

Morozov, E. (2013) *To save everything, click here: The folly of technological solutionism*. PublicAffairs.

Morris, S. and Dobson, A.S. (2023) Tinder marketing and transnational postfeminist media cultures: "Modern" women as single, not sorry? *Feminist Media Studies*, 23(8), 4269–84.

Mosco, V. (2009) *The political economy of communication*. Sage.

Mowlabocus, S. (2010) *Gaydar culture: Gay men, technology and embodiment in the digital age*. Ashgate.

Mowlabocus, S. (2016) The "mastery" of the swipe: Smartphones, transitional objects and interstitial time. *First Monday*, 21(10). https://doi.org/10.5210/fm.v21i10.6950

Mowlabocus, S. (2020) A kindr Grindr: Moderating race(ism) in techno-spaces of desire. In Ramos, R. and Mowlabocus, S. (eds.) *Queer sites in global contexts*. Routledge, pp. 33–47.

Murdoch, C. (2017a) Tinder's new gender options have led to matches for 250,000 trans people. *Mashable*. https://mashable.com/article/tinder-trans-matches

Murdoch, C. (2017b) Are you beautiful or not? Tinder hires James Blunt to critique your profile. *Mashable*. https://mashable.com/article/james-blunt-tinder

Murdock, G. and Wasko, J. (2007) *Media in the age of marketization*. Hampton Press.

Myles, D., Duguay, S., and Dietzel, C. (2021) #DatingWhileDistancing: Dating apps as digital health technologies during the COVID-19 pandemic. In Lupton, D. and Willis, K. (eds.) *The COVID-19 crisis: Social perspectives*. Routledge.

Nader, K. (2024) The gamification of dating online. *Theoria*, 91(3), 1–17.

Nakamura, L. (2002) *Cybertypes: Race, ethnicity, and identity on the Internet*. Routledge.

Nash, C.J. and Gorman-Murray, A. (2014) LGBT neighbourhoods and "new mobilities": Towards understanding transformations in sexual

and gendered urban landscapes. *International Journal of Urban and Regional Research*, 38(3), 756–72.
Neff, G. and Stark, D. (2004) Permanently beta: Responsive organization in the Internet era. In Howard, P.N. and Jones, S. (eds.) *Society online: The Internet in context.* Sage, pp. 173–88.
Newett, L., Churchill, B., and Robards, B. (2017) Forming connections in the digital era: Tinder, a new tool in young Australian intimate life. *Journal of Sociology*, 54(3), 346–61.
Nickenig, A. (2024) The market of love. In Schomacher, E. and Söffer, J. (eds.) *The culture of money: Implications for contemporary economics.* Routledge, pp. 117–35.
Nieborg, D.B. and Poell, T. (2018) The platformization of cultural production: Theorizing the contingent cultural commodity. *New Media & Society*, 20(11), 4275–92.
Noble, S.U. (2018) *Algorithms of oppression: How search engines reinforce racism.* New York University Press.
Noonlight. (n.d.) Noonlight: America's no. 1 safety app. https://www.noonlight.com/noonlight-app
NPR. (2007) Ethics of NBC's sting show "To Catch a Predator." *NPR.* https://www.npr.org/2007/01/16/6870926/ethics-of-nbcs-sting-show-to-catch-a-predator
Nudd, T. (2024) Tinder ads reimagine swipe-rights as romcom-style meet cutes. *AdAge.* https://adage.com/creativity/work/tinder-ads-reimagine-swipe-rights-romcom-style-meet-cutes/2568736/
O'Brien, S.A. (2023) Match Group and background-checking nonprofit end safety partnership. *Wall Street Journal.* https://www.proquest.com/docview/2851956872/citation/DB4420DB4C1741D9PQ/1
Ofcom. (2024) Online nation 2024 report. https://www.ofcom.org.uk/siteassets/resources/documents/research-and-data/online-research/online-nation/2024/online-nation-2024-report.pdf?v=386238
O'Gorman, K., Wilson, M., and Seidler, Z. (2024) Swiping into the void: Tears, fears, and motivations of young men on dating apps. In Seidler, Z. (ed.) *Masculinities and mental health in young men.* Springer, pp. 229–62.
O'Hear, S. (2016) Tinder rival Bumble is majority-owned by European dating behemoth Badoo. *TechCrunch.* https://techcrunch.com/2016/03/25/bumble-meet-badoo/
OkCupid. (n.d.) Privacy controls for the LGBTQ+ community. https://okcupid-app.zendesk.com/hc/en-us/articles/23546659683995-Privacy-controls-for-the-LGBTQ-community
Orchard, T. (2024) *Sticky, sexy, sad: Swipe culture and the darker side of dating apps.* University of Toronto Press.

Ortega, J. and Hergovich, P. (2018) The strength of absent ties: Social integration via online dating. *arXiv Physics and Society*. doi:10.48550/arXiv.1709.10478

Paasonen, S., Jarrett, K., and Light, B. (2019) *#NSFW: Sex, humor, and risk in social media*. MIT Press.

Pambakian, R. (2017) In commemoration of National Pig Day ... *Tinder Newsroom*. https://www.tinderpressroom.com/in-commemoration-of-national-pig-day

Parham, J. (2025) Dating apps promise to remain a rare haven following Trump's executive order. *Wired*. https://www.wired.com/story/dating-apps-promise-to-be-a-haven-following-trumps-executive-order/

Parsons, V. (2019) Tinder has 50 gender options but transgender people are being banned for their gender identity. *PinkNews*. https://www.thepinknews.com/2019/10/25/tinder-50-gender-options-transgender-people-banned-gender-identity/

Parthasarathi, V. and Agarwal, S., 2023. Platformisation of matchmaking: Reconfiguring social economies in India. In Bouquillion, P. et al. (eds.) *Digital platforms and the Global South: Reconfiguring power relations in the cultural industries*. Routledge.

Paul, A., Ahmed, S., and Zaluski, K. (2022) Does online dating promotion vary across cultures? A cross-cultural analysis of homepage advertisements of online dating services in 51 countries. *Journal of Creative Communications*, 17(2), 179–98.

Paul, K. (2014) Swipe right for spambots: Fake Tinder profiles still seduce users. *Mashable*. http://mashable.com/2014/07/15/tinder-spambots-still-happening/#WVu26WRxzSqn

Peck, A.J., Berkowitz, D., and Tinkler, J. (2021) Left, right, Black, and White: How White college students talk about their inter- and intra-racial swiping preferences on Tinder. *Sociological Spectrum*, 41(4), 304–21.

Peetz, T. (2024) Intimate valuation devices: Doing valuation while doing dating in Tinder texts. *Journal of Cultural Economy*, 17(5), 605–25.

Perez, S. (2018) Dating app Hinge is ditching the Facebook login requirement. *TechCrunch*. https://techcrunch.com/2018/06/01/dating-app-hinge-is-ditching-the-facebook-login-requirement/

Perez, S. (2019) Tinder is preparing to launch a lightweight version of its dating app called "Tinder Lite." *TechCrunch*. https://techcrunch.com/2019/05/10/tinder-is-preparing-to-launch-a-lightweight-version-of-its-dating-app-called-tinder-lite/

Perez, S. (2022) Tinder is launching a new feature called Festival

Mode. *TechCrunch*. https://techcrunch.com/2022/04/14/tinder-adds-a-festival-mode-for-making-connections-ahead-of-concerts-and-events/

Perrin, A. and Anderson, M. (2019) Share of U.S. adults using social media, including Facebook, is mostly unchanged since 2018. Pew Research Center. https://www.pewresearch.org/short-reads/2019/04/10/share-of-u-s-adults-using-social-media-including-facebook-is-mostly-unchanged-since-2018/

Pinch, T.J. and Bijker, W.E. (1984) The social construction of facts and artefacts: Or how the sociology of science and the sociology of technology might benefit each other. *Social Studies of Science*, 14(3), 399–441.

Plummer, K. (2003) *Intimate citizenship: Private decisions and public dialogues*. McGill–Queen's University Press.

Poell, T., Nieborg, D., and van Dijck, J. (2019) Platformisation. *Internet Policy Review*, 8(4). https://doi.org/10.14763/2019.4.1425

Poell, T., Nieborg, D., and Duffy, B. (2021) *Platforms and cultural production*. Polity.

Pond, T. and Farvid, P. (2017) "I do like girls, I promise": Young bisexual women's experiences of using Tinder. *Psychology of Sexualities Review*, 8(2), 6–24.

Porter, A., et al. (2024) Swipe left on sexual harassment: Understanding and addressing technology-facilitated sexual violence on dating apps. *Journal of Interpersonal Violence*, 40(13–14), 2964–83.

Portolan, L. and McAlister, J. (2022) Jagged love: Narratives of romance on dating apps during COVID-19. *Sexuality & Culture*, 26, 354–72.

Prendergast, C. (2024) Forbes health survey: 79% of Gen Z report dating app burnout. *Forbes*. https://www.forbes.com/health/dating/dating-app-fatigue/

Quiroz, P.A. (2013) From finding the perfect love online to satellite dating and "Loving-the-one-you're near": A look at Grindr, Skout, Plenty of Fish, Meet Moi, Zoosk and Assisted Serendipity. *Humanity & Society*, 37(2), 181–5.

Race, M. (2023) Tinder swipes left on Russia a year after invasion. *BBC News*. https://www.bbc.com/news/business-65457098

Rad, S. (2015) IAMA Sean Rad, cofounder & CEO of Tinder. AMA! *r/IAmA, Reddit*. https://www.reddit.com/r/IAmA/comments/2zmms5/iama_sean_rad_cofounder_ceo_of_tinder_ama/

Rambukkana, N. (2023) Platform intimacies. *Canadian Journal of Communication*, 48(1), 175–90.

Ramos, R. (2023) Tinder killer Damon Benson sentenced in Rocklin man's murder, woman's torture. *CBS News*. https://www.cbsnews.com/sacramento/news/tinder-killer-damon-benson-sentenced-in-rocklin-mans-murder-womans-torture/

Ramšak, M. (2022) Femininity, online practices of drinking and women in alcohol industry. In Ramšak, M. (ed.) *Social impact of wine marketing: The challenge of digital technologies to regulation*. Springer, pp. 81–90.

Ranzini, G. and Lutz, C. (2016) Love at first swipe? Explaining Tinder self-presentation and motives. *Mobile Media & Communication*, 5(1), 80–101.

Ranzini, G. and Rosenbaum, J.E. (2020) It's a match (?): Tinder usage and attitudes toward interracial dating. *Communication Research Reports*, 37(1–2), 44–54.

Rao, L. (2014) With moments, Tinder decides photos shouldn't always last forever. *TechCrunch*. https://techcrunch.com/2014/06/05/with-moments-tinder-too-decides-photos-shouldnt-always-last-forever/

Reade, J. (2020) Keeping it raw on the 'gram: Authenticity, relatability and digital intimacy in fitness cultures on Instagram. *New Media & Society*, 23(3), 535–53.

Recode. (2016) Full video: Tinder CEO Sean Rad at Code 2016. http://www.recode.net/2016/6/17/11966748/sean-rad-tinder-full-video-code

Reuters. (2025) Anson Funds names its 3 candidates in board fight at Match Group. https://www.reuters.com/markets/wealth/anson-funds-names-its-3-candidates-board-fight-match-group-2025-04-04/

Rhode Island Government. (2015) Health releases new data on infectious syphilis, gonorrhea, and HIV. http://www.ri.gov/press/view/24889

Richardson, D. (2005) Desiring sameness? The rise of a neoliberal politics of normalisation. *Antipode*, 37(3), 515–35.

Richardson, D. (2018) *Sexuality and citizenship*. Polity.

Rösner, L. and Krämer, N.C. (2016) Verbal venting in the social web: Effects of anonymity and group norms on aggressive language use in online comments. *Social Media + Society*, 2(3). https://doi.org/10.1177/2056305116664220

Rubin, G. (1993) Thinking sex: Notes for a radical theory of the politics of sexuality. In Abelove, H., Barale, M.A., and Halperin, D.M. (eds.) *The gay and lesbian studies reader*. Routledge, pp. 3–44.

Safronova, V. (2018) Tinder and Bumble are seriously at war. *The New York Times*, April 4. https://www.nytimes.com/2018/04/04/style/tinder-bumble-lawsuit-explainer.html

Sales, N.J. (2015a) Tinder and the dawn of the "dating apocalypse." *Vanity Fair*. https://www.vanityfair.com/culture/2015/08/tinder-hook-up-culture-end-of-dating?srsltid=AfmBOoqjWSzzocjYYvn7s8MHJBAlCMxlld5O1EXdkTml_LtHwBwDOzWf

Sales, N.J. (2015b) An open letter to Tinder's Sean Rad from V.F.'s Nancy Jo Sales. *Vanity Fair*. https://www.vanityfair.com/news/2015/11/sean-rad-tinder-open-letter-nancy-jo-sales?srsltid=AfmBOoonAKr_E6E_DChbQ4Rgfl41w3Mkg5LWor4IkqBuvToqXoIybf6V

Sales, N.J. (2021) *Nothing personal: My secret life in the dating app inferno*. Hachette Books.

Sanchez, S. (2023) Tinder's 'It Starts with a Swipe' campaign boosts quarterly results. https://www.campaignlive.com/article/1833010?utm_source=website&utm_medium=social

Schaffer, M. (n.d.) Gillette – Tinder Experiment. https://matthewschaffer.com/Gillette-Tinder-Experiment

Schwartz, B. (2008) Jim Safka to replace Jim Lanzone as CEO of Ask.com. *Search Engine Land*. https://searchengineland.com/jim-safka-to-replace-jim-lanzone-as-ceo-of-askcom-13101

Seals, G. (2014) Hacking your way to a date: The weird world of Tinder auto-liking. *The Daily Dot*. https://www.dailydot.com/debug/tinder-hacking-auto-likers/

Senft, T.M. (2013) Microcelebrity and the branded self. In Harley, J., Burgess, J., and Bruns, A. (eds.) *A companion to new media dynamics*. Blackwell, pp. 346–54.

Senft, T.M. and Baym, N.K. (2015) What does the selfie say? Investigating a global phenomenon. *International Journal of Communication*, 9, 1588–606.

Serrano, J. (2022) Tinder breaks up with CEO, dumps plan for virtual "Tinder Coins." *Gizmodo*. https://gizmodo.com/tinder-dumps-ceo-and-plans-for-virtual-tinder-coins-1849366091

Sharabi, L.L., Ryder, C.V., and Niess, L.C. (2023) A space of our own: Exploring the relationship initiation experiences of lesbian, gay, bisexual, transgender, queer, intersex, and asexual dating app users. *Journal of Social and Personal Relationships*, 40(7), 2277–97.

Sharma, S. (2022) Introduction: A feminist medium is the message. In Sharma, S. (ed.) *Re-understanding media: Feminist extensions of Marshall McLuhan*. Duke University Press, pp. 1–22.

Shaw, A. (2017) Diversity without defense: Reframing arguments for diversity in games. *Kinephanos: Journal of Media Studies and Popular Culture*, July, 54–76.

Shield, A. (2018) Grindr culture: Intersectional and socio-sexual. *Ephemera*, 18(1), 149–61.

Sicart, M. (2017) *Play matters.* MIT Press.
Silverstone, R. and Haddon, L. (1996) Design and the domestication of information and communication technologies. In Mansell, R. and Silverstone, R. (eds.) *Communication by design: The politics of information and communication technologies.* Oxford University Press, pp. 44–77.
Silverstone, R., Hirsch, E., and Morley, D. (1992) Information and communication technologies and the moral economy of the household. In Hirsch, E. and Silverstone, R. (eds.) *Consuming technologies: Media and information in domestic spaces.* Routledge.
Simpson, L. (2017) *As we have always done: Indigenous freedom through radical resistance,* 3rd ed. University of Minnesota Press.
Sky News. (2016) Victim of alleged "Tinder killer" Gable Tostee "had 80 injuries." *Sky News.* https://news.sky.com/story/victim-of-alleged-tinder-killer-gable-tostee-had-80-injuries-10615252
Smith, A. (2016) 15% of American adults have used online dating sites or mobile dating apps. Pew Research Center. https://www.pewresearch.org/internet/2016/02/11/15-percent-of-american-adults-have-used-online-dating-sites-or-mobile-dating-apps/
Sobieraj, S. and Humphreys, L. (2022) The Tinder games: Collective mobile dating app use and gender conforming behavior. *Mobile Media & Communication,* 10(1), 57–75.
Sohail, S.A., et al. (2019) Tinder use among Pakistani adults: A socio-psychological need perspective. *Jurnal Studi Komunikasi,* 3, 316–31.
Soper, T. (2015) Tinder founder Sean Rad explains why the dating app is so popular. *GeekWire.* https://www.geekwire.com/2015/tinder-founder-sean-rad-explains-why-the-dating-app-is-so-popular/
Spangler, T. (2020) Tinder names Jim Lanzone as CEO. *Variety.* https://variety.com/2020/digital/news/tinder-jim-lanzone-ceo-cbs-interactive-1234717752/
spencerrascoff. (2025) Starting today @Tinder, we're rolling out a new voice AI experience called The Game Game ... *Instagram.* https://www.instagram.com/p/DH6xNcwTaNt/
Spiritual-Station267. (2025) Has anyone used this yet? I just noticed it when I opened tinder. *r/Tinder, Reddit.* https://www.reddit.com/r/Tinder/comments/1jq5lvl/has_anyone_used_this_yet_i_just_noticed_it_when_i/
Spišák, S., et al. (2021) Social networking sites' gag order: Commercial content moderation's adverse implications for fundamental sexual rights and wellbeing. *Social Media + Society,* 7(2). https://doi.org/10.1177/20563051211024962
Stacey, S. (2024) How we fell out of love with dating apps. *Financial*

Times. https://www.ft.com/content/6f28bf28-8378-436f-ac7f-8fd1e2de17e2

Stampler, L. (2014) Inside Tinder: Meet the guys who turned dating into an addiction. *Time.* https://time.com/4837/tinder-meet-the-guys-who-turned-dating-into-an-addiction/

Stanley, E. (2021) *Atmospheres of violence: Structuring antagonism and the trans/queer ungovernable.* Duke University Press.

Stardust, Z., Gillett, R., and Albury, K. (2023) Surveillance does not equal safety: Police, data and consent on dating apps. *Crime, Media, Culture,* 19(2), 274–95.

Stark, L. and Hutson, J. (2022) Physiognomic artificial intelligence. *Fordham Intellectual Property, Media & Entertainment Law Journal,* 32(4), 922–78.

Statista. (n.d.) Online dating worldwide – statistics & facts. https://www.statista.com/topics/7443/online-dating/?srsltid=AfmBOoqtoDLr1pSLBoPE1wqLZMBQ3wDSKYSnlBCoPOMmY4AroQ_PFCno#topicOverview

Steinmetz, K. (2016) The inside story behind Tinder's new gender options. *Time.* https://time.com/4568225/tinder-gender-feature-transgender/

Stewart, R. (2017) Tinder swipes right on programmatic ads in partnership with Facebook Audience Network. *The Drum.* https://www.thedrum.com/news/2017/02/03/tinder-swipes-right-programmatic-ads-partnership-with-facebook-audience-network

Suchman, L. (2023) The uncontroversial "thingness" of AI. *Big Data & Society,* 10(2). https://doi.org/10.1177/20539517231206794

Suenzo, F.N. (2025) The quest for meaningful connections: Navigating scripted sexuality on Instagram amid Grindr and Tinder fatigue. *New Media & Society,* 27(11), 6215–32.

Sunam Audry, A., et al. (2023) Nationwide research on the uses and motivations of dating apps by young adults in the cultural environment of Turkey. *Mobile Media & Communication,* 12(3), 662–87.

Sundén, J. (2002) *Material virtualities: Approaching online textual embodiment.* Linköping University.

Sundén, J., Paasonen, S., Tiidenberg, K., and Vihlman, M. (2022) Locating sex: Regional geographies of sexual social media. *Gender, Place & Culture,* 31(4), 424–40.

Sundén, J., Paasonen, S., and Tiidenberg, K. (2026) *Hot connections: Why sexual platforms matter.* MIT Press.

Sweeney, M.E. and Whaley, K. (2019) Technically white: Emoji skin-tone modifiers as American technoculture. *First Monday,* 24(7). https://doi.org/10.5210/fm.v24i7.10060

Sweney, M. (2022) Tinder chief leaves dating app after less than a year. *The Guardian*, August 3. https://www.theguardian.com/technology/2022/aug/03/tinder-chief-leaves-dating-app-after-one-year-renate-nyborg
Swisher, K. (2014) Sweat equity: Benchmark takes stake in Tinder in exchange for Matt Cohler joining board. *Vox*. https://www.vox.com/2014/10/28/11632384/sweat-equity-benchmark-takes-stake-in-tinder-in-exchange-for-matt
SXSW. (2017) Swiping right on inclusivity with Tinder & GLAAD. https://schedule.sxsw.com/2025/events/PP96586
Szulc, Ł. (2025) Sad dating apps: Emotional technological determinism and agency in late modernity. *Social Media + Society*, 11(4). https://doi.org/10.1177/20563051251380042
Tang, D.T.S. (2017) All I get is an emoji: Dating on lesbian mobile phone app Butterfly. *Media, Culture and Society*, 39(6), 816–32.
Tanner, M. (2024) The actualisation of mobile dating application affordances to support racial digital dating intentions: The case of Tinder. *Behaviour & Information Technology*, 43(5), 831–44. doi:10.1080/0144929X.2023.2190417
Team Coco. (2014) Dave Franco & Conan Join Tinder | CONAN on TBS. *YouTube*. https://youtu.be/YkiR1KjIw7k?si=KdCCQJu-mO7tSyGv
TEDx Talks. (2019) Can online dating lead to more successful marriages? | Philipp Hergovich | TEDxThessaloniki. *YouTube*. https://youtu.be/ij0F50_Vd-0?si=HwvD8UlCyV5qHVyS
Tepper, F. (2016) Bumble invests in gay dating app Chappy. *TechCrunch*. https://techcrunch.com/2016/12/14/bumble-invests-in-gay-dating-app-chappy/
The Backroom Sydney. (2013) Tinder Launch @ The Backroom Sydney. *YouTube*. https://youtu.be/DlUg8ptaz3U?si=GYmthbYTs16O4m2z
The General. (2017) Swipe right. *YouTube*. https://youtu.be/svv1Qz_LeY8?si=WH29ijm2PR_3SdaJ
The Global Advisory Board for Sexual Health and Wellbeing. (2020) Working definition of sexual pleasure. https://www.gab-shw.org/our-work/working-definition-of-sexual-pleasure/
Thompson, L. (2018) "I can be your Tinder nightmare": Harassment and misogyny in the online sexual marketplace. *Feminism & Psychology*, 28(1), 69–89.
Thompson, R. (2017) Face it, Super Liking on Tinder is for losers. *Mashable*. https://mashable.com/article/super-like-tinder-losers
Tierney, A. (2017) Why are trans people being banned from Tinder? *Vice*. https://www.vice.com/en/article/why-do-trans-people-keep-being-banned-from-tinder/

Tiffany, K. (2018) Alexis Ohanian and Tinder are petitioning Unicode for interracial couple emoji. *The Verge*. https://www.theverge.com/2018/2/27/17057694/tinder-interracial-family-emoji-petition-unicode-jennifer-8-lee

Tiidenberg, K. (2018) *Selfies: Why we love (and hate) them*. Emerald.

Tiidenberg, K. and van der Nagel, E. (2020) *Sex and social media*. Emerald.

Timmermans, E. and Courtois, C. (2018) From swiping to casual sex and/or committed relationships: Exploring the experiences of Tinder users. *The Information Society*, 34(2), 59–70.

Timmermans, E. and De Caluwé, E. (2017) Development and validation of the Tinder Motives Scale (TMS). *Computers in Human Behavior*, 70, 341–50.

Tinder. (2013) Tinder – A fun way to break the ice. Internet Archive. https://web.archive.org/web/20130403040153/http:/www.gotinder.com/

Tinder. (2014) FAQ. Internet Archive. https://web.archive.org/web/20140920185443/http:/www.gotinder.com/faq

Tinder. (2015a) Tinder stories. Internet Archive. https://web.archive.org/web/20220120122633/https:/swipedright.gotinder.com/

Tinder. (2015b) We just revamped your Tinder profile. Tinder Blog. http://blog.gotinder.com/we-just-revamped-your-tinder-profile/

Tinder. (2015c) Keeping Tinder real. Internet Archive. https://web.archive.org/web/20160429131309/http:/blog.gotinder.com/keeping-tinder-real/

Tinder. (2016a) Introducing Tinder Stacks for iMessage – swipe on everything. *Tinder Newsroom*. https://www.tinderpressroom.com/introducing-tinder-stacks-for-imessage-swipe-on-everything

Tinder. (2016b) Tinder is swiping up the volume with Spotify. *Tinder Newsroom*. https://www.tinderpressroom.com/tinder-is-swiping-up-the-volume-with-spotify

Tinder. (2016c) Introducing Smart Photos – for the most swipe-worthy you. *Tinder Newsroom*. https://www.tinderpressroom.com/introducing-smart-photos-for-the-most-swipeworthy-you

Tinder. (2016d) Introducing more genders on Tinder. *Tinder Newsroom*. https://www.tinderpressroom.com/genders

Tinder. (2016e) #AllTypesAllSwipes | Introducing More Genders | Product Release | Tinder. *YouTube*. https://youtu.be/XP90QAnmaA4?si=ecTnP2hdPzD6CtPy

Tinder. (2016f) Hey! VINA, Tinder's got your back. *Tinder Newsroom*. https://www.tinderpressroom.com/hey-vina-tinders-got-your-back

Tinder. (2016g) Tinder launches Swipe Ventures. *Tinder Newsroom*. https://www.tinderpressroom.com/tinder-launches-swipe-ventures

Tinder. (2017) The Menprovement initiative. *Facebook*. https://www.facebook.com/watch/?v=1413515552051559

Tinder. (2018) The Interracial Couple Emoji Project. *YouTube*. https://youtu.be/tWrKrn7t2wo?si=lHsMjYh_PaGhPF_b

Tinder. (2019a) Taking care of everyone in our community. *Tinder Newsroom*. https://www.tinderpressroom.com/taking-care-of-everyone-in-our-community

Tinder. (2019b) Introducing Swipe Night: An original adventure built for the Swipe® feature. *Tinder Newsroom*. https://www.tinderpressroom.com/introducing-swipe-night

Tinder. (2020a) A message from our CEO: Connecting in the time of COVID-19. *Tinder Newsroom*. https://www.tinderpressroom.com/Connecting-in-the-time-of-COVID-19

Tinder. (2020b) Tinder introduces safety-focused updates. *Tinder Newsroom*. https://www.tinderpressroom.com/tinder-introduces-safety-updates

Tinder. (2020c) Tinder releases face to face video. *Tinder Newsroom*. https://www.tinderpressroom.com/Tinder-Begins-Testing-Face-to-Face-Video

Tinder. (2020d) The future of dating is fluid. *Tinder Newsroom*. https://www.tinderpressroom.com/futureofdating

Tinder. (2020e) Tinder and Megan Thee Stallion partner to challenge members to flaunt their authenticity. *Tinder Newsroom*. https://www.tinderpressroom.com/Put-Yourself-Out-There

Tinder. (2021a) Match Group partners with Garbo to make ground-breaking background check technology accessible to users, starting with Tinder. *Tinder Newsroom*. https://www.tinderpressroom.com/news?item=122491

Tinder. (2021b) Tinder introduces Are You Sure?, an industry-first feature that is stopping harassment before it starts. *Tinder Newsroom*. https://www.tinderpressroom.com/2021-05-20-Tinder-Introduces-Are-You-Sure-,-an-Industry-First-Feature-That-is-Stopping-Harassment-Before-It-Starts

Tinder. (2021c) Tinder orders more Swipe Night following transformative 20 million member turnout and 26% increase in matches. *Tinder Newsroom*. https://www.tinderpressroom.com/2021-08-11-Tinder-Orders-More-Swipe-Night-Following-Transformative-20-Million-Member-Turnout-and-26-Increase-in-Matches

Tinder. (2021d) Tinder wins entertainment grand prix for Swipe Night at Cannes Festival 2021. *Tinder Newsroom*. https://www.tinderpressroom.com/2021-06-25-Tinder-Wins-Entertainment-Grand-Prix-for-Swipe-Night-at-Cannes-Festival-2021

Tinder. (2021e) Introducing Vibes, a new way for members to

express themselves on Tinder. *Tinder Newsroom*. https://www.tinderpressroom.com/2021-05-04-Introducing-Vibes,-a-New-Way-for-Members-to-Express-Themselves-on-Tinder

Tinder. (2022a) Garbo launches background check platform to public and on Tinder. *Tinder Newsroom*. https://www.tinderpressroom.com/2022-03-09-Garbo-Launches-Background-Check-Platform-To-Public-and-On-Tinder

Tinder. (2022b) Tinder wins three 2022 Comparably Awards, including best career growth. *Tinder Newsroom*. https://www.tinderpressroom.com/2022-07-14-Tinder-wins-three-2022-Comparably-Awards,-Including-Best-Career-Growth

Tinder. (2023a) HelloFresh and Tinder launch "Date Night Delights" recipe series helping new couples enter their forking season. *Tinder Newsroom*. https://www.tinderpressroom.com/2023-11-06-HelloFresh-and-Tinder-Launch-Date-Night-Delights-Recipe-Series-Helping-New-Couples-Enter-Their-Forking-Season

Tinder. (2023b) Tinder redefines expectations with new brand campaign that celebrates Gen Z's authentic, fluid and beautiful connections. *Tinder Newsroom*. https://www.tinderpressroom.com/2023-02-27-TINDER-REDEFINES-EXPECTATIONS-WITH-NEW-BRAND-CAMPAIGN-THAT-CELEBRATES-GEN-ZS-AUTHENTIC,-FLUID-AND-BEAUTIFUL-CONNECTIONS

Tinder. (2023c) Tinder creates "Single Summer Series" for uncuffing season. *Tinder Newsroom*. https://www.tinderpressroom.com/2023-05-23-TINDER-CREATES-SINGLE-SUMMER-SERIES-FOR-UNCUFFING-SEASON

Tinder. (2024a) Real messages, real romance: Tinder's new campaign inspired by couples' first chats. *Tinder Newsroom*. https://www.tinderpressroom.com/Real-Messages,-Real-Romance-Tinders-New-Campaign-Inspired-by-Couples-First-Chats

Tinder. (2024b) Frequently asked questions. https://tinder.com/faq

Tinder. (2024c) Big Tinder® Wedding: Two Tinder® couples walk down the aisle and say yes in the ultimate celebration of queer love. *Tinder Newsroom*. https://au.tinderpressroom.com/BigTinderWeddingCelebratesQueerLove

Tinder. (2024d) Tinder singles could shift the November elections results with bold new "Take Action Center" initiative. *Tinder Newsroom*. https://www.tinderpressroom.com/2024-09-17-Tinder-Singles-Could-Shift-the-November-Elections-Results-with-Bold-New-Take-Action-Center-Initiative

Tinder. (2024e) Tinder terms of use. https://policies.tinder.com/terms/intl/en/?lang=en

Tinder. (2024f) Flávia Saraiva abre o coração sobre relacionamentos e erros em primeiro episódio do 'Match o Papo' em collab com o 'Clube do Erro'. *Tinder Newsroom Brazil.* URL https://br.tinderpressroom.com/FLAVIA-SARAIVA-ABRE-O-CORACAO-SOBRE-RELACIONAMENTOS-E-ERROS-EM-PRIMEIRO-EPISODIO-DO-MATCH-O-PAPO-EM-COLLAB-COM-O-CLUBE-DO-ERRO

Tinder. (2024g) Tinder apresenta: MTV Beija Sapo: Nova temporada estreia dia 29 de agosto na Pluto TV. *Tinder Newsroom Brazil.* https://br.tinderpressroom.com/TINDER-APRESENTA-MTV-BEIJA-SAPO-NOVA-TEMPORADA-ESTREIA-DIA-29-DE-AGOSTO-NA-PLUTO-TV

Tinder. (2024h) Tinder จับมือ Clawset เปิดตัวคอลเลกชันเสื้อผ้าคู่สัตว์เลี้ยง รับเทรนด์ Pet Humanization มาแรง. *Tinder Newsroom Thailand.* https://th.tinderpressroom.com/TinderxClawset

Tinder. (2025a) Interracial Couple Emoji Project. https://emoji.tinder.com

Tinder. (2025b) Subscription tiers. https://tinder.com/feature/subscription-tiers

Tinder. (n.d.-a) About Tinder. *Tinder Newsroom.* https://www.tinderpressroom.com/about

Tinder. (n.d.-b) Powering Tinder® – the method behind our matching. https://www.help.tinder.com/hc/en-us/articles/7606685697037-Powering-Tinder-The-Method-Behind-Our-Matching

Tinder. (n.d.-c) Community guidelines. https://policies.tinder.com/community-guidelines/intl/en/

Tinder. (n.d.-d) How does photo verification work? https://www.help.tinder.com/hc/en-us/articles/4422771431309-How-Does-Photo-Verification-Work

Tinder. (n.d.-e) Privacy policy. https://policies.tinder.com/privacy/intl/en/#how-we-use-data

Tinder. (n.d.-f) Photo Check data and privacy information. https://www.help.tinder.com/hc/en-us/articles/26147205007885-Photo-Check-data-and-privacy-information

Tinder. (n.d.-g) Dating safety tips. https://policies.tinder.com/safety/intl/en/?lang=en

Tinder. (n.d.-h) Dating safety tips. https://www.gotinder.com/safety?locale=en

Tinder. (n.d.-i) Noonlight. https://www.help.tinder.com/hc/en-us/articles/360039260031-Noonlight

Tinder. (n.d.-j) BrightCheck. https://www.help.tinder.com/hc/en-us/articles/25826520654221-BrightCheck

Tinder. (n.d.-k) Privacy FAQs. https://www.help.tinder.com/hc/en-us/articles/5349453268877-Privacy-FAQs
Tinder. (n.d.-l) Priority Likes. https://www.help.tinder.com/hc/en-us/articles/360046802931-Priority-Likes
Tinder. (n.d.-m) Tinder SELECT Membership. https://www.help.tinder.com/hc/en-us/articles/15408075254797-Tinder-SELECT-Membership
Tinder. (n.d.-n) Super Boost. https://www.help.tinder.com/hc/en-us/articles/360029087891-Super-Boost
Tinder Australia. (2024) Ep 1 – Big Tinder Wedding: When he left me on "read" *YouTube*. https://youtu.be/LlAUsbf6JYc?si=QpTjSiFH_txDNsyb
Toor, A. (2015) Tinder throws a Twitter fit over Vanity Fair article. *The Verge*. https://www.theverge.com/2015/8/12/9136287/tinder-twitter-vanity-fair-meltdown
Tran, C.H. (2024) Room with a viewership: Visibility work & Twitch.tv in the domestic context. *Information, Communication & Society*, 27(12), 2281–96.
Travis, A. (2022) Why do we call internet liars "catfish"? The term actually dates back to the '90s. *Distractify*. https://www.distractify.com/p/where-did-the-term-catfish-come-from
United Nations. (1948) Universal Declaration of Human Rights. https://www.un.org/en/about-us/universal-declaration-of-human-rights
van der Nagel, E. (2017) From usernames to profiles: the development of pseudonymity in Internet communication. *Internet Histories*, 1(4), 312–31.
van Dijck, J. (2013) *The culture of connectivity: A critical history of social media*. Oxford University Press.
van Dijck, J. (2021) Seeing the forest for the trees: Visualizing platformization and its governance. *New Media & Society*, 23(9), 2801–19.
van Dijck, J., Poell, T., and de Waal, M. (2018) *The platform society*. Oxford University Press.
van Grove, J. (2014) IAC stakes bigger claim over dating app Tinder. *CNET*. https://www.cnet.com/tech/services-and-software/iac-stakes-larger-claim-over-tinder/
van Oorschot, J. (2015) Tender – It's how people meat. *YouTube*. https://youtu.be/9EPXVN5IMhQ?si=_HwCQYoAEZ_hocsc
Vasani, S. (2023) Tinder Select is a $499 per month plan for Tinder's 1 percent. *The Verge*. https://www.theverge.com/2023/9/25/23889285/tinder-select-match-group-dating-apps

Veix, J. (2014) I joined Tinder as a dog. *Death and Taxes*. http://www.deathandtaxesmag.com/220826/i-joined-tinder-as-a-dog/

Venturini, T. (2009) Diving in magma: How to explore controversies with actor-network theory. *Public Understanding of Science*, 19(3), 258–73.

Villarreal, Y. (2015) Tinder is allegedly banning transgender users because they're trans. *Advocate*. https://www.advocate.com/politics/transgender/2015/06/05/tinder-allegedly-banning-transgender-users-because-theyre-trans

Violet Blue. (2020) We need to talk about sex, tech and COVID-19. *Engadget*. https://www.engadget.com/2020-03-13-we-need-to-talk-about-sex-tech-and-covid-19.html

Vlessing, E. (2024) Grace Millane murder documentary lands at brainstorm media (exclusive). *The Hollywood Reporter*. https://www.hollywoodreporter.com/movies/movie-news/grace-millane-tinder-murder-documentary-brainstorm-media-1235788137/

Vogels, E. and McClain, C. (2023) Key findings about online dating in the U.S. Pew Research Center. https://www.pewresearch.org/short-reads/2023/02/02/key-findings-about-online-dating-in-the-u-s/

Vonderau, P. (2019) The Spotify effect: Digital distribution and financial growth. *Television & New Media*, 20(1), 3–19.

Wade, L. (2017) *American hookup: The new culture of sex on campus*. W.W. Norton.

Wagner, K. (2016) Tinder's Sean Rad is stepping down as CEO to become chairman. *Vox*. https://www.vox.com/2016/12/8/13880424/tinder-sean-rad-stepping-down-ceo-chairman-swipe-ventures

Wajcman, J. (2010) Feminist theories of technology. *Cambridge Journal of Economics*, 34(1), 143–52.

Walther, J.B. (1992) Interpersonal effects in computer-mediated interaction: A relational perspective. *Communication Research*, 19(1), 52–90.

Ward, J. (2017) What are you doing on Tinder? Impression management on a matchmaking mobile app. *Information Communication and Society*, 20(11), 1644–59.

Warner, M. (2002) *Publics and counterpublics*. Zone Books.

Wasko, J. (2014) The study of the political economy of the media in the twenty-first century. *International Journal of Media & Cultural Politics*, 10(3), 259–71.

Weltevrede, E. and Burton, A. (forthcoming) App time: The dual-layered logic of appification. *International Journal of Communication*.

Weltevrede, E. and Jansen, F. (2019) Infrastructures of intimate data: Mapping the inbound and outbound data flows of dating apps. *Computational Culture*, 7. http://computationalculture.net/infrastructures-of-intimate-data-mapping-the-inbound-and-outbound-data-flows-of-dating-apps/

Weltevrede, E., et al. (2025) Gatekeepers of the mobile ecosystem: Understanding app store moderation. In Rogers, R. (ed.) *Content moderation across social media platforms*. Amsterdam University Press.

Werning, S. (2015) Swipe to unlock. *Digital Culture & Society*, 1(1), 53–69.

Wilken, R., Burgess, J., and Albury, K. (2019) Dating apps and data markets: A political economy of communication approach. *Computational culture*, 7. http://computationalculture.net/dating-apps-and-data-markets-a-political-economy-of-communication-approach/

Williams, A. (2024) *Not my type: Automating sexual racism in online dating*. Stanford University Press.

Williams, R. (1974) *Television: Technology and cultural form*. Routledge.

Williams, R. (1977) *Marxism and literature*. Oxford University Press.

Wingman Plus. (2025) Tinder's new AI dating game (full breakdown). *YouTube*. https://youtu.be/NIMQtQF3LkU?si=WyxOZvoRkmxpEXi_

Woll, S. (1986) So many to choose from: Decision strategies in videodating. *Journal of Social and Personal Relationships*, 3(1), 43–52.

World. (2025a) Experience real connections with World ID and Match Group. https://world.org/blog/announcements/experience-real-connections-with-world-id-and-match-group

World. (2025b) FAQ: Frequently asked questions about World. https://world.org/faqs

World. (2025c) What is an iris code, and how does it preserve privacy? https://world.org/blog/world/what-is-iris-code-how-does-it-preserve-privacy

World. (2025d) At last: Keynote summary and big announcements. *YouTube*. https://www.youtube.com/watch?v=ktGI5MOPUQs

World Health Organization. (n.d.) Defining sexual health. https://www.who.int/teams/sexual-and-reproductive-health-and-research/key-areas-of-work/sexual-health/defining-sexual-health

Wu, S. and Liu, S. (2024) When the hunter plays the hunted: Heterosexual Chinese women's negotiations with hegemonic sexual scripts on dating apps. *Feminist Media Studies*, 25(8), 1975–90.

Wu, S. and Trottier, D. (2021) Constructing sexual fields: Chinese gay men's dating practices among pluralized dating apps. *Social Media + Society*, 7(2). https://doi.org/10.1177/20563051211009014

Wyatt, S. (2021) Metaphors in critical Internet and digital media studies. *New Media & Society*, 23(2), 406–16.

Xie, T. (2024) Dating events are on the rise as young people abandon the apps. *Bloomberg*. https://www.bloomberg.com/news/articles/2024-06-28/gen-z-revives-singles-events-as-many-abandon-dating-apps

Zelenko, M. (2015) A brilliant Tinder hack made hundreds of bros unwittingly flirt with each other. *The Verge*. https://www.theverge.com/2015/3/25/8277743/tinder-hack-bros-swiping-bros

Zimmer, M. (2010) Facebook's Zuckerberg: "Having two identities for yourself is an example of a lack of integrity." *MichaelZimmer.org*. https://michaelzimmer.org/2010/05/14/facebooks-zuckerberg-having-two-identities-for-yourself-is-an-example-of-a-lack-of-integrity/

Index